TEACHING VOLLEYBALL

Steps to Success

Barbara L. Viera, MS
Bonnie Jill Ferguson, MS
University of Delaware, Newark

Leisure Press
Champaign, Illinois

Library of Congress Cataloging-in-Publication Data

Viera, Barbara L., 1941-
    Teaching volleyball: steps to success / Barbara L. Viera, Bonnie
Jill Ferguson.
        p.   cm.—(Steps to success activity series)
    Bibliography: p.
    ISBN 0-88011-316-2
    1. Volleyball—Study and teaching.   I. Ferguson, Bonnie Jill,
1957-   . II. Title. III. Series.
GV1015.15V54 1989
796.32'5'07—dc19   88-9430
                                                         CIP

ISBN: 0-88011-316-2

Developmental Editor: Judy Patterson Wright, PhD
Production Director: Ernie Noa
Copy Editor: Peter Nelson
Assistant Editors: Kathy Kane, Holly Gilly, and Robert King
Proofreader: Laurie McGee
Typesetters: Brad Colson and Yvonne Winsor
Text Design: Keith Blomberg
Text Layout: Tara Welsch
Cover Design: Jack Davis
Cover Photo: Bill Morrow
Illustrations By: Sharon Barner and Gretchen Walters
Printed By: United Graphics, Inc.

Printed in the United States of America

10 9 8 7 6 5 4 3 2

Leisure Press
A Division of Human Kinetics Publishers, Inc.
Box 5076, Champaign, IL 61825-5076
1-800-747-4457

Contents

Series Preface

The Steps to Success Activity Series is a breakthrough in skill instruction through the development of complete learning progressions—the *steps to success*. These *steps* help students quickly perform basic skills successfully and prepare them to acquire advanced skills readily. At each step, students are encouraged to learn at their own pace and to integrate their new skills into the total action of the activity, which motivates them to achieve.

The unique features of the Steps to Success Activity Series are the result of comprehensive development—through analyzing existing activity books, incorporating the latest research from the sport sciences and consulting with students, instructors, teacher educators, and administrators. This groundwork pointed up the need for three different types of books—for participants, instructors, and teacher educators—which we have created and together comprise the Steps to Success Activity Series.

The *participant book* for each activity is a self-paced, step-by-step guide; learners can use it as a primary resource for a beginning activity class or as a self-instructional guide. The unique features of each *step* in the participant book include

- sequential illustrations that clearly show proper technique for all basic skills,
- helpful suggestions for detecting and correcting errors,
- excellent drill progressions with accompanying *Success Goals* for measuring performance, and
- a complete checklist for each basic skill for a trained observer to rate the learner's technique.

A comprehensive *instructor guide* accompanies the participant's book for each activity, emphasizing how to individualize instruction. Each *step* of the instructor's guide promotes successful teaching and learning with

- teaching cues (*Keys to Success*) that emphasize fluidity, rhythm, and wholeness,

- criterion-referenced rating charts for evaluating a participant's initial skill level,
- suggestions for observing and correcting typical errors,
- tips for group management and safety,
- ideas for adapting every drill to increase or decrease the difficulty level,
- quantitative evaluations for all drills (*Success Goals*), and
- a complete test bank of written questions.

The series textbook, *Instructional Design for Teaching Physical Activities*, explains the *steps to success* model, which is the basis for the Steps to Success Activity Series. Teacher educators can use this text in their professional preparation classes to help future teachers and coaches learn how to design effective physical activity programs in school, recreation, or community teaching and coaching settings.

After identifying the need for participant, instructor, and teacher educator texts, we refined the *steps to success* instructional design model and developed prototypes for the participant and the instructor books. Once these prototypes were fine-tuned, we carefully selected authors for the activities who were not only thoroughly familiar with their sports but also had years of experience in teaching them. Each author had to be known as a gifted instructor who understands the teaching of sport so thoroughly that he or she could readily apply the *steps to success* model.

Next, all of the participant and instructor manuscripts were carefully developed to meet the guidelines of the *steps to success* model. Then our production team, along with outstanding artists, created a highly visual, user-friendly series of books.

The result: The Steps to Success Activity Series is the premier sports instructional series available today. The participant books are the best available for helping you to become a master player, the instructor guides will help you to become a master teacher, and the teacher educator's text prepares you to design your own programs.

This series would not have been possible without the contributions of the following:

- Dr. Joan Vickers, instructional design expert,
- Dr. Rainer Martens, Publisher,
- the staff of Human Kinetics Publishers,
- the following volleyball teachers and coaches who, as recognized outstanding volleyball teachers by their colleagues, helped shape this book and others in the series with their questionnaire responses: Barbara Viera, Bonnie Jill Ferguson, Annalies Knoppers, Connie Fox, Sandy Gibbons, Leigh Goldie, Laurel and John Kessel, Sandy Stewart, March Krotee, Diane Jacoby, JoAnn Atwell-Scrivner, Patricia Sheldon, M. Elizabeth Verner, Carl McGowen, Scott McQuilkin, Debbie Holzapfel, Peggy Rees, Walter Versen, Stew McDole, Nancy Chapman, Dorothy Wells, Jody Clasey, and
- the *many* students, teachers, coaches, consultants, teacher educators, specialists, and administrators who shared their ideas—and dreams.

Judy Patterson Wright
Series Editor

Preface

In *Volleyball: Steps to Success* the focus is, naturally, on the player. Our experience has taught us that learning the game can be quite different from the player's point of view than from the teacher/coach's point of view. Actual game experience often enhances your growth as a teacher/coach, but it is not essential. Some of the best coaches have never participated in their sports as players.

Most important to your development as a teacher/coach is learning to correctly analyze poor performance and to communicate the proper corrections to the learner. This text, *Teaching Volleyball: Steps to Success*, provides the information you need for instructing beginning players in the skills and strategies of volleyball. For each skill we describe typical errors made by beginning players and suggestions for correcting them. All drills include easy-to-follow instructions, student options for drill variety, suggestions for adapting drills to varying ability levels, and two ways to evaluate your students (Student Keys to Success and Success Goals).

The most interesting aspect of teaching and coaching for us is that every player is different. Often you will find a teaching cue or a "Student Key to Success" to be quickly understood by one learner, but not well received by another. Your challenge as a teacher is to have as many approaches as possible to help you meet each individual's needs.

This instructor's manual provides the variety you need to achieve teaching success.

Typically students will vary in performance levels, both within and among your classes. This book outlines different methods of teaching individual students and ways to vary drills for groups. *Teaching Volleyball* can help teachers of all experience levels because of its systematic approach to teaching skills in game play situations.

As in any project of this magnitude, many people have contributed to its successful completion. We would like to thank Karen Woodie for the help she has rendered in word processing and computer technology; David Barlow, PhD, for his help in the filming presented to the artist for sketching diagrams; and our subjects, Jeanne Dyson, Nancy Griskowitz, Maggie Hennigan, Sue Sowter, Pat Castagno, John Aiello, and Clare Wisniewski. We would also like to extend our sincere appreciation to the illustrators, Sharon Barner and Gretchen Walters, who transformed photos and diagrams into expert drawings.

We would like to thank each other for sharing ideas and for the patience necessary to complete this book. Finally, we are very grateful to the people around us for their support and understanding.

Barbara L. Viera
Bonnie Jill Ferguson

Implementing the Steps to Success Staircase

This book is meant to be flexible for not only your students' needs but for your needs as well. It is common to hear that students' perceptions of a task change as the task is learned. However, it is often forgotten that teachers' perceptions and actions also change (Goc-Karp & Zakrajsek, 1987; Housner & Griffey, 1985; Imwold & Hoffman, 1983).

More experienced or master teachers tend to approach the teaching of activities in a similar manner. They are highly organized (e.g., they do not waste time getting groups together or using long explanations); they integrate information (from biomechanics, kinesiology, exercise physiology, motor learning, sport psychology, cognitive psychology, instructional design, etc.); and they relate basic skills into the larger game or performance context, succinctly explaining why the basic skills, concepts, and tactics are important within the game or performance setting. Then, usually within a few minutes, they place their students into gamelike practice situations that progress in steps that follow logical manipulations of factors such as

- the number of skills used in combination;
- the number of people used in tactical combinations;
- the velocity of a served or tossed ball;
- the achievement required by success goals;
- the restrictions of space or time allotted; and
- the variation of directions for tossed or served balls.

This book will show you how the basic volleyball skills, tactics, and selected physiological, psychological, and other pertinent knowledge are interrelated (see Appendix A for an overview). You can use this information not only to gain insights into the various interrelationships but also to define the subject matter for volleyball. The following questions offer specific suggestions for implementing this knowledge base and help you evaluate and improve your teaching methods, which include class organization, drills, objectives, progressions, and evaluations.

1. Under what conditions do you teach?
   - How much space is available?
   - What type of equipment is available?
   - What is the average class size?
   - How much time is allotted per class session?
   - How many class sessions do you teach?
   - Do you have any teaching assistants?

2. What are your students' initial skill levels?
   - Look for the rating charts located in the beginning of most steps (chapters) to identify the criteria that discriminate between beginning, intermediate, and advanced skill levels.

3. What is the best order to teach volleyball skills?
   - Follow the sequence of steps (chapters) used in this book.
   - See Appendix B.1 for suggestions on when to introduce, review, or continue practicing each step.
   - Based on your answers to the previous questions, use the form in Appendix B.2 to put into order the steps that you will be able to cover in the time available.

4. What objectives do you want your students to accomplish by the end of a lesson, a unit, or a course?
   - For your technique or qualitative objectives, select from the Student Keys to Success (or see the Keys to Success Checklists in *Volleyball: Steps to Success*) that are provided for all basic skills.
   - For your performance or quantitative objectives, select from the Success Goals provided for each drill.

- For written questions on safety, rules, technique, tactics, and psychological aspects of volleyball, select from the ''Test Bank'' of written questions.
- See the Sample Individual Program (Appendix C.1) for selected technique and performance objectives for a 16-week unit.
- For unit objectives, adjust your total number of selected objectives to fit your unit length (use the form in Appendix C.2).
- For organizing daily objectives, see the Sample Lesson Plan in Appendix D.1 and modify the basic lesson plan form in Appendix D.2 to best fit your needs.

5. How will you evaluate your students?
- Read the section ''Evaluation Ideas.''
- Decide on your type of grading system; you could use letter grades, pass-fail, total points, percentages, skill levels (bronze, silver, gold), and so forth.

6. Which activities should be selected to achieve student objectives?
- Follow the drills for each step because they are specifically designed for large groups of students and are presented in a planned, easy-to-difficult order. Avoid a random approach to selecting drills and exercises.

- Modify drills as necessary to best fit each student's skill level by following the suggestions for decreasing and increasing the difficulty level of each drill.
- Ask your students to meet the Success Goal listed for each drill.
- Use the cross-reference to the corresponding step and drill in the participant's book, *Volleyball: Steps to Success*, for class assignments or makeups.

7. What rules and expectations do you have for your class?
- For general management and safety guidelines, read the section ''Preparing Your Class for Success.''
- For specific guidelines, read the subhead ''Group Management and Safety Tips'' included with each drill.
- Let your students know what your rules are during your class orientation or first day of class. Then post the rules and discuss them often.

Teaching is a complex task, requiring you to make many decisions that affect both you and your students (see Figure 1). Use this book to create an effective and successful learning experience for you and everyone you teach. And remember, have fun, too!

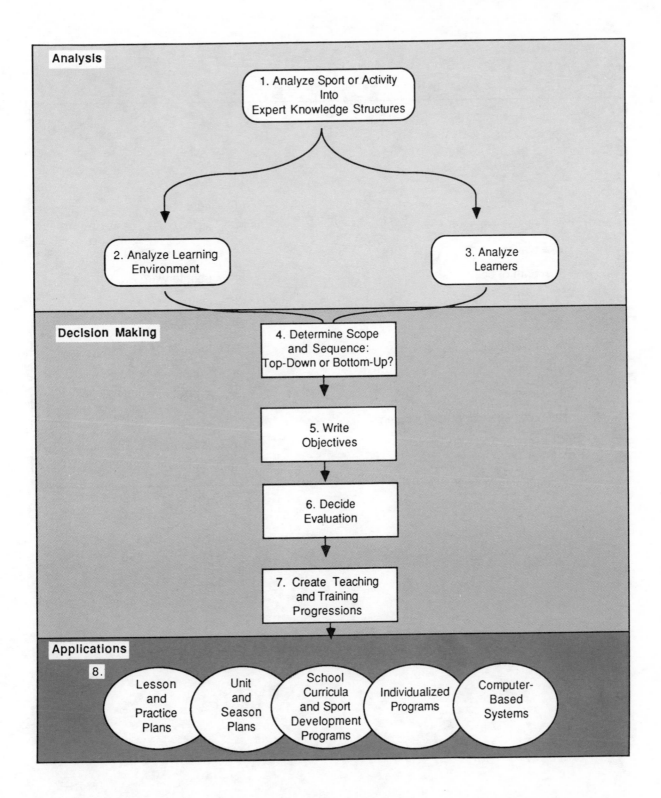

Figure 1 Instructional design model utilizing expert knowledge structures. *Note.* From *Instructional Design for Teaching Physical Activities* by J.N. Vickers, in press, Champaign, IL: Human Kinetics. Copyright by Joan N. Vickers. Reprinted by permission. This instructional design model has appeared in earlier forms in *Badminton: A Structures of Knowledge Approach* (p. 1) by J.N. Vickers and D. Brecht, 1987, Calgary, AB: University Printing Services. Copyright 1987 by Joan N. Vickers; and ''The Role of Expert Knowledge Structures in an Instructional Design Model for Physical Education'' by J.N. Vickers, 1983, *Journal of Teaching in Physical Education,* **2**(3), p. 20. Copyright 1983 by Joan N. Vickers.

KEY

C = coach

^o_x = player with ball

x = player

- - ➤ = path of ball

——➤ = path of player

△ = target player

⌒ = rolled ball

S = setter

T = tosser

⊓ = box, chair, or official's stand

▦ = feeder and ball supply

RB = right back

CB = center back

LB = left back

RF = right forward

CF = center forward

LF = left forward

R = receiver or retriever

B = blocker

D = digger

F = feeder

So = setter with the ball

Before you begin teaching your class, you need to make many procedural decisions. The following suggestions will give you guidance in creating an effective learning environment.

GENERAL CLASS MANAGEMENT

Volleyball is a sport that is basically safe for participation. Even though two teams compete against each other, they are physically separated onto different halves of the court, which greatly limits the possibility of physical contact between opponents. Teammates, however, do play close to one another and occasionally collide, which may cause injury. Several class rules can be established to aid in making the playing environment safe. The following safety rules are suggested:

1. Players should call for the ball every time they intend to contact it.
2. Players should honor a teammate's signal of intent to play the ball.
3. In all movement drills, individuals or teams should be set up to move parallel to one another.
4. During the drills there should be an established verbal signal, easily recognized by all players, that will stop action immediately. This signal is to be used any time there is a danger that a ball will roll under the feet of jumping players.
5. Players should not be allowed to kick volleyballs; besides being dangerous, kicking is not good for volleyballs.
6. Generally, players who hold a ball in a gymnasium, regardless of what kind of ball, may be tempted to use it as a basketball. It is highly recommended for volleyball classes that you establish a rule of no basket shooting. If any player desires to put the ball in the basket, a volleyball skill, such as an overhead pass or a set, must be used.

7. During practice, players should be aware of the location of other players around them. Players practicing spiking or serving must be sure that the opposite side of the court is free of players, unless performing a drill designed to accommodate others.
8. It is highly recommended that players wear knee pads.
9. Long-sleeved shirts add to the comfort of beginners learning the forearm pass and the dig.
10. Have equipment out well before the beginning of class so that early arrivers may practice skills. A list of suggested preclass activities posted on the wall helps guide these early students.

CLASS ORGANIZATION TECHNIQUES

In order to make the best use of available space, you need to decide how to set up the gym in order to have as many courts as possible. The size of the court can be adjusted in both its length and its width. It is also important that you make efficient use of total class time. Following are several considerations to assure that your students learn as much as possible in every class.

1. You should have at least one net for every 12 players, even if it means that each court is slightly smaller than regulation size. If a court is smaller, its attack line should still be the legal distance from the net. The attack line should be 9 feet 10 inches (3 meters) from the centerline. This line determines the take-off point for a legal spike by a back line player. Regardless of a court's size, all appropriate lines (end lines, sidelines, etc.) should be present. The drills in this book are designed for a class of approximately 30 students with the use of two courts.

2. If you don't have enough nets, ropes or nets from other sports adapt well.
3. If net standards are not available, attach nets to the wall.
4. The more a student contacts a ball, the more learning takes place. Drills using only one, two, or three players per ball are the most beneficial. Having several balls available allows drills to continue uninterrupted between trials.
5. Volleyball is a highly competitive sport with definite skill methodology. In an educational setting, students are expected to perform with the correct skill techniques as much as possible.
6. You should have a signal that will quickly bring your students to a central location to receive additional instructions.
7. Make all skill descriptions as brief and concise as possible. Initial descriptions should contain only enough information for players to be able to initiate performance.
8. As your players practice, you should analyze their performance and give as much feedback as possible.
9. Stop all activity and give group feedback whenever the same error appears in the performance of several players.
10. Try to get your students into a competitive situation as soon as possible. Once your students learn the underhand serve and the forearm pass, they are capable of playing a modified game.
11. In most drills, the players must begin in different positions to perform a specific task together. It is your responsibility to make sure that everyone rotates to practice at all the various positions.

CLASS WARM-UPS

The following warm-up drills prepare your class for success in the game of volleyball. Make the drills as gamelike as possible, in order to enhance the carryover into competitive play. It is not expected that all of these drills will be completed for each class. Depending on the time available and the objectives of the day, you should select the drills that you feel will be most appropriate.

1. Court Sprints With a Partner

Two players begin on the end line with one ball. The first player runs quickly to the attack line with the ball, puts the ball down, and backpedals to the end line. The second player runs, picks up the ball, and backpedals to the end line, returning the ball to the first player. This action continues with the players running and backpedaling to and from the centerline, the attack line on the other side of the court, and the other end line. The entire sequence should be completed twice. Although the diagram below shows the four phases of movement at different locations, in reality, all four phases take place at the same location for each pair of players.

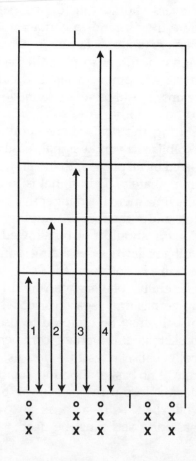

2. Ball Exchange

Two partners stand back to back about 3 feet apart. Both players turn at the same time to their right and exchange the ball between them. Then, quickly turning to their left, they exchange the ball again. They continue exchanging the ball with right and left turns for 30 to 60 seconds.

3. Over and Under

Two partners start in the same position as in the previous drills. With their legs in a slight straddle, the players bend forward and reach back between their legs. The player with the ball gives it to the other. Then both players stand up, reaching high and back over their head, again exchanging the ball. These alternating actions are continued for 30 to 60 seconds.

4. Over Net Ball Exchange

Two players stand facing each other on opposite sides of the net, one player with the ball. Both players jump together, exchange the ball over the top of the net, land on both feet, and repeat, continually exchanging the ball without pause. Action is continued for 30 exchanges. The players must be careful not to touch the net before, during, or after the exchange. The net may be lowered for shorter players, though, if necessary.

5. Blocking Along Net

Many players may stand single file in two lines. One line starts at the net on the right side, and the second line starts at the opposite side of the net on the left side (the players first in each line facing one another). The two players jump and, with a blocking motion, clap their hands together over the top of the net. After landing, the players slide two steps toward the middle of the net, jump and clap, continuing this action along the entire length of the net. Upon reaching the opposite sideline, they turn and run to the end of their respective lines. The second pair of players should not begin the action until the first two have jumped twice. Everyone should perform the action twice. The two lines then trade places, and everyone repeats two more times.

drill twice. Then move the lines to the right side of the court and repeat.

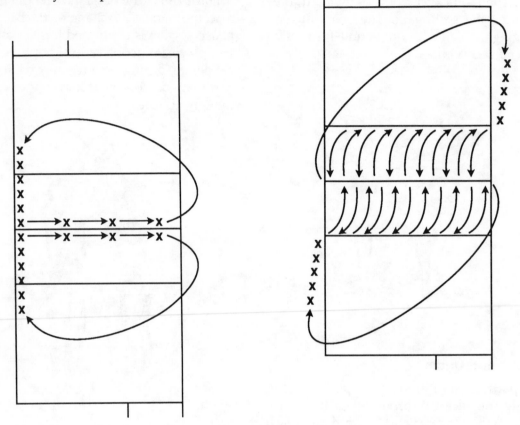

6. Attack Approaches

Many players may stand single file in two lines. One line starts at the attack line on the left sideline of each side of the court. The first player in each line approaches the net and completes an attack motion. Upon landing he or she backpedals to the attack line and repeats the attack action, traveling along the entire length of the net, and returns to the end of the line. The second player in each line should not begin until the first player has performed two attacks. Each player should perform this

7. Court Perimeter

The students line up in two single-file lines again. This time they start at the right back corner of the court and run to the net in a medium body posture. Arriving at the net, they execute four block jumps. They use sliding steps to move along the net between jumps. At the left sideline, they backpedal to the end line. At the end line, they move to the end of the line by using the cross-step, with the crossing action in front of the feet only. They repeat this sequence three times.

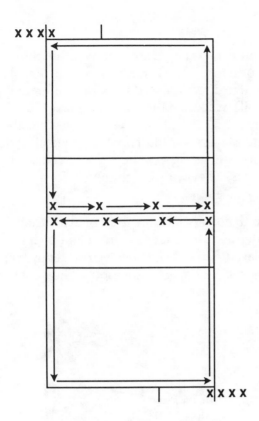

9. Consecutive Overhead Passes

Every player has a ball and overhead passes to him- or herself continuously for 30 seconds, takes a 15-second rest, and repeats the action. The player goes through four trials.

This drill can be adjusted to the number of balls and players. If there aren't enough balls for every player, one player can work while another rests.

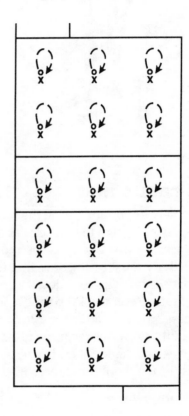

8. Elastic Rope Jumps

Stretch an elastic rope 1 to 3 feet high across the width of a court. Use elastic rope only, as other rope may cause injuries. The height of the rope should vary according to the ability of the students. The players stand all along the rope, facing it. Using a two-footed takeoff and landing, the players jump over the rope, land, turn, and jump back. Action is continuous for 25 repetitions.

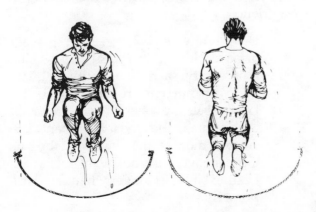

10. Consecutive Forearm Passes

This is the same as the previous drill, except that the player executes forearm passes (see Warm-up 9).

11. Wall Sit

Your players stand with their backs against the wall. They slide down into a sitting position, with knees bent, thighs parallel to the floor, and lower legs perpendicular to the floor. This position should be held for 25 seconds.

CLASS COOL-DOWNS

It is extremely important during the cool-down that the players stretch the muscles as they did when warming up. The muscles most used during activity must be the ones that the cool-down focuses on. The cool-down also lowers the heart rate. Refer to ''Preparing Your Body for Success'' in *Volleyball: Steps to Success* for the flexibility exercises recommended for the head, arms, back, legs, and feet. Here are some additional cool-down activities:

1. Ball Rubdown

One student lies down on his or her stomach. A partner kneels alongside and rolls a ball over the student's body, massaging muscles used during the session's activity. After approximately 2 minutes, the partners trade places.

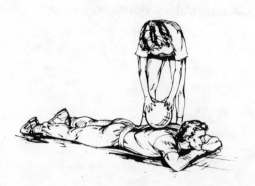

2. Court Walk

Your players begin anywhere within the court boundaries. They walk slowly to any line, change direction, and walk to a different line. While walking, they gently shake out their arms and concentrate on slow, deep breathing. The players should constantly watch where they are going so they don't collide with others. They walk continuously for 1 minute.

3. Leg Shake

Your players sit on the floor with their legs extended straight out in front and their ankles relaxed. They shake their legs by gently bouncing the legs against the floor. They continue for 1 minute.

EQUIPMENT

Equipment needs are determined by the number of players and the space available. Certain types and brands of equipment are better than others when it comes to ease of use, safety, and longevity. The most expensive equipment is not necessarily the best in quality. It is important that you learn as much about equipment as possible before ordering any. The following suggestions are based upon our past experience:

1. Have one volleyball for every player, or be as close to this ideal as possible. If necessary, sacrifice quantity for quality. *Never* purchase rubber volleyballs. Leather balls are softer for play, are easier to the touch, and, most important, are enjoyed more by the players—if the ball hurts, players do not want to use it. Leather balls last longer when cared for properly.

If you have a shortage of volleyballs, use any other available balls that are lighter in weight than volleyballs (but only for teaching the basic skills). Sponge-type balls, beach balls, playground balls, kickballs, and multicolored, discount store playballs all work extremely well. In fact, they are often more effective at the beginning level because they are lighter and larger in size. Two concepts to keep in mind are that

- the more contacts the player has on the ball, the more the learning and the enjoyment; and
- players refrain from any activity that causes pain.

2. It is desirable to have one net for every 12 players. The size of each court is not as important as the number of them. It is better to have two courts reduced in size than only one regulation court.

3. Nets should have a cable at the top and at least a rope through the bottom. They must be set up so that the top of the net is the same height above the floor the entire width of the court.

4. The best net standards, especially when you consider safety factors, are those that have no base and fit into a sleeve placed in the floor. This eliminates the need for guide cables and the base that gets underfoot. One standard per court should be equipped with a crank for raising the net.

5. It is recommended that each player wear knee pads for safety and that each provide his or her own for health reasons.

6. For competitive purposes, an official's stand, net antennae, and scoreboards are also recommended; however, they are not essential. You would often use an official's stand when running drills.

EQUIPMENT PREPARATION

If possible, all nets should be set up before the beginning of class. Although setting up nets is not difficult, it does require a certain amount of expertise to do it correctly as well as effi-

ciently. The standards can be dangerous if not handled correctly, due to their weight and lack of stability. It is recommended that a crew of students be trained in the proper setup and care of nets. This crew will be responsible for setup and takedown each day.

Make sure that all volleyballs are inflated to the correct pressure. The acceptable range of pressure, such as 4 to 6 pounds per square inch (PSI), is usually stamped on the volleyball. For beginning-level players, the inflation level should be kept at the lower end of the range.

Valuable time is often lost by the players' changing clothes and preparing for class. It is highly suggested that volleyballs be made available for skill practice to players who are ready early. Also, it is important that players be supervised even during this time.

SAFETY

When you teach volleyball, there are several things you should consider in order to make the class as safe as possible. If students are instructed in safety from the beginning, their consciousness about safety concerns is heightened. An injury procedure should be set up and all students must be familiar with it. Students must report all accidents and injuries to you. The items numbered 1 through 5 and 7 through 9 in the "General Class Management" section all have important safety implications. In addition, the following safety rules are suggested:

1. You should try to keep all participants in view at all times.

2. When equipment is available for practice at the beginning of class, that practice should be limited to volleyball skills. This rules out the possibility of students' throwing or kicking the ball at each other, and it also enhances skill development.

3. At the conclusion of class, the volleyballs should be picked up and put away until you are ready for the next class.

4. When adjoining courts are used, the players should be restricted from entering an adjoining court to play the ball.

A ball entering an adjoining court should be considered unplayable or dead.

5. No student with any known injury that would prevent normal skill performance should be allowed to participate actively without medical approval.
6. Any time a court area gets wet for any reason, play should stop until the area is dried off.
7. Players should not wear any type of jewelry during class.
8. All players must wear sneakers.
9. Gum should not be allowed.
10. Eyeglasses should be firmly attached; safety glass is recommended for the lenses.
11. Any area outside the court that is dangerous should be called unplayable; the players should not be allowed to enter that area when playing a ball.
12. Standards should be padded, if at all possible.
13. Playing surfaces must be clear of excessive amounts of loose dirt.

PRECLASS CHECKLIST

An inordinate amount of time can be lost to you because of insufficient planning. Accomplishing various tasks before the class arrives allows for more practice time; you must constantly keep this fact in mind.

One of the most important advance considerations for you is how your students will progress from one class activity to the next. For example, how will they shift from a drill requiring two people to work together to a drill requiring three to work together? If thought out in advance, the transition can be made efficiently.

In addition, the following suggestions will help:

1. Be prepared with additional activities to substitute for the planned activity if students are bored with it, if the level of skill required is too difficult, or if it is finished in less time than expected.

2. Keep as many players involved as possible at all times. Idle players can become disruptive.
3. Use all the equipment available as efficiently as possible. A drill with two players working with a ball provides for many more contacts than one with three or more players working with a single ball.
4. Always use the same two signals for starting and stopping activity.
5. Your volleyball facility should be set up and ready before the class enters. Train your net crew in the proper setup and takedown procedures.
6. Post a list of suggested activities for preclass skill practice.
7. You should give as much feedback as possible during class. Positive feedback is much more effective than negative feedback.
8. Always end the class on a positive note so that players will be eager to return for more activity.
9. Don't be afraid to modify the official volleyball rules (as well as drill and exercise rules) by establishing ''class rules.'' Make sure, however, that your students are aware of any difference and its purpose. For example, a class rule is often established that requires the server to announce the score before serving. Often a penalty is assessed against a player who fails to do this. This rule allows the teams to keep reliable track of the score.
10. Learn and use your players' names at all times.

NINE LEGAL DUTIES

As a teacher you are responsible to provide students with a safe learning environment. The following nine duties are appropriate for consideration when teaching a class in volleyball. Adhering to these suggested rules will protect you from being liable.

1. Adequate Supervision

You should make every attempt to be in a gym location from which all your players are visible at all times.

2. Sound Planning

You must make sure that the activities planned for your class are within the level of capability of the students. Expecting students to perform skills above their physical capabilities can be dangerous.

3. Inherent Risks

One of the biggest hazards during a volleyball class is the chance that a stray ball will roll under a jumping student's feet. You must establish a signal recognized by all students that immediately stops activity in case of imminent danger.

4. Safe Environment

Refer to the "Safety" section for items that should be considered to ensure a safe volleyball environment. Also, the surface of the court must be clean, because accumulated dust is slippery.

5. Evaluating Students' Fitness for the Activity

The activities and drills in this book are appropriate for average high school or college students. Many of these activities and drills may also be used at lower levels. At any level you must be aware of the element of fatigue. If drills continue for such a long time that your students begin to show fatigue or soreness, you should stop or change the activity, allowing them to recover. For example, when first learning the forearm pass, students often experience soreness and redness in the forearm area. By interspersing other skill practice with forearm pass practice, these symptoms will be alleviated.

6. Matching or Equating Students

In most of the drills, the students working together can be of varying levels of ability and still have a successful experience. However, three skills—blocking, spiking, and digging—would be executed more efficiently when performed by students of equal ability due to the advanced level of these skills. For example, a highly proficient spiker practicing against a beginning blocker could cause a dangerous situation.

7. Emergency First Aid Procedures

Almost every school or institution has its own procedures to follow in case of an injury or an accident. You should be aware of these procedures and make sure they are followed when a problem arises. You must always be ready to provide adequate first aid until further medical assistance arrives.

8. Other Legal Concerns

In all teaching situations, you must respect the civil rights of your students.

9. General Legal Concerns

There is always a chance that in spite of taking all precautions, an accident may occur. With it, there is the possibility of a lawsuit against you. Keeping accurate and complete records of all accidents and injuries is essential for your legal protection. These records must be kept for a period of 5 years. You should consider having personal liability insurance as further protection against lawsuits.

Step 1   Movement Patterns

One basis for success in any sport is knowing and understanding the proper movement patterns in that activity. Movements and skills in volleyball are generally executed in three body postures: high, medium, and low. Performing a skill in an incorrect posture can be inefficient and, in some cases, can cause injury. Your players need to practice movement patterns in order to make them automatic reactions. They must master the movement patterns to be able to successfully master the skills.

In analyzing a player's performance in relation to movement patterns, the following questions are important:

1. Was the player in the correct body posture—high, medium, or low—when executing the skill?
2. Did the player move correctly to the point where execution was to begin,

that is, by using cross-steps, slide steps, or running steps?
3. Did the player arrive at the execution point soon enough to set the body in position before executing the skill?
4. Did the player quickly return to a ready position after completing the skill?

How a player moves to an execution point is determined by the distance to be covered and the time available. Slide steps are used for a short distance and ample time. Cross-steps are used for a greater distance and less time. Running steps are used when the distance is great and time is very limited. A player also has to decide whether time allows maintaining eye contact with the ball or whether he or she must turn away, move quickly, then regain eye contact with the ball in order to complete the skill.

Movement Pattern Rating

CRITERION	BEGINNING LEVEL	INTERMEDIATE LEVEL	ADVANCED LEVEL
Preparation	• Caught in incorrect position, not thinking in advance about where to locate	• Consistently positions based on formation learned and not on opponent's play	• Reads opponent's play well, positions accordingly

CRITERION	BEGINNING LEVEL	INTERMEDIATE LEVEL	ADVANCED LEVEL
Execution	• Same body posture for most skills, often high position, even if inappropriate • Moves upper body without moving feet first; attempts to move feet but has low level of body control • Reaches execution point same time as ball	• Generally correct body posture for the required skill but often does not set before execution • Usually correct movement method • Reaches execution point prior to ball but without time to set position	• Always correct body posture[a] • Correct movement method • Reaches execution point before ball and usually has time to set position
Follow-Through	• Considers one spot on court as correct position and doesn't adjust • After executing skill, forgets to either cover or get into position for next play	• Tries to remain an integral part of action but often hesitates before reacting. • Remembers to cover team's play but often is caught as spectator and does not react to opponent's play	• Constantly moving on court and reacting • Covers team's play and anticipates opponent's play very well

[a]Correct body posture differs depending upon the skill being performed. For example, correct body posture for a block is high, but for a dig is low.

Error Detection and Correction for Movement Patterns

As you observe your students, you will find many errors typical to their performance. Look for the following errors in particular. If you find one, refer to the corresponding correction for suggestions to give the performer. Remember that it is difficult to concentrate on correcting more than one error at a time; a correction should be mastered before you and the performer work on another.

ERROR	CORRECTION
1. The hands are too close to the body.	1. The hands and arms need to be held parallel to the thighs. The player should have the feeling of reaching for the ball.
2. The player keeps the hands joined.	2. The player must move quickly with the hands apart, then join them just before contacting the ball.
3. The player hits the floor hard following a dig.	3. The player must remember that defensive moves are always made from a low body posture. Tell the player to make the last step before execution a giant, reaching step, which usually puts him or her in a low enough posture, making contact with the floor less forceful.
4. The defensive player stops his or her motion after playing the ball.	4. After contacting the ball, the defensive player must continue to move in the direction of the play.
5. The player arrives at the execution point late.	5. Make sure the player is using the appropriate movement pattern for the distance to be covered in time. When running steps are used, it may be necessary for the player to turn away from the ball, run forward to the execution point, and turn again to play the ball. Players find it easier to do this than to backpedal.

Movement Pattern Drills

1. Mirror Drill

[Corresponds to *Volleyball*, Step 1, Drill 1]

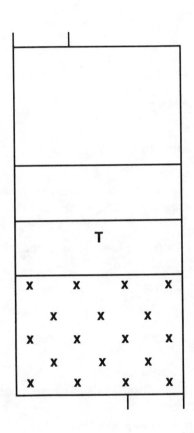

Equipment

- None

Instructions to Class

"I will stand in front of you. You get in the medium body posture. When I move forward, backward, left, or right, you must follow along, mirroring my actions. Maintain the medium body posture throughout the drill."

- "I will rehearse all three body postures and all three movement patterns."
- "Respond to my verbal command with the appropriate body posture and movement pattern. For example, to a command of 'middle blocker low set,' you should respond with high body posture and cross-step movement. To a command of 'back court defensive player,' you should respond with low body posture."

Student Option

- None

Student Keys to Success

- Quick movement
- High, medium, or low posture
- Set and execute

Student Success Goal

- 60 seconds continuous movement combining
    high posture, cross-step
    medium posture, running steps
    low posture, slide step

To Decrease Difficulty

- Emphasize correct movement at a slow pace.
- Change direction infrequently.
- Move for a shorter period of time.

To Increase Difficulty

- Increase the pace of the movement.
- Change direction frequently.
- Change the body posture frequently.
- Move for a longer period of time.

Group Management and Safety Tips

- Make sure all students are facing in the same direction.
- You should face your students and move in the same compass direction. For example, when you move to your left, the students move to their right. Be careful with giving directions verbally. If you were to direct your students to move to their right, and you also move right, some students would follow the spoken directions, while others would mirror your actions. This could cause collisions and injuries.
- Make sure your students have sufficient space between them to allow for freedom of movement; arm's length on all sides is the minimum spacing.

2. Forward and Backward Movement Drill

[Corresponds to *Volleyball*, Step 1, Drill 2]

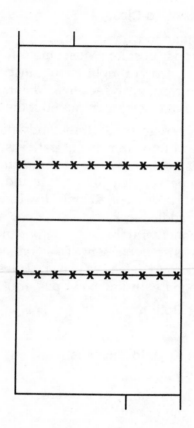

Equipment

- None

Instructions to Class

"Stand in the medium body posture on the attack line, facing the net. Move forward with a step-hop, touch the centerline with your foot, and backpedal to the attack line."

- "Try to move as quickly as possible in a controlled manner."

Student Option

- "Move with either a high or a low body posture."

Student Keys to Success

- Quick movement
- Maintain single body posture throughout movement
- Bend at knees to touch line

Student Success Goal

- 30 seconds continuous movement with the medium body posture

To Decrease Difficulty

- Don't make the player touch the line.
- Continuous movement could last for a shorter period of time.
- Shorten the distance.

To Increase Difficulty

- Have player touch the line with the palm of a hand.
- Lengthen the time.
- Lengthen the distance.

Group Management and Safety Tips

- Make sure your students have sufficient space for freedom of movement.
- Your students should begin with a low or medium body posture when backpedaling so that if a player falls, there is less chance of injury.

3. *Block and Roll Drill*
[Corresponds to *Volleyball*, Step 1, Drill 3]

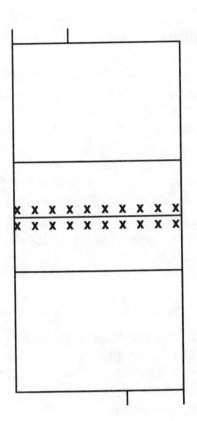

Equipment

- 2 courts
- 2 nets
- 1 ball for every two players

Instructions to Class

"Stand at the net in a high body posture with your elbows bent close to your body and your hands in front of your shoulders. Jump and reach over the net, then quickly withdraw your hands, attempting not to touch the net. Return to the floor in a low body posture, sit and roll onto your back, and quickly return to the starting position."

- "Be careful not to touch the net when you penetrate the net."
- "You must return to your feet as quickly as possible."

Student Option

- "Either roll onto your back and return to your feet, or continue the roll over your shoulder."

Student Keys to Success

- Quick withdrawing of hands after penetrating net
- Buttocks to floor first
- Quick roll and return to feet

Student Success Goal

- 10 consecutive jumps and rolls without touching the net

To Decrease Difficulty

- Lower the net.
- Lower the Success Goal.

To Increase Difficulty

- Lower the height of the ball on the opposite side of the net.
- Raise the Success Goal.

Group Management and Safety Tips

- It is often helpful to have a player standing on the opposite side of the net, holding a ball near the top of the net. The blocker should attempt to penetrate and touch the ball, then quickly withdraw the hands and return to the floor.
- Emphasize that the buttocks contact the floor first before the player rolls onto the back.
- It is best for beginning players to use only one side of the net until gaining body control. All blockers should be on the same side of the net.

4. *Low to Floor Sit Drill*

[Corresponds to *Volleyball*, Step 1, Drill 4]

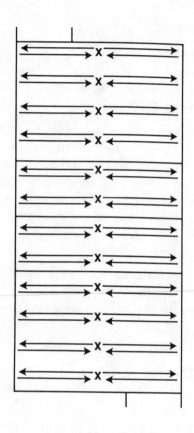

Instructions to Class

"Begin single file at the center of the court, lined up from the net to the end line, facing the net in a low body posture, your hands touching the floor. Maintaining the low posture, slide to the right sideline. At the sideline take a big step to the side, sit on the floor, then stand quickly and return to your starting position. Repeat this movement to the left. Continue this drill, alternating right and left."

- "Reach as far as possible when taking the step to ensure low body posture before touching the floor."
- "Return to your feet as quickly as possible."

Student Options

- "You may choose to move only to the left or only to the right."
- "If you want, continue the rolling motion until returning to your feet."

Student Keys to Success

- Low body posture
- Quick movement
- Large last step
- Buttocks to floor first

Student Success Goal

- 5 floor sits in 30 seconds

To Decrease Difficulty

- Lower the Success Goal.

To Increase Difficulty

- Make the student roll rather than just sit.
- Increase the number of floor sits per 30 seconds.
- Shorten the time allowed for a given number of sits.

Group Management and Safety Tips

- Make sure the players are at least 5 feet apart.
- The players should take a large step, lowering their bodies to the floor before attempting to sit. Trying to sit from a high body posture is dangerous.

Equipment

- 2 courts

Step 2   Forearm Pass

In teaching volleyball, there is always the question as to the order the skills should be taught. Some teachers feel that the best progression is similar to the order that the skills are used in an actual game. Thus, the serve would be the first skill taught.

However, we feel that the forearm pass is the most critical skill for players to learn, so we prefer to teach this skill first. Learning the forearm pass is not easy, because using the forearms to propel a ball is unique to volleyball. Players initially find it difficult to use their forearms as the ball-contact point because using the hands seems more natural and comfortable. It is essential that players learn to receive an opposing serve effectively with their forearms; otherwise, they will never gain the serve for their team.

Forearm Pass Rating

CRITERION	BEGINNING LEVEL	INTERMEDIATE LEVEL	ADVANCED LEVEL
Preparation	• Attempts forearm pass on most serve receptions; occasionally, when not in correct position, attempts overhead pass	• Anticipates where to be for efficient serve reception and moves to that position, often arriving at same time as ball	• Anticipates where to be to receive serve, arrives there ahead of ball, and sets position before playing ball
Execution	• Too much arm swing • Arm swing instead of leg extension to impart force • Feet too far apart; gets low by bending at hips; plays ball too close to body • Misjudges ball, often reaching before moving into correct position	• Contacts ball with poking action • Pass usually setable but not always to the desired target area • Feet shoulder width apart; bends at knees; plays the ball too close to the body and too soon • Eyes focus on ball but switch to target prior to contact	• Contacts ball low and generally directs ball high to target area • Passes to target area perfect most of time • Feet shoulder width apart; waits for ball to drop low; keeps arms parallel to thighs and uses body well to provide force • Eyes concentrate on ball before, during, and after contact

Forearm Pass Rating

CRITERION	BEGINNING LEVEL	INTERMEDIATE LEVEL	ADVANCED LEVEL
Follow-Through	• Hands often come apart • Weight transfer often backward • Arms finish higher than shoulder level	• Hands remain joined • Weight transfer more upward than forward • Platform follows ball to target	• Platform always directed toward target • Weight transfer forward • No follow-through of arms

Error Detection and Correction for the Forearm Pass

Analyzing the forearm pass skills of your players is very important. The following questions should be considered: (a) What is the action of the player's arms, and where is the ball contact point? (b) Is the player in the correct position in relation to the ball when attempting to play it? (c) How does the player provide force to the ball? and (d) Does the player wait for and play the ball from a low position?

ERROR

CORRECTION

1. The arms follow through above shoulder height.	1. Tell the player to allow the ball to drop to a lower position. The arms will then be at an angle that will project the ball forward toward the target.

ERROR

CORRECTION

2. The ball is contacted near the elbows and too close to the body.

2. The player needs to play the ball out in front and slightly to the left of the body to obtain a left to right ball movement, which is used for passing to a setter. The contact point should be closer to the wrists than to the elbows.

3. Player gets into a low position by spreading the feet farther apart and bending at the waist.

3. The feet should be no more than shoulder width apart. Also, bending at the knees puts the arms at an angle that projects the ball high and easy to the target area.

4. Force is imparted to the ball by the arms' swinging.

4. The force of the pass should come from the extension of the knees and the forward, upward action of the body as the weight transfers to the forward foot.

5. The ball is not directed toward the target.

5. The platform made by the arms should provide an even, flat surface.

Forearm Pass Drills

1. *Passing a Held Ball Drill*
[Corresponds to *Volleyball*, Step 2, Drill 1]

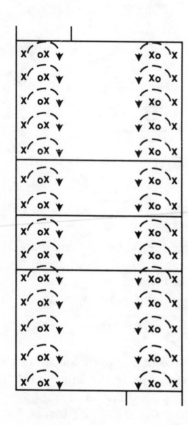

in front of the ball. Using the forearm pass technique, the second partner hits the ball out of the other's hands so that it flies back over the partner's head. The holder then retrieves the ball, and the drill continues.''

- ''Make sure the holder holds the ball lightly so that it is easily hit out of the hands.''
- ''The passer must be close enough to the holder to be able to get under the ball so that it is directed up and forward.''
- ''The passer's transfer of weight must be forward.''

Student Options

- ''You may vary the height of your passes.''
- ''You may be involved in reciprocal teaching; if you are the holder, watch and analyze the passer's movements and offer suggestions for improvement.''

Student Keys to Success

- Poking contact motion
- Ball contact near wrists
- Platform directed to target
- Leg extension
- Weight transfer
- No follow-through

Student Success Goal

- 25 good forearm passes in 30 attempts

To Decrease Difficulty

- Lower the Success Goal.

To Increase Difficulty

- Raise the Success Goal.

Group Management and Safety Tips

- When performing this drill, the holder must hold the ball far enough in front of his or her body that the passer will not hit the ball into his or her face.
- A third person can enhance this drill by receiving the ball behind the passer.

Equipment

- 1 ball for every pair of players

Instructions to Class

''One partner loosely holds the ball at waist level, and the second partner stands directly

2. *Partner Pass Drill*
[Corresponds to *Volleyball*, Step 2, Drill 2]

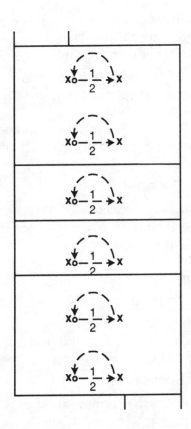

of 10 feet or more, passes the ball back to the tosser. The tosser must be able to catch the pass without taking more than one step in any direction.''

- ''The passing players should all face the same direction.''
- ''The tosser should allow the passer enough preparation time between tosses.''
- ''The toss should be underhand, with little force and a medium trajectory.''
- ''The toss should arrive slightly in front of the passer.''
- ''Passers maintain eye contact with the ball, pass high and easy to target.''

Student Option

- ''The tosser may toss the ball to the side, making the reception and pass more difficult, when the passer begins to show mastery.''

Student Keys to Success

- Reach for ball
- Maintain eye contact with ball
- Easy contact
- Pass high and easy
- Platform directed to target

Student Success Goal

- 20 good forearm passes off of 25 tosses

To Decrease Difficulty

- Have the tosser throw the ball higher.
- Require fewer repetitions.
- Shorten the distance between partners.

To Increase Difficulty

- Have the tosser throw the ball lower and harder, to either side of the passer, or out in front of the passer.

Group Management and Safety Tips

- Players need adequate space to perform this drill. Each pair of partners (a tosser and a passer) should be 5 to 10 feet away from the next pair.
- You should circulate through the class, giving as much feedback as possible.
- Players can be taught to correct the action of their partners.

Equipment

- 1 ball for every pair of players

Instructions to Class

''One partner tosses a ball. The other partner, using the forearms and standing at a distance

3. Continuous Bumping Drill
[Corresponds to *Volleyball*, Step 2, Drill 3]

continuously to yourself. Bump the ball 8 to 10 feet high, using the net as a height guide. Stay within a 10-foot square."

- "The drill is easier if you allow the ball to drop and bounce up before contacting it."
- "Call for the ball before each contact."
- "Bump the ball in a fairly perpendicular manner."

Student Options

- "You may occasionally need to contact the ball with an overhead pass in order to maintain control."
- "You may vary the height of your bumps."

Student Keys to Success

- Let ball drop low
- Weight transfer forward and up
- Platform directed to target

Student Success Goal

- 25 consecutive, nonstop bumps while remaining in the 10-foot square

To Decrease Difficulty

- Have the player let the ball bounce on the floor between contacts.
- Make the playing area larger than a 10-foot square.

To Increase Difficulty

- Make the playing area smaller than a 10-foot square.
- Have the player make a quarter-turn between each contact.
- Have the player touch the floor with a hand between each contact.

Group Management and Safety Tips

- Players need at least 6 feet on all sides.
- If the ball leaves the 10-foot square, the player should stop and begin again.
- You should circulate through the class, giving as much feedback as possible.

Equipment

- 1 ball for every player

Instructions to Class

"To start, gently toss the volleyball underhand. Use forearm passes to bump the ball

4. Passing to Target Drill

[Corresponds to *Volleyball*, Step 2, Drill 4]

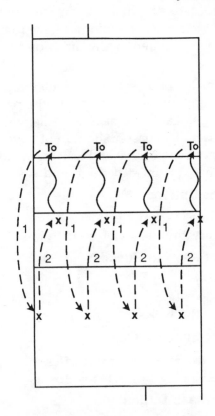

Instructions to Class

"Divide into teams of three. One person in each team tosses the ball over the net to a second person in the backcourt. This receiver keeps the ball moving with a forearm pass to the third person, who is at the net."

- "A two-handed overhead throw by the tosser is usually most effective."
- "The receiver should call for every ball."
- "The person at the net should raise the right hand high as a target for the passer."

Student Options

- "The tosser may throw the ball to the left, to the right, or in front of the receiver."
- "The passer may vary the height of the pass."

Student Keys to Success

- Call for ball
- Use low body posture
- Square shoulders to target
- Impart force with body
- Make eyes follow ball to target

Student Success Goal

- 20 accurate forearm passes off of 25 tosses

To Decrease Difficulty

- Allow high, easy tosses.
- Have the tosser lengthen the time between throws.

To Increase Difficulty

- Require hard, low tosses.
- Have the tosser shorten the time between throws.

Group Management and Safety Tips

- Have no more than five teams (3 persons each) on a court at a time.
- All tossers stand on the same side of the net.

Equipment

- 2 courts
- 2 nets
- 1 ball for every three-person team

5. Pass and Move Drill

[Corresponds to *Volleyball*, Step 2, Drill 5]

Group Management and Safety Tips

- Use the attack lines and the end lines, one partner on each, as a guide in establishing the 20-foot spacing.
- Only two or three teams should work on half of a court at a time.

- If ball availability is a problem, teams of four can successfully work this drill by using two passers simultaneously. The passers must decide which one will move in front of the other when they cross paths.

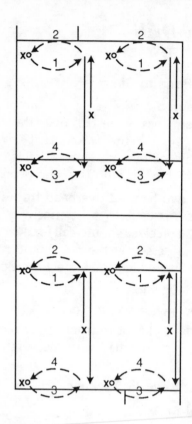

aligned with it tosses the ball. The moving player receives the ball by forearm passing it back at least 2 feet higher than the height of the net. The tosser should not have to move more than one step in any direction to catch the pass.''

- ''The tosser must time the underhand toss to allow the passer to get to the passing spot, but at the same time challenging the passer. The passer should not have time to get into position and wait for the toss.''
- ''The pass must be high and easy.''

Student Options

- ''Vary the types of tosses.''
- ''Vary the height of your passes.''

Student Keys to Success

- Move
- Set position
- Play the ball

Student Success Goal

- 20 accurate forearm passes off of 25 challenging but playable tosses

To Decrease Difficulty

- Have the tosser throw the ball higher and easier.
- Have the tosser wait for the passer to get into position before tossing the ball.

To Increase Difficulty

- Have the tosser throw the ball lower and sooner.
- Increase the distance between the tossers.

Equipment

- 2 balls for every three-person team

Instructions to Class

''Divide into teams of three. Two of the three stand 20 feet apart, one on the attack line, and one on the end line. The third person begins between and facing the other two and moves laterally (from side to side) to the spots directly in front of the other two players. As the player approaches one of the spots, the partner

6. Forearm Pass for Accuracy Drill

[Corresponds to *Volleyball*, Step 2, Drill 6]

Group Management and Safety Tips

- Put only two teams on each court.
- A couple of players could serve as ball retrievers in the target areas.
- Because it requires much space for only a few participants, this drill could run in conjunction with another activity that in-

volves more participants, for instance, the Pass and Move Drill (Drill 5) or the Passing to Target Drill (Drill 4).
- If passer needs additional accuracy feedback, place a physical target such as a bedsheet or laundry cart in the target area.

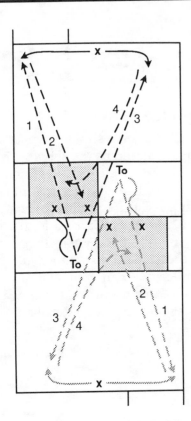

Equipment

- 2 courts
- 2 nets
- Tape for outlining target area, bedsheet or laundry cart
- 1 ball for every student pair

Instructions to Class

"A tosser stands on attack line. A receiver stands near the middle of the backcourt on the other side of the net. The tosser throws the ball to either side of the receiver. The receiver moves to receive and forearm passes the ball to a 10-foot-square target area between the attack line (on the *same* side of the net) and the centerline. (The target area begins 5 feet from the right sideline and extends 10 feet into the center of the court.) The forearm pass should reach a height of 2 feet above the net."

- "This drill is important because it emphasizes passing accuracy."
- "The tosser should face the direction he or she is about to toss the ball, in order to help the receiver judge in what direction to move."
- "The receiver must judge where the tossed ball is going, move to that position, and get set in a ready position before the ball arrives."

Student Options

- "The receiver may work on moving to only one particular side if there is a perceived weakness to that side."
- "The receiver may request that the tosses go to alternate sides or to the same side three or five times in a row."

Student Keys to Success

- Call for ball
- Move to position
- Square to target
- Platform directs ball to target
- Use a high trajectory
- Eyes follow ball to target

Student Success Goal

- 20 on-target forearm passes off of 25 tosses

To Decrease Difficulty

- Enlarge the target area.
- Have the tosser throw the ball closer to the receiver.
- Have the tosser lengthen the time between tosses.

To Increase Difficulty

- Decrease the size of the target.
- Have the tosser throw the ball farther from the receiver.
- Have the tosser shorten the time between tosses.

Step 3   Serve

The first priority of the server is to be consistent, to serve the ball into the opponent's court as often as possible. The server's second priority is to be accurate, to place the serve to a desired location on the opponent's court. Once these serve facets have been mastered, the server can think about serving with more power or putting more action on the ball. Beginning servers often believe that power should be the first priority; when attempting to serve with power, they sacrifice consistency and accuracy. Consistency *must* be the top priority because holding on to service is crucial: no one scores points in volleyball without serving.

UNDERHAND SERVE

The underhand serve should be mastered by all players. It should be the serve with which all players have the greatest consistency. It is valuable not only as a high-percentage play but also as a skill that is utilized in many drills. When the objective of a drill is to work on passing, pass-set-spike combinations, or teamwork, more can be accomplished with the underhand serve than with overhand serves because it is easier to receive, resulting in more attempts at the emphasized skills.

Underhand Serve Rating

CRITERION	BEGINNING LEVEL	INTERMEDIATE LEVEL	ADVANCED LEVEL
Preparation	• Holds ball too high • One shoulder points at the net • Eyes not concentrating either on target or ball • Uses fist	• Holds ball at waist level • Shoulders square to net • Eyes on target • Uses open hand	• Ball at waist level • Shoulders square to net • Eyes on ball • Uses open hand
Execution	• Arm swings up • Weight shifts back • Holding hand moves forward • Contact point above waist	• Arm swings forward but too early • Weight shifts forward • Holding hand moves very little, but ball is tossed • Ball contacted at waist level, hand contact on bottom of ball	• Allows ball to drop before swinging arm • Weight transfer with ball contact • Ball held just before contact, then holding hand drops (Figure 3.1) • Ball contacted just below center back, heel of hand the main contact point

CRITERION	BEGINNING LEVEL	INTERMEDIATE LEVEL	ADVANCED LEVEL
Follow-Through	• Weight on back foot • Follow-through high and to the ceiling • Player watches result	• Weight on front foot • Arm swings to top of net • Player remains in serving area	• Player smoothly moves onto the court • Allows arm swing and weight transfer to carry him or her into ready defensive position • Prepares for next play

Figure 3.1 Ball release for underhand serve.

Error Detection and Correction for the Underhand Serve

Errors in the underhand serve can generally be traced to (a) the hitting hand and arm swing, (b) the holding hand, or (c) weight transfer. As with any skill, it is highly recommended that only one problem area be dealt with at a time.

ERROR  **CORRECTION**

1. The ball is held too high.	1. The ball should be held and contacted at waist level.

ERROR ⊘	CORRECTION
2. Contact with the ball is not solid.	2. The holding hand should not move forward as the hitting hand swings to hit the ball. The heel of the hand must cut into the ball.
3. The server's weight transfers onto the back foot.	3. Arm swing and weight transfer should be smooth, united, and in a forward direction.

OVERHAND FLOATER SERVE

The overhand floater serve is more powerful than the underhand serve and can impart a floating action on the ball, both of which make it very difficult to receive. A floater serve travels in an unpredictable manner because of its reaction to the air currents. The two keys to making a serve float are tossing the ball without spin and hitting the ball with as little hand-ball contact time as possible. Players often learn the concept of why a serve floats before they have the ability to actually execute the technique. Continued practice usually allows them to attain the necessary feel for making a serve float.

Overhand Floater Serve Rating

CRITERION	BEGINNING LEVEL	INTERMEDIATE LEVEL	ADVANCED LEVEL
Preparation	• Toes pointed toward sideline; shoulders not square to net • Eyes not concentrating either on target or on ball	• Shoulders are squared to net as the ball is played • Eyes on target	• Shoulders square to net before ball contact, toes of forward foot point toward intended target • Eyes on ball

CRITERION	BEGINNING LEVEL	INTERMEDIATE LEVEL	ADVANCED LEVEL
Execution	• Ball toss in-consistent, usually behind hitting shoulder and too high • Player takes steps before con-tact and contacts ball with fingers • Extraneous body movements	• Toss too far in front of hitting shoulder but to good height • Contact made with open hand, but arm not fully extended • Forward move-ment limited to weight transfer	• Ball tossed so that contact con-sistently occurs in front of hit-ting shoulder and close to body (Figure 3.2) • Contact made by cutting into ball with heel of open hand, arm at full extension, and hand-ball contact time low • Body movement efficient
Follow-Through	• Arm swings around and across body • Weight transfers from hitting side to nonhitting side • Player stands, watches result	• Little follow-through of arm • Weight transfers onto forward foot • Some movement toward court position	• No follow-through of arm • Weight transfer emphasized in hip area • Player quickly moves onto court, ready for defense

Figure 3.2 Toss for overhand serve.

Error Detection and Correction for the Overhand Floater Serve

A player's success in overhand serving can largely be attributed to the ability to make an accurate and consistent toss. Therefore, it is suggested that players spend a high percentage of the time allotted for this serve in practicing the toss by itself.

ERROR

CORRECTION

ERROR	CORRECTION
1. The ball goes into the net.	1. Have your student toss the ball slightly ahead of the hitting shoulder and directly in front of it.
2. The ball goes out of bounds, over the end line, or over a sideline.	2. Again, have your student toss the ball directly in front of the hitting shoulder. Also, the ball must be contacted just below center back.
3. Player makes too much nonessential body movement.	3. No steps should be taken. There should be only a transfer of weight; this and all other movement should be directed toward the intended target.
4. There is a lack of power on the serve.	4. The toss must be directly in front, and slightly ahead, of the hitting shoulder. The ball must be contacted with the heel of a wide-open hand. Weight transfer takes place at contact.

Serving Drills

1. Ball Toss Drill
[Corresponds to *Volleyball*, Step 3, Drill 1]

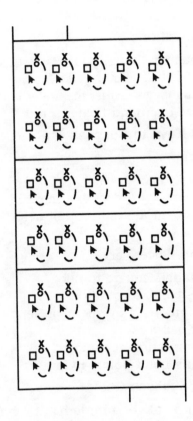

Instructions to Class

"Place a 12-inch-square target on the floor in front, and slightly to the center, of your forward foot. Stand in the overhand floater serving position and hold your hitting arm fully extended. Toss the ball so that it goes higher than your hitting hand and lands on the target."

- "Your success is enhanced when you feel that you have not so much tossed as *placed* the ball in position for the serve."
- "Make your ball-tossing motion as efficient and consistent as possible."
- "Toss the ball without spin."

Student Option

- "You may choose not to use a target."

Student Keys to Success

- Concentrate on ball
- Reach high with arm that places ball
- Place ball consistently

Student Success Goal

- 9 out of 10 accurate tosses

To Decrease Difficulty

- Make the target larger.

To Increase Difficulty

- Make the target smaller.

Group Management and Safety Tip

- Players should practice the ball toss while standing at least one arm's distance away from one another.

Equipment

- 1 ball for every player
- A 12-inch-square target for each player

2. *Wall Serve Drill*
[Corresponds to *Volleyball*, Step 3, Drill 2]

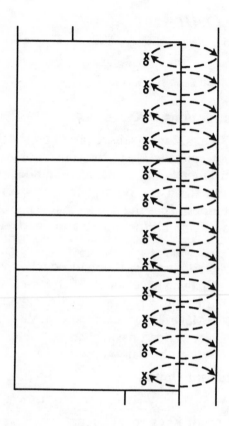

- "Select a target on the wall and attempt to hit that target as often as possible."
- "You should make an effort to gain consistency without being concerned about power."

Student Options

- "You may change your wall target, serving the ball higher or lower."
- "You may use either the underhand serve or the overhand floater serve."

Student Keys to Success

Underhand serve

- Contact ball at waist
- Holding hand does not move
- Follow through to "top of net" (line on wall)

Overhand floater serve

- Shoulders square to net
- Place ball into position
- Continuous movement of serving arm after ball toss
- Poking action at contact
- Hitting hand points to target

Student Success Goals

- 9 out of 10 good underhand serves
- 9 out of 10 good overhand floater serves

To Decrease Difficulty

- Move the student closer to the wall.

To Increase Difficulty

- Assign a specific target above the wall line.
- Move the student farther from the wall.

Group Management and Safety Tips

- Make sure the players are at least 20 feet from the wall and 5 feet apart.
- Players must watch out for other players when retrieving stray balls.
- Tape or mark a line at the proper net height on a wall.

Equipment

- Tape for line on wall
- 1 ball for every player

Instructions to Class

"Stand in a serving position approximately 20 feet away from the wall. Toss and serve the ball into the wall above the line."

3. *Partner Serve at the Net Drill*

[Corresponds to *Volleyball*, Step 3, Drill 3]

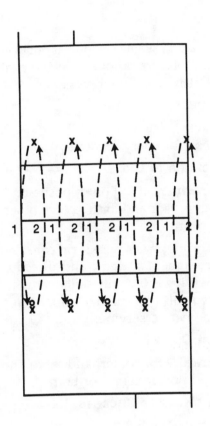

Instructions to Class

"Two partners stand in opposite sides of the court, each 20 feet from the net. One serves the ball over the net to the other. This partner should be able to catch the ball without moving more than one step in any direction."

- "Serving a distance of 40 feet is relatively easy, requiring little force. Therefore, your emphasis should be on consistency in execution."
- "Use your partner as the target."

Student Options

- "You may experiment with either the underhand serve or the overhand floater serve."
- "You may slightly vary the direction of your serves—a little to the right or a little to the left—if such variance is intentional."

Student Keys to Success

Underhand serve

- Accuracy before all else

Overhand floater serve

- Consistent toss
- Consistent movement
- Eliminate excess body movements

Student Success Goals

- 9 out of 10 good underhand serves
- 9 out of 10 good overhand floater serves

To Decrease Difficulty

- Reduce the distance between partners.
- Lower the net.
- Allow the receiver more than one step in any direction.

To Increase Difficulty

- Increase the distance between partners.
- Make the receiver stand without moving to receive the ball.

Group Management and Safety Tips

- Players on the same side of the net should stand at least 5 feet apart.
- Players may serve at their own pace unless a real lack of control in the group is apparent, in which case it is suggested that all players serve simultaneously at your signal.

Equipment

- 2 nets
- 1 ball for every student pair

4. *End Line Serve Drill*
[Corresponds to *Volleyball*, Step 3, Drill 4]

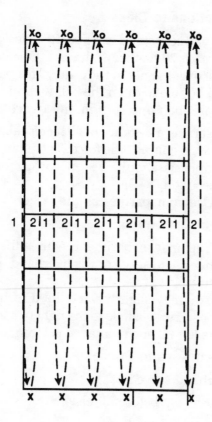

- If the drill seems somewhat out of control, have players on one side serve simultaneously upon your signal.

Equipment

- 2 nets
- 1 ball for every student pair

Instructions to Class

"Two partners stand on opposite end lines. They serve back and forth to each other's side of the court."

- "The emphasis here is on consistency of technique, accuracy, and direction."
- "Serving is the only skill over which you have full control. Therefore, take your time before serving."

Student Option

- "Practice the underhand serve, the overhand floater serve, or both."

Student Keys to Success

- Same as Drill 3

Student Success Goals

- 7 out of 10 accurate underhand serves
- 7 out of 10 accurate overhand floater serves

To Decrease Difficulty

- Reduce the distance between server and receiver.
- Use a lighter ball.

To Increase Difficulty

- Increase the distance.
- Have the receiver change position at the end line, creating a new angle of serve.

Group Management and Safety Tips

- Players can serve from anywhere behind the end lines.
- Players on the same side of the court should be approximately 5 feet apart.
- Players must watch out for balls coming at them from servers other than their own partners.

5. Consistency Drill

[Corresponds to *Volleyball*, Step 3, Drill 5]

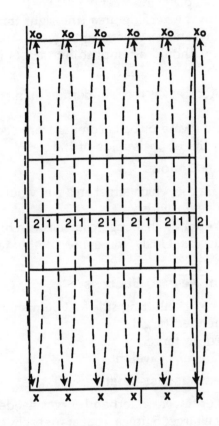

Instructions to Class

''This is the same as the previous drill, but with different Success Goals.''

Student Option

- ''Practice the underhand serve, the overhand floater serve, or both.''

Student Keys to Success

- Same as Drill 3

Student Success Goals

- 25 consecutive good underhand serves
- 25 consecutive good overhand floater serves

To Decrease Difficulty

- Require fewer consecutive serves (lower the Success Goals).

To Increase Difficulty

- Require more consecutive serves.
- Have student serve to one half of the court, divided across either the width or the length.

Group Management and Safety Tip

- Same as Drill 4

Equipment

- 2 nets
- 1 ball for every student pair

6. Serve for Accuracy Drill
[Corresponds to *Volleyball*, Step 3, Drill 6]

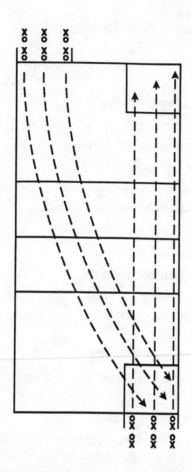

Instructions to Class

"Place a 10-foot-square target in one of the six rotational positions on either side of the court. Stand in the serving area (the right third of the court) and serve, attempting to hit the target. You should attempt to hit targets in all six areas in this drill."

- "Accuracy is more important than power here."
- "Be aware of balls coming from servers on the opposite side of the net."

Student Options

- "Choose which target area you would like to begin with."
- "You may challenge yourself with higher Success Goals for some of the target areas."

Student Keys to Success

- Toe of nonhitting-side foot points toward intended target
- Arm to target
- Transfer of weight

Student Success Goal

- 20 or fewer underhand serves needed to hit a target 5 times; repeat for each target

To Decrease Difficulty

- Enlarge the target.
- Increase the number of attempts allowed for meeting the Success Goal.

To Increase Difficulty

- Reduce the size of the target.
- Reduce the number of attempts allowed for meeting the Success Goal.
- Make the drill competitive: Challenge the servers on one end line to reach the Success Goal before those on the other end line.

Group Management and Safety Tips

- Servers should serve only from the legal serving area. This means that only three servers on each side of the net should serve at a time.
- Targets can be placed on both sides of the net, allowing both sides to serve at the same time.
- It is easier to score this drill if the Success Goal applies to group, rather than individual, effort. Each time a ball hits a target, it counts as a hit. Conceivably, the 5-hit Success Goal could be met at once.

Equipment

- 2 nets
- 2 courts
- 10-foot-square target or tape for marking court
- 1 ball for every player

7. Call and Serve Drill

[Corresponds to *Volleyball*, Step 3, Drill 7]

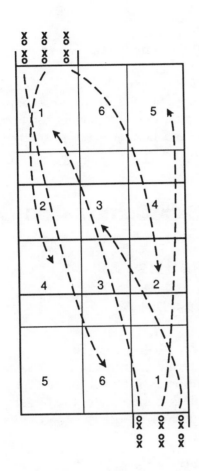

Instructions to Class

"Each side of the volleyball court is divided into six equal areas—three by the end line, three along the net. These areas are numbered counterclockwise, beginning with Area 1 in the right back position. *Short* (net) areas are numbered *2, 3,* and *4,* and *long* areas are *5, 6,* and *1.*

"Indicate to which area you will serve by calling out its number. Serve using either the underhand or overhand floater method. Points are awarded as follows: 3 points for hitting the target called, 2 points if the target is missed but the serve hits an adjacent target at the same distance (both short or both long), and 1 point for a serve to an opposite-distance area."

- "Each player should keep track of his or her own score."

Student Options

- Student can choose into which target area they want to serve first and in what order.
- Student can decide what type of serve to use first.

Student Keys to Success

- Change direction by changing body position, not ball toss or arm swing.
- Short serves as close to top of net as long serves.

Student Success Goals

- 20 points on 10 underhand serves
- 20 points on 10 overhand floater serves

To Decrease Difficulty

- Lower the Success Goals.
- Enlarge each target area, making fewer target areas per court.

To Increase Difficulty

- Decrease the size of each target area.
- Add a time limitation.
- Raise the Success Goals.

Group Management and Safety Tips

- Be sure that all players serve from the service area.
- Have no more than three players serve at one time from each side.
- Remind players that they must be cognizant of errant balls from the servers on the opposite side.
- Players could work in pairs, one partner serving and the other keeping score.

Equipment

- 2 courts
- 2 nets
- 1 ball for every student pair

Step 4 Two-Skill Combination

It is highly recommended that when your students begin to combine the serve and the forearm pass, they should use the underhand serve exclusively. At this point beginners have better control and accuracy with the underhand serve. Thus, time is not wasted due to bad serves.

In the following drills, a player starts in one of a few specific roles. It is your responsibility to make sure that the players rotate so that everyone practices at every position.

Two-Skill Combination Drills

1. *Simulated Serve and Pass Drill*
[Corresponds to *Volleyball*, Step 4, Drill 1]

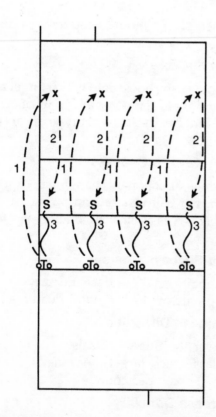

Group Management and Safety Tips

- Have no more than four teams on a court at a time.
- The tosser should throw the ball overhand using two hands.

- If the receiver does not call for the ball before receiving it, his or her pass will not count, even if it is accurate.
- If a pass is inaccurate, the target person should look before chasing the ball.

Equipment

- 2 courts
- 2 nets
- 2 balls for every three-player team

Instructions to Class

''Divide into teams of three players. Each team has two balls. A tosser is on one side of the net at the attack line. The other two players are on the other side of the net. A receiver stands in the backcourt midway between the attack line and the end line. The third player is a target person standing near the net and to the receiver's right.

''The tosser, using a two-handed overhand throw, sends one ball over the net toward the receiver. The receiver calls for the ball and forearm passes it higher than (but not over) the net to the target person, who should not have to move more than one step in any direction. Meanwhile, the target person has already delivered the second ball to the tosser. The tosser immediately tosses the second ball, then receives and tosses the first ball, and so on, making the drill continuous.''

- ''The tosser should allow the receiver sufficient time between tosses.''
- ''The trajectory of the toss should simulate that of a serve.''
- ''The target person should raise the hand closer to the net as a target for the passer.''

Student Options

- ''The tosser may slightly vary the direction, length, and force of the tosses.''
- ''The receiver could request that the tosser send only one particular type of toss if the receiver needs additional work on it.''

Student Keys to Success

- Anticipate well
- Call for ball before it crosses net
- Move, set, execute

Student Success Goal

- 20 accurate forearm passes off of 25 tosses

To Decrease Difficulty

- Have the tosser decrease the force of the toss.
- Have the tosser throw directly at the receiver.
- Have the tosser lengthen the time between tosses.
- Lower the Success Goal.

To Increase Difficulty

- Have the tosser increase the force of the toss.
- Have the tosser send the toss farther away from the receiver.
- Have the tosser shorten the time between tosses.
- Make a more stringent Success Goal.

2. *Serve and Forearm Pass Drill*

[Corresponds to *Volleyball*, Step 4, Drill 2]

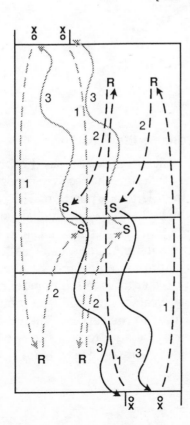

Group Management and Safety Tips

- Have teams of three players on each court. Two teams serve from the service area on one side of the net; the other two teams serve from the opposite side.
- Two receivers and two targets will equally divide the court in half.
- All four servers may serve at the same time.
- Receiver should not attempt to pass a ball that is not served to his or her half of the court.

Equipment

- 2 courts
- 2 nets
- 2 balls for every three-player team

Instructions to Class

''Divide into teams of three players each. Each team uses two balls and the same basic formation as in the previous drill. Now, though, the tosser moves back to the service area and serves the ball with an underhand serve. The receiver calls for the ball and forearm passes it with proper height and accuracy to the target player, who returns it to the server. When switching into the serving position, pay close attention to your service techniques.''

- ''The receiver calls for the ball before it crosses the net.''
- ''The target person should raise the hand closer to the net as a target for the passer.''

Student Options

- ''Choose which side of the court you prefer to work from.''
- ''The receiver may ask for a serve to come to a particular area, in order to work on a perceived weakness.''
- ''The server may increase or decrease the trajectory of the ball.''

Student Keys to Success

- Anticipate well
- Call for ball before it crosses net
- Move, set, execute

Student Success Goals

- 30 good forearm passes off of 50 serves
- 25 out of 30 good underhand serves
- 25 out of 30 good overhand floater serves

To Decrease Difficulty

- Have the server use a high trajectory.
- Have the server serve directly at the receiver.
- Have the server lengthen the time between serves.

To Increase Difficulty

- Have the server use a lower trajectory.
- Have the server serve farther away from the receiver.
- Have the server shorten the time between serves.

3. Serve and Forearm Pass for Accuracy Drill

[Corresponds to *Volleyball*, Step 4, Drills 3 and 4]

Group Management and Safety Tips

- Four teams of three students each can be on a court.
- One server serves to the right side, and another server alongside the first serves to the left side.
- These two servers on the same side of the court alternate serving.
- Servers and receivers should change places after 12 serves.

Equipment

- 2 courts
- 2 nets
- Tape or other material for targets
- 2 balls for every three-player team

Instructions to the Class

''This is basically the same as the previous drill, except that now the receiver is positioned in the right or left back position. The receiver calls for the ball and passes the ball so that it goes higher than the net and falls to the court in a 10-foot-square target area. This target is bounded by the centerline and the attack line, and begins 5 feet from the right sideline. The target person catches the ball after it bounces, then returns it to the server. When it is your turn to serve, be sure to serve to the half of the opposite court where your team's receiver is standing.''

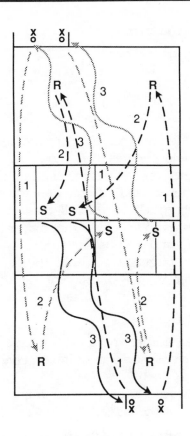

- ''The receiver should call for the ball before it crosses the plane of the net.''
- ''The receiver should not attempt to pass a ball that is not served to the correct half of the court.''
- ''The receiver should not play a ball that seems to be going out of bounds. Instead, the receiver should call 'Out!' ''

Student Options

- ''You may choose which side of the court you want to work from first.''
- ''The passer may ask for a particular serve in order to work on a perceived weakness.''
- ''The server may increase or decrease the trajectory of the ball.''

Student Keys to Success

- Anticipate well
- Call for ball before it crosses net
- Move, set, execute

Student Success Goals

- 10 out of 12 legal underhand serves
- 10 out of 12 legal overhand floater serves
- 12 out of 20 good forearm passes

To Decrease Difficulty

- Have the server use a high trajectory.
- Have the server serve directly at the passer.
- Have the server lengthen the time between serves.

To Increase Difficulty

- Have the server use a lower trajectory.
- Have the server serve farther away from the passer.
- Have the server shorten the time between serves.

4. Calling the Pass Drill
[Corresponds to *Volleyball*, Step 4, Drill 5]

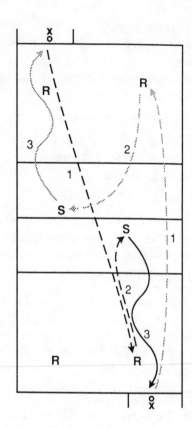

Group Management and Safety Tips

- Have two teams of four players on each court.
- In a large class, this drill should be done in conjunction with another activity to keep more players active.
- With a large class, three servers can be on each team, taking turns serving.

Equipment

- 2 courts
- 2 nets
- 1 ball for every four-player team

Instructions to Class

"Divide into teams of four each. Two receivers in the left back and right back positions; one target person stands in the right third of the court near the net; and the fourth serves from the other side of the net. The server should vary the serves and hit them into each of the three deep positions. One or the other of the receivers should call for each serve and pass it to the target as in Drills 2 and 3."

- "Underhand serves are recommended."
- "One of the receivers should call for the ball before it crosses the plane of the net."
- "When one back (receiver in deep [back] position) calls for the ball, the second back should move behind that player to be in position if help is needed."
- "The target person rolls the ball to the server on the same side of the court, not to the one who just served that ball."

Student Options

- "The server needs to decide which receiver to serve to, trying to serve equitably to them."
- "The server can vary the trajectory and force of the serve."

Student Keys to Success

- Call for ball
- Move, set, execute
- Cover for partner

Student Success Goals

- 10 out of 12 legal underhand serves into each of the three deep positions
- 10 out of 12 legal overhand floater serves into each of the three deep positions
- 60 good forearm passes off of 72 serves

To Decrease Difficulty

- Have the server use a higher trajectory.
- Have the server serve directly at the receiver.
- Have the server lengthen the time between serves.

To Increase Difficulty

- Have the server use the overhand floater serve.
- Have the server use a lower trajectory and more force.
- Have the server serve to the space between the backs (the "seam").
- Have the server shorten the time between serves.

Step 5 Overhead Pass

The overhead pass is one of the most difficult skills for beginners to learn. This is because they seem to fear playing the ball with the fingers of open hands. Due to this fear, beginners seem to be tense when they attempt to play the ball. This tenseness is one of the main causes of injuries to fingers: tense fingers do not give with ball impact. It is recommended to initially use drills in which the ball is allowed to bounce between contacts. Thus, the beginner can play a ball that is not dropping from a great height, does not have time to accelerate, and tends to feel lighter.

Players often find it difficult to impart the necessary force to the ball. This is usually a result of their trying to play the ball in a completely extended position rather than bending the arms and legs and allowing the ball to drop lower. When this bending is done along with the transfer of weight at contact, the weight of the body propels the ball.

Overhead Pass Rating

CRITERION	BEGINNING LEVEL	INTERMEDIATE LEVEL	ADVANCED LEVEL
Preparation	• Fails to get totally behind ball	• Gets body behind ball but often does not set position before contact	• Gets to required position early
	• Does not raise arms and hands, with thumbs back, quickly enough	• Hands in position early and waiting, with thumbs back	• Hands up and ready, with thumbs back
	• Does not allow ball to drop by bending arms and legs	• Arms usually bent, legs sometimes bent	• Body low, allowing ball to drop

Overhead Pass Rating

CRITERION	BEGINNING LEVEL	INTERMEDIATE LEVEL	ADVANCED LEVEL
Execution	• Too much hand on ball, palms often contacting ball • Arms and legs extended prior to contact • Hands behind ball • Weight transfer upward	• Ball contacted with upper two joints of fingers • Arms extend during contact, no extension of legs • Hands wrap around ball, with thumbs back (Figure 5.1) • Weight transfer usually forward	• Hand position is correct; on side of ball with thumbs back • Total body action used and timed to occur during ball contact • Soft touch • Total body action is up and forward
Follow-Through	• No follow-through toward target • No weight transfer toward target • Stands and watches result	• Hands follow through toward target sometimes • Weight transfer toward target usually • Begins movement in direction of pass	• Extension of arms toward target • Weight transfer forward • Quick movement in direction of pass

Figure 5.1 Hands wrapped around ball for overhead pass.

Error Detection and Correction for the Overhead Pass

Errors in the overhead pass are generally due to (a) how the ball contacts the hands, (b) how the body imparts force, or (c) the direction of the weight transfer. Often beginners erroneously attempt to play the ball with too much hand, extend before contact, and transfer the weight in a vertical, rather than forward, direction.

ERROR

CORRECTION

1. The ball remains in contact with the hands too long.

1. The ball must not contact the palms of the hands. Contact should come on the upper two finger joints only. You should not use the terminology "contact the ball with your fingertips," because this leads to incorrect technique. The thumbs should be back, and the hands placed on the sides of the ball rather than directly behind it.

2. The ball travels straight up instead of forward toward the intended target.

2. The player must direct the ball forward by properly transferring the weight, keeping the upper body at a slight incline, and directing the hands and arms toward the target.

3. The player does not send the ball the desired distance.

3. It is extremely important, especially with a weaker player, that the player wait for the ball low, with both arms and legs bent. As the ball is contacted, the arms and legs are extended, transferring the force of the body weight into the ball.

Overhead Pass Drills

1. Pass-Bounce-Pass Drill
[Corresponds to *Volleyball*, Step 5, Drill 1]

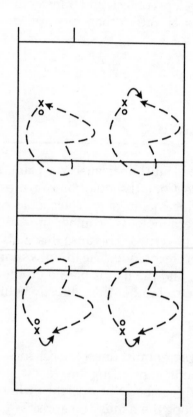

Equipment

- At least 2 courts
- 2 nets
- 1 ball for every player

Instructions to Class

"Overhead pass the ball at least 5 feet into the air, let it drop to the floor, and pass the ball again as it rebounds from the floor. Keep the ball in your half of one side of the court."

- "When you pass the ball upward, try to stay within as confined an area as possible."
- "Work on good hand contact and extension of arms and legs."

Student Options

- "Work on varying heights."
- "Make a quarter-turn after each pass."

Student Keys to Success

- Let ball drop
- Contact with upper two joints of fingers
- Extend arms and legs with contact

Student Success Goal

- 25 consecutive overhead passes

To Decrease Difficulty

- Increase the allowed space.
- Lower the Success Goal.

To Increase Difficulty

- Reduce the allowed space.
- Raise the Success Goal.

Group Management and Safety Tips

- There are only two players per side of the net.
- Players should be aware that when the ball goes out of the assigned area, they should not attempt to continue playing it.
- Due to the fact that only eight players can work on two courts, you should allow a certain amount of time for each trial.

2. *Partner Toss and Pass Drill*
[Corresponds to *Volleyball*, Step 5, Drill 2]

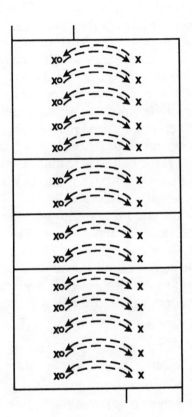

Instructions to Class

"Get a partner. One player tosses the volleyball high and easy toward the other. This partner overhead passes the ball back so the other can catch it without moving more than one step in any direction."

- "Call for the ball before contacting it."
- "Work on setting the ball high and forward."
- "Be as accurate as possible."

Student Option

- "Toss the ball in front of, behind, or to either side of the receiver without being deceptive."

Student Keys to Success

- Let ball drop
- Contact with upper two joints of fingers
- Extend arms and legs with contact

Student Success Goal

- 8 good overhead passes to partner

To Decrease Difficulty

- Allow the receiver to move more than one step to catch the ball.
- Have the tosser lengthen the time between tosses.
- Lower the Success Goal.

To Increase Difficulty

- Have the tosser vary the direction and height of the toss; the lower the toss and the farther away from the passer, the more difficult.
- Have the tosser shorten the time between tosses.

Group Management and Safety Tips

- All players should be tossing and passing in the same direction.
- The tosses must be high and easy; underhand tosses are recommended.

Equipment

- 1 ball for every student pair

3. Free Ball Passing Drill

[Corresponds to *Volleyball*, Step 5, Drill 3]

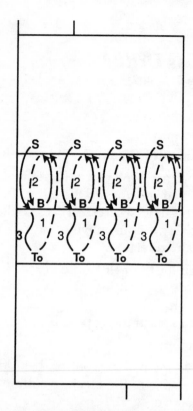

the opponents in a manner other than a spike. Upon hearing 'Free,' the receiver moves off the net to the attack line and the setter moves to the net, remaining on the right of the blocker. Having delayed, the tosser throws the ball over the net high and to the attack line. The receiver passes the ball overhead to the setter. The pass should be 2 or 3 feet higher than the net, and the setter shouldn't have to adjust his or her new net position more than one step to receive the pass. The setter catches the ball and returns it to the tosser. Everyone returns to the starting position for more practice.''

- "Every free ball pass should be perfect.''
- "The overhead pass is the best method of receiving a free ball.''
- "Passes should *never* go over the net.''
- "Deception is not the purpose of this drill.''
- "The tosser should always indicate the direction of the toss by squaring the shoulders in that direction.''

Student Option

- "The tosser may throw the ball in front of, behind, or to either side of the receiver.''

Student Keys to Success

- Square shoulders to direction of pass
- Pass ball high
- Transfer weight in direction of target

Student Success Goal

- 8 good overhead passes off of 10 tosses

To Decrease Difficulty

- Have the tosser toss the ball easily.
- After the free ball signal, the tosser could wait until the receiver is at the attack line before tossing the ball.
- Allow the setter to move more than one step to receive the pass.

To Increase Difficulty

- Have the tosser vary the direction and force of the toss.
- Raise the Success Goal.

Group Management and Safety Tips

- Place no more than four teams of three students each on a court.
- The tosser must be sure to delay between yelling "Free!" and tossing the ball; he or she should not yell and toss simultaneously.
- The passer should square the shoulders to the setter before making the pass.

Equipment

- 2 courts
- 2 nets
- 1 ball for every three-player team

Instructions to Class

"Divide into teams of three players each. One player, a tosser, stands near the attack line. A receiver stands on the other side in a blocking position—close to the net, hands up in front of the shoulders, fingers spread. The third player, a setter, stands at the receiver's attack line to the right of the blocker.''

- "The tosser yells 'Free!' and delays a moment. This simulates a ball returned by

4. *Short Pass, Back Pass, Long Pass Drill*
[Corresponds to *Volleyball*, Step 5, Drill 4]

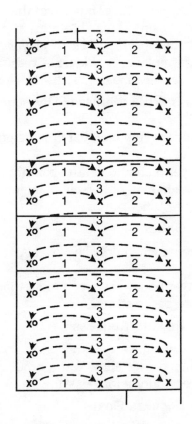

Group Management and Safety Tips

- All teams should be working in the same direction.
- The sidelines are good places for the two outside passers.
- Every player should drill in all three positions.

Equipment

- 1 ball for every three-player team

Instructions to Class

"Divide into teams of three players each. Stand approximately 10 feet apart in a line, two players facing the third, who is facing them. The player facing the other two sends an overhead pass to the middle player, who back sets the ball to the third player, who then long passes the ball back to the starting player. Without catching the ball, the starting player again sends an overhead pass, keeping the drill running continuously."

- "The middle player should arch the back while pushing the back set to the ceiling."
- "Players should not have to back set a distance greater than 10 feet."
- "Arm and leg extension are extremely important in executing the long pass."
- "It is important that each player calls for the ball. A player making a bad pass *must* call for the ball if planning to hit it a second time."
- "A forearm pass may be used to keep the ball going."

Student Options

- "Select your starting position."
- "Use a forearm pass when the ball is too low for you to execute an overhead pass."

Student Keys to Success

- Back pass action same as overhead pass except that the back is arched at contact
- In back pass, ball passed more upward than back
- Leg and arm extension for long pass

Student Success Goal

- 15 consecutive three-pass sequences

To Decrease Difficulty

- Shorten the distance between the three players.
- Have the players increase the height of the passes.
- Lower the Success Goal.

To Increase Difficulty

- Lengthen the distance between the three players.
- Raise the Success Goal.

5. Pass, Move, Pass Drill

[Corresponds to *Volleyball*, Step 5, Drill 5]

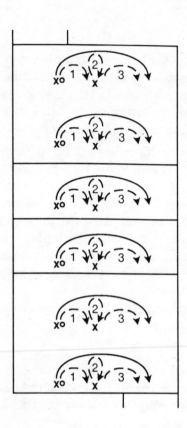

Group Management and Safety Tips

- The partner pairs should be set up parallel to each other and should move in the same direction.
- Allow at least 10 feet between pairs, if possible.

Equipment

- 1 ball for every student pair

Instructions to Class

''Start this drill facing a partner. Player A overhead passes to player B and runs to a position behind player B. Player B receives the pass by overhead passing the ball to him- or herself. Player B then back passes to player A and turns to face player A. Player A receives the pass by overhead passing the ball back to player B, starting the whole sequence over. This drill can continue indefinitely.''

- ''Call for every ball that you are going to receive.''
- ''Player B should set the ball high when setting to him- or herself, allowing player A more time to move.''

Student Options

- ''Choose whether to be player A or player B.''
- ''Player B may set to self more than once before back setting.''

Student Keys to Success

- Pass and move quickly
- Higher passes allow more time
- Set position before passing

Student Success Goal

- 10 consecutive front-back pass sequences

To Decrease Difficulty

- Have the students pass the ball higher, allowing more time for movement.
- Have player B set more than once to self before back setting.
- Lower the Success Goal.

To Increase Difficulty

- Have the students pass the ball lower, allowing less time for movement.
- Have player B not pass to him- or herself before back setting.
- Raise the Success Goal.

6. *Pass Around and Back Drill*
[Corresponds to *Volleyball*, Step 5, Drill 6]

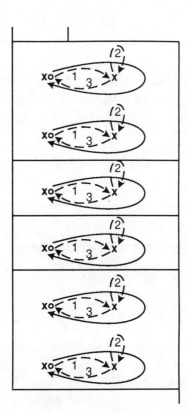

Instructions to Class

"Face a partner as in the previous drill. Player A overhead passes the ball to player B. This time, though, player A runs all the way around player B and back to the starting position. Player B, meanwhile, overhead passes the ball to him- or herself. When player A gets back to the starting position, player B overhead passes back to player A. Keeping the ball moving, player A starts the sequence over."

- "Call for every ball that you are going to receive."
- "Player B should set the ball high when self-setting, allowing player A more time to move."

Student Options

- "Choose whether to be player A or player B."
- "Player B may set to self more than once before setting back to Player A."
- "The moving player may decide whether to circle the stationary player in a clockwise or in a counterclockwise direction."

Student Keys to Success

- Pass and move quickly
- Set position before passing

Student Success Goal

- 10 consecutive pass-and-go sequences

To Decrease Difficulty

- Have the students pass the ball higher, allowing more time for movement.
- Have player B set more than once to self before setting to player A.
- Lower the Success Goal.

To Increase Difficulty

- Have the students pass the ball lower, allowing less time for movement.
- Don't let player B pass to self before setting to player A.
- Raise the Success Goal.

Group Management and Safety Tips

- All partner pairs should be set up parallel to each other and should move in the same direction.
- Allow at least 10 feet between pairs if possible.
- If space is a problem, have all the player A's move in the same direction around the stationary player B's, either clockwise or counterclockwise.
- Because of the running and turning, the players may become dizzy; they should switch positions frequently.

Equipment

- 1 ball for every student pair

Step 6   Set

The set is an overhead pass that places the ball in position for the attack. It is usually performed by a setting specialist, during all the rotations. It is very important that you select as setter a player with excellent overhead passing skills. The set must be one of the most consistent plays in the game.

Setting Rating

CRITERION	BEGINNING LEVEL	INTERMEDIATE LEVEL	ADVANCED LEVEL
Preparation	• Difficulty getting to setting position before ball • Does not square shoulders to target	• Gets to position at the same time as ball • Does not square shoulders to target when off the net	• Gets to target area and waits for ball • Shoulders square to target, right hand held high as target for passer
Execution	• Hands positioned more behind than beside ball; too much palm contact • No arm or leg extension; does not set ball far enough to outside positions • No weight transfer toward target, ball travels straight up	• Contacts ball on lower back with upper two joints of fingers • Extends arms and legs upward but not forward • Set sometimes too high and not forward enough	• Hand position on sides of ball, thumbs back contact with upper two joints of fingers • Extends arms and legs forward toward target • Consistently puts ball high to outside positions

CRITERION	BEGINNING LEVEL	INTERMEDIATE LEVEL	ADVANCED LEVEL
Follow-Through	• Weak arm extension toward target • Weight back instead of transferring forward • Does not follow set for coverage	• Arms extend toward target and away from body • Weight transfer more upward than forward • Follows set for coverage but does not assume a low body posture	• Arms extend and point toward target (Figure 6.1) • Weight transfer forward and upward • Follows set for coverage and is low and ready

Figure 6.1 Arms point to target for set.

Error Detection and Correction for the Set

When the overhead pass is used as a set, it needs to be very accurate in height, distance, and placement. The setter needs to have a feel for the location of the pass in relation to the court boundaries in order to efficiently make the set. It is particularly important that the setter square the shoulders toward the target so that the attacker, the net, and the sideline are all clearly in view. The setter should also be able to observe what is happening on the opponent's side of the net, in order to take advantage of any errors that the opponent makes.

ERROR

1. The ball contacts the palms.

2. The ball travels too much vertically and not directly to the target.

3. The set is not high enough and does not reach the sideline.

CORRECTION

1. The hands must be placed on the ball so that the upper two joints of the fingers are all that actually make contact.

2. The arm extension and the weight transfer must be forward toward the target. The shoulders must be positioned square to the target. The right foot of the setter must be forward.

3. Both the weight transfer and the arm and leg extension must be done in a forward and upward direction.

Setting Drills

1. High Outside Set Drill
[Corresponds to *Volleyball*, Step 6, Drill 1]

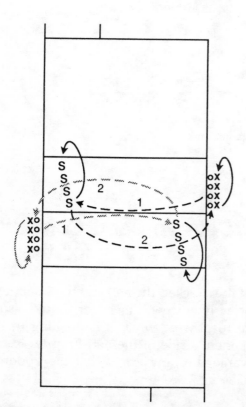

Group Management and Safety Tips

- In order to have more players involved in this drill, you may have a line of four receivers and a line of four setters rotating in a shuttle pattern: After each set or toss, the player goes to the end of their own line.
- Have one line of receivers and one line of setters on each side of the net.
- Working on a court near the net is most important in this drill.

Equipment

- 2 courts
- 2 nets
- 1 ball for every student pair (or pair of lines)

Instructions to Class

"Stand 5 feet in from the right sideline, while your partner stands just outside the left sideline. Your partner tosses you the ball. You must set the ball to a height of at least 6 feet above the top of the net, and it should land within 1 foot of the left sideline.''

- ''The toss to the setter must be underhand, easy, and high.''
- ''The set needs to be at a distance of 1 to 3 feet away from the net and at least 6 feet above the top of the net.''

Student Option

- ''Vary the height of the set.''

Student Keys to Success

- Move to position
- Square to target
- Set forward and upward
- Follow for coverage

Student Success Goal

- 15 good sets off of 20 tosses

To Decrease Difficulty

- Lower the Success Goal.

To Increase Difficulty

- Have the tosser vary the closeness of the toss to the net.
- Increase the distance of the setter away from the target area.
- Raise the Success Goal.

2. *High Back Set Drill*
[Corresponds to *Volleyball*, Step 6, Drill 2]

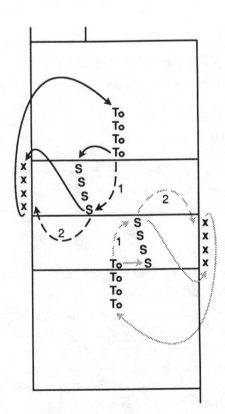

Group Management and Safety Tips

- In order to have more players involved in this drill, you may have three lines: four tossers, four setters, and four receivers. After the tossers toss the ball, they go to the end of the setting line; after the setters set, they go to the end of the receiving line; and after the receivers catch the ball, they take it to the end of the tossing line.
- Have one three-line group on each side of the net.
- The setter's being positioned near the net is important.

Equipment

- 2 courts
- 2 nets
- 1 ball for every three-player team (or three-line group)

Instructions to Class

''Divide into teams of three players each (or into three lines of four players each). The tosser stands at the middle of the attack line, the setter 5 feet in from the right sideline, and the receiver just outside the right sideline.

"The tosser sends a high toss to the setter, who back sets the ball at least 5 feet higher than the top of the net. The back set must land within 1 foot of the right sideline, where the receiver catches it after the bounce."

- "The goal is to make high, accurate sets."

Student Options

- "The setter may vary the height of the set."
- "The tosser may vary the closeness of the toss to the net."

Student Keys to Success

- Move to position
- Square to target
- Set upward while arching back
- Turn to cover

Student Success Goal

- 15 good sets off of 20 tosses

To Decrease Difficulty

- Move the tosser closer to the setter.
- Lower the Success Goal.

To Increase Difficulty

- Have the tosser vary the distance of the toss from the net.
- Have the tosser vary the height of the toss.
- Raise the Success Goal.

3. *Quick Set Drill*
[Corresponds to *Volleyball*, Step 6, Drill 3]

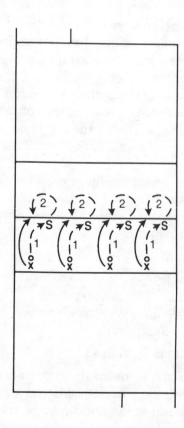

Group Management and Safety Tips

- Place no more than four student pairs on each court.
- Make sure that the attacker approaches as if to spike, extending the hitting hand high as a target for the set.
- The attacker should land on both feet simultaneously.

Equipment

- 2 courts
- 2 nets
- 1 ball for every student pair

Instructions to Class

"With a partner, one of you be an attacker, the other a setter. The attacker begins at the attack line; the setter stands close to the net, holding the hand closer to the net up as a target. The attacker overhead passes the ball to the setter and quickly runs to the net. The attacker jumps just before or as the setter contacts the ball, raising the hitting hand as a target for the set. The setter quick sets the ball 1 foot in front of him- or herself and 1 or 2 feet higher than the top of the net. The attacker catches the ball, lands on both feet, and returns to the attack line. After several attempts, switch places.''

- ''Attacker and setter should communicate with each other throughout the drill.''
- ''The higher the pass to the setter, the more time the attacker has to approach.''
- ''The attacker moves with his or her pass.''
- ''The attacker jumps as or before the ball leaves the setter's hands.''
- ''The setter is responsible for getting the ball directly to the attacker, who has no time to adjust position.''

Student Option

- ''Choose whether to set or attack first.''

Student Keys to Success

- Setter's hand up as pass target
- Setter calls for pass
- Attacker makes quick approach and uses quick shortened arm swing
- Attacker swings hitting arm high as set target

Student Success Goal

- 5 out of 10 sets

To Decrease Difficulty

- The pass to the setter could go higher.
- Lower the Success Goal.

To Increase Difficulty

- The pass to the setter could go lower.
- Raise the Success Goal.

4. Setting a Bad Pass Drill
[Corresponds to *Volleyball*, Step 6, Drill 4]

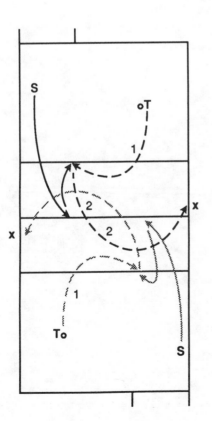

Group Management and Safety Tips

- Place three-player teams on each court.
- Using two balls aids in making the drill continuous.

Equipment

- 2 courts
- 2 nets
- 2 balls for every three-player team

Instructions to Class

''Divide into teams of three players each. A tosser stands in the backcourt, a setter in the right back position, and a target on the left sideline, 1 or 2 feet off the net.

''The tosser calls 'Go!' and tosses the ball high and at least 10 feet away from the net, simulating an inaccurate pass. The setter, having run into the setting position at the net on the 'Go!' signal, reacts to the toss by moving off the net, squares the shoulders to the left side of the court, and sets high outside to the target person. The set should be at least 6 feet higher than the net, and the target should not have to take more than one step to catch it.''

- ''The setter moves quickly to the net.''
- ''The setter must get around the ball and square the shoulders to the target.''
- ''The setter must set the ball at an angle and approximately 2 feet off the net.''

Student Options

- ''The tosser may choose where to toss the ball—toward the right sideline or the left sideline.''
- ''Decide who will start in which role.''

Student Keys to Success

- Establish position before setting ball
- Setter's shoulders square to target
- Set off net

Student Success Goal

- 8 out of 10 high, outside sets caught

To Decrease Difficulty

- The toss could go closer to the setter.
- The toss could go higher to the setter.
- Lower the Success Goal.

To Increase Difficulty

- The toss could go lower to the setter.
- The toss could go farther from the setter.
- Raise the Success Goal.

Step 7 Three-Skill Combination

This combination of three skills—the serve, the pass, and the set—prepares your players for competitive game situations. Players often find it easy to execute an isolated skill but find it difficult to combine skills in ways that are typical of actual game play. It is important that each new skill learned be combined with the previously learned skills as your players climb the staircase to success.

Three-Skill Combination Drills

1. Serve, Forearm Pass, and Set, or Back Set Drill
[Corresponds to *Volleyball*, Step 7, Drills 1 and 2]

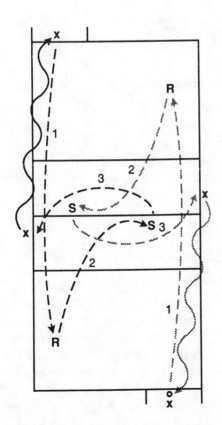

Group Management and Safety Tips

- Place two four-player teams on each court.
- In a larger class, you can work this drill with eight-player teams, two players alternating at each position.
- Both teams may serve simultaneously.

Equipment

- 2 courts
- 2 nets
- 1 ball for every four-player team

Instructions to Class

''Divide into teams of four players each. A receiver stands in the left back position; a setter in the front at the net, at least 5 feet in from the right sideline; a target person just outside either sideline; and a server in the service area on the other side of the net.

''The server sends an underhand serve to the left back. The receiver forearm passes the ball to the setter, who should not have to move more than one step to play the ball. The setter sets the ball high outside, at least 5 to 7 feet higher than the top of the net and landing within a foot of the left or right sideline. The target person lets the ball bounce to check its accuracy, then returns it to the server.''

- ''When running any drill, accuracy is extremely important.''
- ''The servers should use the underhand serve.''
- ''The receiver should call for the ball before it crosses the net.''
- ''The target person should roll the ball back to the server.''

Student Options

- ''The server may vary trajectory or force of the serve.''
- ''The receiver may vary the height of the pass.''
- ''The setter may vary the set's height and distance from the net.''

Student Keys to Success

- Anticipate
- Call for ball before it crosses net
- Move, set, and cover

Student Success Goals

- 12 out of 15 legal serves
- 10 good forearm passes off of 12 serves
- 8 good sets off of 10 passes

To Decrease Difficulty

- Have the server serve higher in trajectory and with less force.
- Make the server lengthen the time between serves.
- Have the server serve directly at the receiver.
- Permit *only* an underhand serve.

To Increase Difficulty

- Have the server serve away from the receiver.
- Have the passer pass away from the setter.
- Raise the Success Goals.

2. *Reception Decision Drill*
[Corresponds to *Volleyball*, Step 7, Drill 3]

Group Management and Safety Tips

- Place two five-player teams on each court.
- In larger classes, you can use ten-player teams, two players alternating at each position.
- Both teams may serve simultaneously.

Equipment

- 2 courts
- 2 nets
- 2 balls for every five-player team

Instructions to Class

''Divide into teams of five players each. Two receivers stand in the back left and back right halves; a setter at the net, at least 5 feet in from the right sideline; a target person just outside the left sideline; and a server in the service area on the other side of the net.

''The server serves underhand, alternating in the general direction of one receiver or the other. The receivers determine who will play the ball and call for it prior to its crossing the net. The receiver forearm passes the ball to the setter, who, as always, shouldn't have to move more than a step. The setter sets the ball high outside, at least 6 feet higher than the net and within 1 foot of the left sideline. The target person returns the ball to the server after letting it bounce.''

- ''The receiver should call for the ball before it crosses the plane of the net.''
- ''When one receiver calls for the ball, the second receiver should cover.''
- ''The setter should attempt to set every ball.''

Student Options

- ''The server may use the overhand floater serve.''
- ''The server may choose which back to serve toward.''
- ''The backs must decide who will play the ball.''
- ''The setter may vary the height of the set.''

Student Keys to Success

- Team decision making critical
- Communication essential
- Accuracy the goal

Student Success Goals

- 6 out of 10 legal serves toward each receiver
- 5 good forearm passes off of 6 good serves
- 8 good sets off of 10 good passes

To Decrease Difficulty

- Have the server serve high and easy.
- Have the server serve directly at a receiver.
- Have the receiver pass high and easy.
- Have the server lengthen the time between serves.

To Increase Difficulty

- Have the receiver pass off the net.
- Have the receiver pass with a lower trajectory.
- Raise the Success Goal.

3. Serve, Pass, and Set Game Drill

[Corresponds to *Volleyball*, Step 7, Drill 4]

Group Management and Safety Tips

- Place two four-player teams on each court.
- When the target person rolls the ball to the server on the opposite side of the net, the ball must stay outside the court's boundary lines.
- The more balls used, the more efficiently this drill will run.

Equipment

- 2 courts
- 2 nets
- 4 balls for each four-player team

Instructions to Class

''Two teams of four players each compete against each other in this drill. Each team has a server on one side of the net and a forearm passer, a setter, and a target person on the opposite side of the net. Both teams start at the same time, but then race to accumulate points. A team scores 1 point each time it completes the combination of a legal serve, a good forearm pass, and a good set. A legal serve crosses the net without touching it and would land within the boundaries of the court. A good pass allows the setter to set without moving more than one step in any direction. A good set goes at least 6 feet higher than the net and lands within 1 foot of the left sideline. The target person catches the ball after it bounces and returns it to the serving teammate.''

- ''The server should make sure the receiver is ready before serving.''

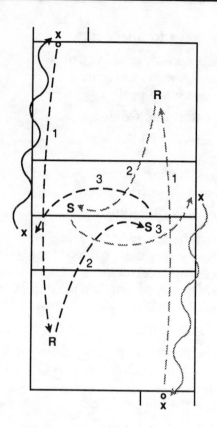

- "The server is encouraged to take his or her time even while attempting to serve as often as possible in order to beat the opponents."
- "The receiver should call for the ball before it crosses the plane of the net."

Student Options

- "The server may direct the serve to any area of the court but should indicate the selected target before serving."
- "The server may choose what type of serve to use."
- "The setter may use a back set instead of a front set."

Student Keys to Success

- Calling early for ball
- Receiver moves toward every serve
- Pass to setter 4 to 5 feet higher than net
- Setter calls for pass to indicate his or her location on the court

Student Success Goal

- 20 points scored before the other team

To Decrease Difficulty

- The server should use only the underhand serve.
- The server should serve directly at the receiver.
- Increase the size of the target area for the pass.
- Increase the size of the target area for the set.
- Lower the Success Goal.

To Increase Difficulty

- Have the server vary the type of serve.
- Do not let the server indicate to the receiver which target area has been selected.
- Raise the Success Goal.

Step 8   Attack

Your students must realize that all three methods of attack—the dink, the off-speed spike, and the hard-driven spike—are important. They must also recognize that varying the attack is the best method to throw off the opponent's defensive timing in a competitive situation. Unfortunately, many players do not consider an off-speed attack or a dink as valuable as a hard-driven spike. However, the best attackers are keenly aware of their opponent's defensive positions and have the ability to take advantage of the defensive weaknesses by using all three attacks.

DINK

When you teach the dink, you need to emphasize that this skill is an offensive maneuver like the hard-driven spike, which has always been the "glamour play" of the game. Players enjoy making the hard-driven spike because they receive more recognition for it than for any other play. Therefore, it is often forgotten that the dink is a valuable offensive weapon. Encourage your players to think of the dink as an offensive play equal in value to the hard-driven spike. When used correctly, the dink can score points; even more importantly, the dink demoralizes opponents.

Dink Rating

CRITERION	BEGINNING LEVEL	INTERMEDIATE LEVEL	ADVANCED LEVEL
Preparation	• Begins approach before set reaches highest point • Does not watch set to highest point • Does not begin at attack line near or outside the sideline	• Weight forward, anticipating approach • Concentrates on ball • Begins approach with setter's action	• Gets wide, with weight forward, anticipating approach • Concentrates on ball throughout • Begins approach when set is at highest point

Dink Rating

CRITERION	BEGINNING LEVEL	INTERMEDIATE LEVEL	ADVANCED LEVEL
Execution	• Use more than four steps to cover distance • Does not use nonhitting hand in arm swing • Contacts ball behind hitting shoulder with bent arm	• Uses fewer steps to cover distance, but last two steps may not be right, close left • Uses both arms to gain height • Contacts ball with palm instead of upper two joints of fingers, but uses full arm extension	• Times approach well, including right, close left for last two steps (Figure 8.1) • Forceful arm swing to gain height • Contacts ball with full extension in front of hitting shoulder, with upper two joints of fingers (Figure 8.2)
Follow-Through	• Hand does not follow ball to target, but stops • Lands off balance on one foot • Knees not bent to cushion landing	• Hand follows ball to target • Lands slightly unbalanced but on both feet • Knees partially bent to cushion landing	• Hand follows ball to target • Lands balanced on both feet • Knees bent to cushion landing

Figure 8.1 Dink approach.

Figure 8.2 Correct position for ball contact.

Error Detection and Correction for the Dink

The best way to describe the dinking action is to say that the dink is like a one-handed set. The dink is directed slightly upward to clear the block in such a way that it drops quickly close behind or to either side of the block. Recently a new dink referred to as the *power dink* has come into vogue. The power dink is hit with more force and is directed more like a spike. For the purpose of this book, though, we are concerned with only the softer dink.

ERROR    **CORRECTION**

ERROR	CORRECTION
1. The ball goes into the net or does not clear the block.	1. The ball must be contacted close to and just in front of the hitting shoulder. The ball must be contacted on its lower back half, with the arm fully extended.
2. The attacker stops the approach and waits for the set or even has to take steps backward to adjust to the set.	2. The attacker must wait until the set has reached the highest point of its trajectory before predicting where the set will go, then make an approach to that point.
3. The attacker contacts the net.	3. The attacker must use a good heel plant to change forward momentum into upward momentum. The set must be 1 to 3 feet off the net.
4. The dink does not fall to the floor quickly enough.	4. The ball must be contacted on its lower back with full arm extension and must be projected just high enough to clear the block.

OFF-SPEED SPIKE

The more weapons an attacker has in his or her arsenal, the more effective he or she can be in varying the attack. The attacker's key to success is to make the approach, the jump, and the arm swing exactly the same no matter which of the three methods of attack he or she plans to execute. Defensive players should not be able to read what attack is going to be used and, therefore, should have great difficulty in covering their court.

Off-Speed Spike Rating

CRITERION	BEGINNING LEVEL	INTERMEDIATE LEVEL	ADVANCED LEVEL
Preparation	• Begins approach before set reaches highest point • Does not watch set to highest point • Does not begin at attack line near or outside the sideline	• Weight forward, anticipating approach • Concentrates on ball • Begins approach with setter's action	• Gets wide, with weight forward, anticipating approach • Concentrates on ball throughout (Figure 8.3) • Begins approach when set is at highest point
Execution	• Uses more than four steps to cover distance • Does not use nonhitting hand in arm swing • Contacts ball behind hitting shoulder • Contacts ball with bent arm	• Fewer steps to cover distance, but last two steps may not be right, close left • Uses both arms to gain height • Contacts ball with open hand at center back, but does not roll fingers over top of ball or snap wrist • Full arm extension	• Times approach well, including right, close left for last two steps • Forceful arm swing to gain height • Contacts ball in front of hitting shoulder, with full arm extension • Cuts into ball with heel of hand and rolls fingers over top of ball by snapping wrist
Follow-Through	• Hand does not follow ball to target, but stops • Lands off balance on one foot • Knees not bent to cushion landing	• Hand follows ball to target • Lands slightly off balance but on both feet • Knees partially bent to cushion landing	• Hand follows ball to target • Lands balanced on both feet • Knees bent to cushion landing

Figure 8.3 Spiker focuses on ball throughout execution.

Error Detection and Correction for the Off-Speed Spike

Most of the errors committed in performing one method of attack are similar to those of the other methods. The most frequent errors have to do with timing. Especially at the beginning level of play, the attacker tends to be overly anxious and begins the approach much too early. We have found that a good way to alleviate this problem is for you, the teacher or coach, to stand at the attack line either telling the player when to begin or holding onto the player's shirt until the appropriate starting time. If the timing problem can be eliminated, most of the other errors will be easier to correct.

ERROR

CORRECTION

1. The ball goes into the net or does not clear the block.

1. The ball must be contacted close to and just in front of the hitting shoulder. The ball must be contacted on its lower back half, with the arm fully extended.

2. The attacker stops the approach and waits for the set or even has to take steps backward to adjust to the set.

2. The attacker must wait until the set has reached the highest point of its trajectory before predicting where it will go, then making an approach to that point.

ERROR 🚫	CORRECTION
3. The attacker contacts the net.	3. The attacker must use a good heel plant to change forward momentum into upward momentum. The set must be 1 to 3 feet off the net.
4. The hit ball does not fall to the floor quickly enough.	4. The ball must be contacted on its lower back by cutting into the ball with the heel of the hand and rolling the fingers over the top of the ball by snapping the wrist.

HARD-DRIVEN SPIKE

The hard-driven spike is the most exciting play in volleyball. Players who spike well usually receive the greatest amount of attention from teammates and fans. Therefore, it is not diffi-cult to stimulate players to practice this skill. In fact, 95 percent of the time, if a volleyball player walks into a gym where a net is set up, the first skill the player will practice is the spike.

Hard-Driven Spike Rating

CRITERION	BEGINNING LEVEL	INTERMEDIATE LEVEL	ADVANCED LEVEL
Preparation	• Begins approach before set reaches highest point • Does not watch set to highest point • Does not begin at attack line near or outside the sideline	• Weight forward, anticipating approach • Concentrates on ball • Begins approach with setter's action	• Gets wide, with weight forward, anticipating approach • Concentrates on ball throughout • Begins approach when set is at highest point

CRITERION	BEGINNING LEVEL	INTERMEDIATE LEVEL	ADVANCED LEVEL
Execution	• Uses more than four steps to cover distance	• Fewer steps to cover distance, but last two steps may not be right, close left	• Times approach well, including right, close left for last two steps
	• Does not use nonhitting hand in arm swing	• Uses both arms to gain height	• Forceful arm swing to gain height (Figure 8.4)
	• Contacts ball behind hitting shoulder	• Contacts ball at center back with heel of an open hand, but no forceful wrist snap	• Contacts ball in front of hitting shoulder, with solid heel contact and strong wrist snap
	• Contacts ball with bent arm	• Full arm extension	• Full arm extension (Figure 8.5)
Follow-Through	• Hand does not follow ball to target, but stops	• Hand follows ball to target, but without forceful follow-through to waist	• Hand follows ball to target with forceful follow-through to waist
	• Lands off balance on one foot	• Lands slightly unbalanced but on both feet	• Lands balanced on both feet
	• Knees not bent to cushion landing	• Knees partially bent to cushion landing	• Knees bent to cushion landing

Figure 8.4 Forceful arm swing needed for height.

Figure 8.5 Full arm extension and solid contact.

Error Detection and Correction for the Hard-Driven Spike

All volleyball players want to spike the ball as hard as possible. In learning to attack, though, a player's first priority should be learning control. An attacker should be able to hit the ball in such a way as to take advantage of an opponent's defensive weaknesses. Many times players feel that the harder the ball is hit, the better the result of the attack; in fact, it is usually the placement of the attack that determines its effectiveness.

ERROR

CORRECTION

ERROR	CORRECTION
1. The ball goes into the net or does not clear the block.	1. The ball must be contacted close to and just in front of the hitting shoulder. The ball must be contacted on its back lower half, with the arm fully extended.
2. The attacker stops the approach and waits for the set or even has to take steps backward to adjust to the set.	2. The attacker must wait until the set has reached the highest point of its trajectory before predicting where it will go, then making an approach to that point.
3. The attacker contacts the net.	3. The attacker must use a good heel plant to change forward momentum into upward momentum. The set must be 1 to 3 feet off the net.
4. The attacker lacks height on the jump.	4. It is extremely important that when the two-footed takeoff is executed, the heels be planted first to convert horizontal momentum into vertical momentum. Swinging both arms forcibly upward also helps.
5. The spike goes out of bounds over the end line.	5. The ball must be contacted in front of the hitting shoulder, with the heel of an open hand at the center back of the ball and with a forcible wrist snap bringing the fingers over the top of the ball.

Attack Drills

1. Dink to Target Drill
[Corresponds to *Volleyball*, Step 8, Drill 1]

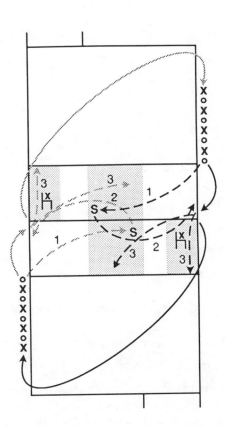

Equipment

- 2 courts
- 2 nets
- Tape for targets, or cloth targets
- 4 chairs or boxes
- 1 ball for every attacker

Instructions to Class

"Divide into teams of three players each. An attacker starts at the attack line, a setter stands at the net, and a blocker stands on a chair on the other side of the net near the sideline. A 5-foot-wide target, stretching from the center-line to the attack line, is on the floor directly behind the blocker. A second target, 10 feet wide and 10 feet in from the sideline, stretches from the centerline to the attack line.

"The attacker tosses the ball to the setter to begin the action. The setter sets the ball high to the sideline of the court. The attacker approaches and dinks over the blocker's hands, which are extended over the top of the net. The attacker should practice dinking onto both targets."

- "The ball should clear the block while remaining as close to the top of the block as possible, falling quickly to the floor."
- "The attacker should attempt 10 dinks to one target before attempting 10 dinks to the other target."
- "The blocker should be active in trying to block each attempt."

Student Options

- "Choose which target to start with."
- "After 10 attempts at each target, choose which target to continue working on."

Student Keys to Success

- Disguise approach
- Arm fully extended
- Direct ball to target
- Land on both feet

Group Management and Safety Tips

- This drill is readily adapted for a large group. Instead of having a single attacker on each team, line up several players with volleyballs at the attack line. After executing a dink, the player retrieves the ball and goes to the end of the attacker line on the other side of the net.
- Remember to rotate the blocker and tosser after every 10 to 15 dinks.
- Use a signal to stop the drill whenever there is danger of a stray ball rolling under a jumper's feet.
- The attacker tosses the ball to the setter to begin the action.

Student Success Goals

- 5 dinks landing in the 5-foot-wide target area off of 10 tosses
- 5 dinks landing in the 10-foot-wide target area off of 10 tosses

To Decrease Difficulty

- Enlarge the targets.
- Do not use a blocker.
- Have the setter stand closer to the attacker.

To Increase Difficulty

- Reduce the size of the targets.
- Use a two-person block.

2. Off-Speed Spike to Center Court Drill

[Corresponds to *Volleyball*, Step 8, Drill 2]

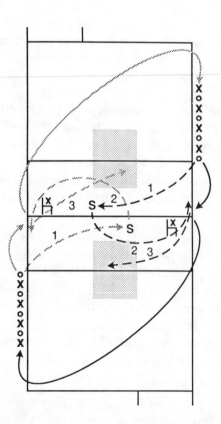

Equipment

- 2 courts
- 2 nets
- Tape for targets, or cloth targets
- 4 chairs or boxes
- 1 ball for every attacker

Instructions to Class

"This drill is about the same as the previous one. Your targets here, though, are both 10-foot squares placed 5 feet from the net; one target is placed 10 feet in from each sideline on both sides of the court. The attacker now hits off-speed spikes over a blocker and onto the targets from both the left and the right sides of the court."

- "The heel of the open hand contacts the ball just below its center back, and the fingers roll over the top of the ball as the wrist snaps."
- "The spike should clear the block and still fall as quickly as possible."
- "The attacker should use the same approach no matter which attack method is used."

Student Option

- "Select which side of the court you want to begin on."

Group Management and Safety Tips

- Set up the same as for a large group in Drill 1.
- Refer to Drill 1, "Group Management and Safety Tips."

Student Keys to Success

- Same approach for every attack method
- Contact ball with heel of hand, rolling fingers over top
- Topspin causes ball to drop sharply

Student Success Goal

- 10 good off-speed spikes off of 15 tosses

To Decrease Difficulty

- Enlarge the targets.
- Do not use a blocker.
- Lower the Success Goal.

To Increase Difficulty

- Reduce the size of the targets.
- Use a two-person block.
- Raise the Success Goal.

3. *Spike Hit Against Wall Drill*

[Corresponds to *Volleyball*, Step 8, Drill 3]

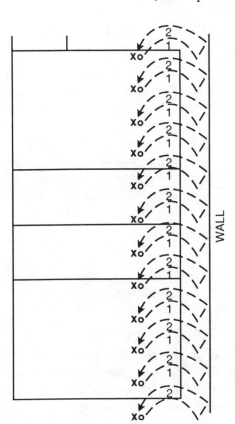

WALL

- A player losing control of the ball should stop and retrieve the ball, being careful not to interrupt another player.
- If less than one ball is available for each attacker, take turns.

Equipment

- As much unobstructed wall space as possible
- 1 ball for every player

Instructions to Class

"Stand with a ball 10 feet away from a wall. Spike the ball forward and into the floor. The ball should bounce sharply off the floor, rebound off the wall, and come back to you on the fly. Continue the action by spiking the ball a second time."

- "The angle you hit the ball into the floor is equal to the angle it bounces off the floor."
- "You must hit the ball forward for it to bounce off the floor and into the wall."
- "The lower you hit the ball into the floor, the lower the return off the wall, and the more difficult it will be to continue consecutive hits."

Student Options

- "Choose which hand to use on each hit; you may want to alternate hands throughout the drill."
- "Move closer to or farther away from the wall if it adds to control."

Group Management and Safety Tips

- Your players should stand approximately 5 feet apart—at a greater distance if there is room.
- Make sure the balls have sufficient air pressure (4 to 6 pounds).
- Make use of all wall area available.

Student Keys to Success

- Wrist snap with arm fully extended
- Hit ball hard into floor
- Follow through by snapping arm to waist
- Position for a rebound

Student Success Goal

- 25 consecutive sharp spike hits

To Decrease Difficulty

- Let the student stand closer to the wall.
- Have the student indicate by a mark on the floor the ideal ball contact spot.
- Lower the Success Goal.

To Increase Difficulty

- Make the student stand farther from the wall.
- Raise the Success Goal.

4. *Spike Hit for Direction Drill*

[Corresponds to *Volleyball*, Step 8, Drill 4]

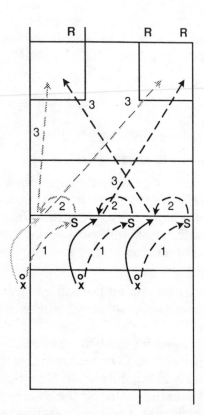

Group Management and Safety Tips

- Put no more than three student pairs on each court.
- All pairs on a court should hit in the same direction.
- A third person could be added to each student pair as a ball retriever.

- Any retriever should remain outside the boundaries of the court so there is less chance of being hit by a spike.
- With a large group, you could have several attackers lined up to take turns working with a single setter.
- You could make a game out of this drill: Each spiker attempts to hit either target 10 times before the other spikers.

Equipment

- 2 courts
- 2 nets
- Material or tape for targets
- 1 ball for every attacker

Instructions to Class

''Get a partner. An attacker stands at the attack line near either sideline. A setter starts near the net. There is a 10-foot-square target area in each back corner of the opponent's court.

''The attacker passes the ball high to the setter, who sets the ball back. Without jumping, the attacker spike hits the ball over the net to either of the two large target areas.''

- ''The spiker should make sure that the shoulders are square to the selected target.''
- ''The spiker should get to the ball before attempting to hit it.''

Student Options

- "The three teams on a court may decide where on the court they will work."
- "The setter may use either a front set or a back set."
- "The spiker may choose which of the corner targets to aim at."

Student Keys to Success

- Shoulders to target
- Get to ball
- Hit at full extension
- Hand snaps over ball to impart topspin

Student Success Goals

- 5 out of 10 spike hits landing in the left back target area
- 5 out of 10 spike hits landing in the right back target area

To Decrease Difficulty

- Enlarge the target areas.
- Lower the Success Goals.

To Increase Difficulty

- Decrease the size of the target areas.
- Raise the Success Goals.

5. *Approach and Throw Drill*
[Corresponds to *Volleyball*, Step 8, Drill 5]

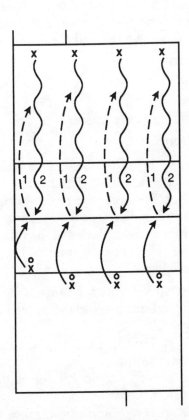

- When returning the ball to the tosser, the retriever must be careful not to roll it under the feet of another tosser. A good way to prevent this from happening is to have the tossing partner step under the net to receive the ball.

Equipment

- 2 courts
- 2 nets
- 1 ball per tosser

Instructions to Class

"Find a partner. One begins with a ball at the attack line; the other stands on the other side of the net. The player with the ball approaches the net carrying the ball, jumps, and throws the ball forcibly over the net, using a two-handed overhead motion with a wrist snap. This thrower tries to hit the front two thirds of the court. The partner retrieves the ball and rolls it back."

- "The retriever could move around as a target for the tosser."
- "The tosser snaps the ball down so that it contacts the floor as close to the net as possible."
- "The tosser must square the shoulders in the direction of the toss."

Group Management and Safety Tips

- All tossers should be throwing from the same side of the net.
- A partner is used for the purpose of retrieving the ball and rolling it back to the tosser.

Student Options

- "Choose which direction to toss the ball."
- "Choose whether to be a tosser or a retriever first."

Student Keys to Success

- Snap the wrists
- Shoulders to target
- Hit floor as close to net as possible

Student Success Goal

- 10 out of 15 good tosses

To Decrease Difficulty

- Enlarge the target to include the full court.
- Lower the Success Goal.

To Increase Difficulty

- Decrease the size of the target.
- Raise the Success Goal.

6. *Bounce and Spike Drill*
[Corresponds to *Volleyball*, Step 8, Drill 6]

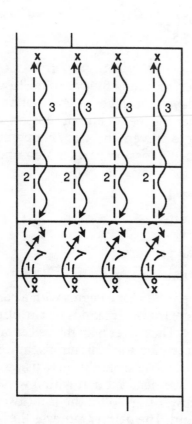

Group Management and Safety Tips

- Make sure the balls have sufficient air pressure (4 to 6 pounds). Any time the ball must be bounced, air pressure is critical.
- All attackers must be on the same side of the net.
- A partner is used as a retriever on the opposite side of the net.

- The retriever must be careful not to roll the ball under the feet of another spiker.
- The spiking partner should step under the net to receive the ball from the retriever.

Equipment

- 2 courts
- 2 nets
- 1 ball for every spiker

Instructions to Class

"Partners set up as in the previous drill. Beginning at the attack line, the attacker bounces the ball forcibly into the floor, jumps, and spikes the rebound over the net. The ball must land within the boundaries of the opponent's court. The retriever rolls the ball back safely to the attacker."

- "The spiker must bounce the ball so that it rebounds straight up rather than forward."
- "The spiker must get to the ball before jumping to hit it."
- "The spiker should hit the ball at full extension."
- "The spiker should not attempt to hit a ball that bounces into the net."

Student Options

- "The spiker may choose in which direction to spike the ball."
- "The spiker may choose whether to hit the ball or not."

Student Keys to Success

- Bounce ball so that it rebounds straight up
- Get to ball before jumping
- Hit ball forcibly and with wrist snap

Student Success Goal

- 10 good spikes off of 15 bounces

To Decrease Difficulty

- Lower the Success Goal.

To Increase Difficulty

- Set up specific targets for the attacker to spike toward.
- Raise the Success Goal.

7. *Spiking From a Set Drill*
[Corresponds to *Volleyball*, Step 8, Drill 7]

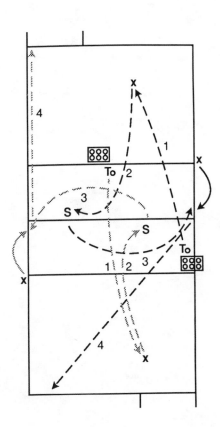

the court. If the attack will be crosscourt, the attacker should stand between the attack line and the net or as close to the right sideline as possible.
- Both attackers should hit either from the right sideline or left sideline simultaneously on their respective courts.

Equipment

- 2 courts
- 2 nets
- 1 ball for every attacker

Instructions to Class

"Divide into teams of four players each. A tosser stands on one side of the net; a passer, a setter, and an attacker set up on the opposite side. The tosser throws the ball hard over the net to the receiver, who is standing in the backcourt. The receiver forearm passes the ball to the setter, who sets the ball high outside to the attacker, who spikes the ball over the net."

- "Accurate passing is essential for success."
- "Each team should communicate the attacker's intended spike direction to the other team on the court."

Student Options

- "Choose the height and the force of the toss."
- "Spike from either the right side or the left side of the net."
- "Decide which type of set to practice."

Group Management and Safety Tips

- Put no more than two teams on each court.
- The tosser should begin with a fairly easy toss; an underhand toss is suggested.
- The tosser needs to be aware of the direction of the attack of the other team on the court. If the attack will be down the line, the tosser should stand in the middle of

Student Keys to Success

- Attacker wide, offcourt
- Attacker waits until set is dropping before beginning approach
- Heel plant
- Powerful arm swing

Student Success Goal

- 8 out of 10 good spikes

To Decrease Difficulty

- The ball could be tossed with less force and higher.
- The ball could be tossed at the receiver.

To Increase Difficulty

- The ball could be tossed with more force and lower.
- The ball could be tossed 3 to 4 feet away from the receiver.

Step 9 Four-Skill Combination

Particularly at the beginning level, your players should make every effort to complete the three-hit attack beginning with the reception of the serve. To do this, they combine the serve, the forearm pass, the set, and the attack.

The three-hit attack frequently breaks down when the attacker cannot execute the spike as the result of a poor performance by the passer, the setter, or his or her own incorrect positioning. The attacking player who is not in an appropriate position to jump and spike should return the ball over the net using a spike hit (an open, overhand contact with the ball, similar to serving). The ball must be returned to the opponents as aggressively as possible. This can be accomplished by hitting the ball forcibly or placing the ball to exploit the opponent's weaknesses.

Four-Skill Combination Drills

1. Serve, Forearm Pass, Set or Back Set and Attack Drill

[Corresponds to *Volleyball*, Step 9, Drills 1 and 2]

Group Management and Safety Tips

- Place teams on each court.
- Make sure that the players rotate to all the drill positions.
- The players should be aware of stray balls on the court that may roll under the feet of the attackers.
- Use a loud verbal signal to warn players of impending danger.

Equipment

- 2 or more courts
- 1 net for each court
- 2 balls for every four-player team

Instructions to Class

"For this drill, you need a team of four players. A server stands in the service area. On the other side of the court, a receiver starts in the left or right back position, a setter in the front of the court at the net, and at least 5 feet in from the right sideline, and an attacker on the attack line on the left or right side of the court.

"The ball is served underhand to the receiver, who accurately forearm passes the ball to the setter. The setter sets the ball at least 5 to 7 feet higher than the net and within 1 foot of the sideline. The attacker hits the ball over the net using any of the three attack methods. This drill should be completed twice, once with the receiver in the right back position and the attacker on the right sideline hitting a back set, and then with the receiver in the left back position and an attacker on the left sideline hitting a front set."

- "Make every effort to receive the serve and complete the three-hit combination."
- "The server should serve the ball directly at the receiver."
- "The receiver should call for every reception prior to the ball's crossing the net."

Student Options

- ''The server may choose what position to serve first.''
- ''The receiver may choose the position on the court where he or she will receive the serve first.''
- ''The attacker may choose the direction of the attack.''

Student Keys to Success

- Receiver calls for ball
- Passes as accurate as possible
- Set high and slightly off net
- Attack approach begins when set has reached highest point

Student Success Goals

- 12 out of 15 legal serves to each back court position.
- 10 accurate forearm passes off of 12 serves in each back court position.

- 8 good sets to each attacker off of 10 passes
- 5 successful attacks off of 8 sets (forward and back)

To Decrease Difficulty

- Have the server serve with a high trajectory.
- Have the server serve with little force.
- Have the server serve directly at the receiver.
- Have the setter use high, outside sets.
- Lower the Success Goal.

To Increase Difficulty

- Have the server use an overhand floater serve.
- Have the server serve away from the receiver.
- Raise the Success Goal.

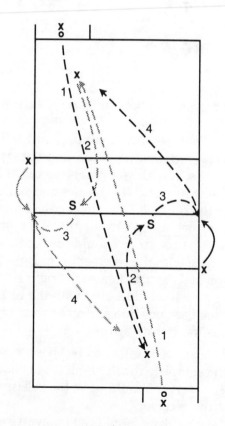

Receiver right back
Attacker right sideline
Back set

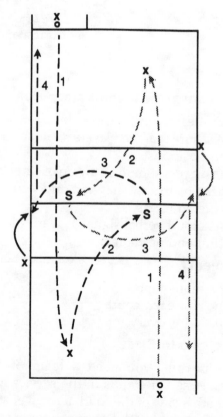

Receiver left back
Attacker left sideline
Front set

2. *Continuous Three-on-Three Drill*

[Corresponds to *Volleyball*, Step 9, Drill 3]

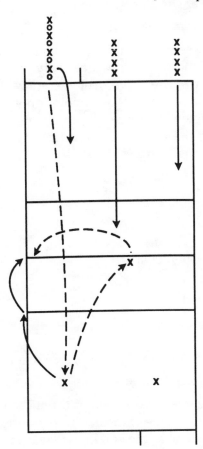

Instructions to Class

"Divide into teams of three players each. One team sets up on the court without a ball. On the end line of the other side of the court, all the other teams line up, one behind the other, each team with a volleyball.

"The first of these teams in line serves the ball and runs out into defensive positions on the court. On receiving the serve, the other team must successfully complete each part of the three-hit combination of pass, set, and attack. If they do, the ball stays in play, although from this time forward it may be returned with less than three hits. Furthermore, at no time may a dink land in front of the attack line, due to the low number of defenders.

"The team winning the rally scores a point, even if they hadn't served. They position themselves on the side opposite the servers. The losing team returns to the end of the serving line. The team now at the head of the line serves immediately, and the game continues. A team's goal is to stay on the court receiving service, winning rallies and points, and being the first team to accumulate [X] points."

- "One player should remain at the net to serve as a setter/blocker. The other two players stay in the backcourt to receive serve, then move in for the attack."
- "All players should call for the ball."
- "The three team members must cover the *entire* court."

Student Options

- "Choose which position to serve at."
- "Decide whether you want to be a setter/blocker or a receiver/attacker."
- "Decide what side of the court you want to play on—left or right."
- "The setter may decide which attacker to set for."
- "The attackers may decide the direction of the attack."

Group Management and Safety Tips

- With a large class, use two courts.
- This game works with as few as five three-player teams. It is best to use two courts with five teams on each to enhance the students' involvement.
- You should serve as an official, telling the teams when to serve and also calling violations.
- Each team should select a person to keep track of the score.
- Encourage the players to use the three-hit combination (forearm pass, set, spike) every time they receive the ball from their opponents, not just on the serve.

Equipment

- 2 courts
- 2 nets
- 1 ball for every three-player team

Student Keys to Success

- Call early for ball
- Pass ball high and easy
- Set ball high because attackers are coming from backcourt
- Cover for each other

Student Success Goal

- Be the first team to reach a certain number of points

To Decrease Difficulty

- Let the server serve only underhand.

- Have the server serve only to the back two thirds of the court.
- Increase the team size to four players.
- Lower the Success Goal.

To Increase Difficulty

- Use teams of only two players each.
- Ask the server to widely vary the placement of the serve over the entire court.
- Have a team receive a point only if they complete the three-hit combination, even after the initial service return.
- Raise the Success Goal.

3. Attack Line Dink Game
[Corresponds to *Volleyball*, Step 9, Drill 4]

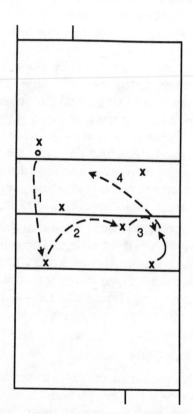

Equipment

- 2 courts
- 2 nets
- 1 ball for every three-player team

Instructions to Class

''Get together two teams of three each, one team on each side of the net. Play a game with the attack line as the end line. Play is initiated with an overhead pass over the net. The receiving team must execute a three-hit combination of pass, set, and dink. The team that wins the rally initiates the next rally with an overhead pass.''

- ''Try to use the three-hit combination at all times.''
- ''Call for the ball before playing it.''
- ''Place the ball to open areas.''
- ''A small court area requires a high level of control.''

Student Options

- ''Choose which side of the court to play on—left or right.''
- ''Choose whether to set or to attack.''
- ''Choose whether to dink or to use the off-speed spike.''

Group Management and Safety Tips

- With a large class, you can set up two games per court, each using half a court.
- When two games are on the same court, the rule must be made that if the ball goes into the adjacent court, it is not playable.

Student Keys to Success

- Call for every ball
- Move to ball
- Set yourself
- Play ball
- Dig ball high
- Place ball to open area

Student Success Goal

- Reach a certain number of points before your opponents

To Decrease Difficulty

- Use four-person teams.
- Lower the Success Goal.

To Increase Difficulty

- Enlarge the court area lengthwise and set up only one game on each court.
- Use two-person teams.
- Raise the Success Goal.

4. One-Third Court Game
[Corresponds to *Volleyball*, Step 9, Drill 5]

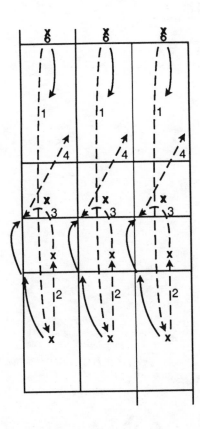

Equipment

- 2 courts
- 2 nets
- 1 ball for every four players
- Tape for the floor

Instructions to Class

"Get together two teams of two players each. Play a regular volleyball game, except that you use only one third of the court's width, along with its regular length. Play is initiated by a serve from the end line. The rally continues until an error is made and the ball is dead. Two points are awarded for each three-hit combination, and 1 point is awarded for winning a rally."

- "Keep track of your score by announcing the score prior to serving."
- "You should call for every ball."
- "Attempt to complete the three-hit combination of pass, set, and attack, especially on serve reception."
- "Placement of the attack is important."

Student Options

- "Play either the front court or the backcourt; otherwise, rotate, experiencing both positions."
- "The attacker selects the method to use."

Group Management and Safety Tips

- It is suggested that tape lines be put on the floor.
- Students should not be allowed to play a ball that goes into an adjacent court.
- Three games can be played on each court.

Student Keys to Success

- Total communication
- Control and placement of attack
- Teamwork
- Read opponent's play

Student Success Goal

- Be the first team to earn a certain number of points

To Decrease Difficulty

- Use three-person teams.
- Have the server use only an underhand serve.
- Play only two games per court, using the two side thirds and allowing the players to move into the middle third to play the ball.
- Lower the Success Goal.

To Increase Difficulty

- Let the server use a variety of serves.
- Raise the Success Goal.

Step 10 Dig

The dig is the volleyball skill that, next to the spike, is the most exciting and appealing to spectators. When the spike goes past the block, it is the responsibility of the backcourt defensive players to dig the ball to keep it in play.

The longer the rallies are between two teams, the more exciting the match. A strong digging team is as exciting for spectators to watch as a strong attacking team.

Dig Rating

CRITERION	BEGINNING LEVEL	INTERMEDIATE LEVEL	ADVANCED LEVEL
Preparation	• Does not get to correct defensive position • Body posture medium to high	• Goes to same defensive position all the time without reading opponent's play • Body posture usually low	• Reads opponent's play and positions self on court in most advantageous area • Body posture always low (Figure 10.1)
Execution	• Reacts only to ball coming directly to him or her • Does not react well to balls directed to either side • Ball contact usually out of control • Too much arm swing	• Reacts well to most balls • Reaches for balls directed away, but fails to step in necessary direction • Usually cushions force of spike but often sends ball over net • Direction of dig is not to center of court	• Steps to every ball • Reads play, gets to position before ball • Cushions force of spike, keeping ball on own side of net • Digs high, toward center of court

Dig Rating

CRITERION	BEGINNING LEVEL	INTERMEDIATE LEVEL	ADVANCED LEVEL
Follow-Through	• Weight transfer back • Arm platform not directed toward target • Arm swing higher than shoulder level	• Weight transfer forward but sometimes upward • Platform usually directed toward target • Arm swing below shoulder level	• Weight transfer forward • Platform directed to target • Little arm swing and quick recovery and preparation for next phase

Figure 10.1 Low body posture for dig.

Error Detection and Correction for the Dig

Digging is a very difficult skill to master. The force of the spike and the limited amount of time that it takes the ball to travel from the spiker's hand to the digger (a half-second) make the dig more of a reaction play than a preparation play. Therefore, when analyzing a player's digging ability, exactness of form is more important to consider than exactness of the result. A dig is considered effective if the digger places the ball with control high and to the general area of the center of the court. Successful digging is more dependent on the player's ability to read the opponent's attack than on the player's overall physical abilities.

ERROR   **CORRECTION**

1. The weight is transferred straight up or away from the target.

1. Have players lean slightly forward from the hips, with their upper bodies in an incline position. Emphasize the teaching cue ''platform to target.'' Make sure that the arms are parallel to the thighs.

2. The dig travels over the net.

2. The receiver must cushion the ball by ''giving'' slightly at reception. The digger can prevent an extreme forward trajectory, especially on low receptions, by ''breaking'' the wrists or the elbows at contact.

3. The ball hits the player's arms and continues out of bounds.

3. When digging a ball to the side of the player's body, the player must drop the shoulder closest to the desired direction of the dig. Thus, the angle of the platform projects the ball back into the playing area.

4. The ball is dug low and into the net.

4. The player must assume the low posture for digging by bending at the knees and keeping the back straight, rather than by bending at the waist. A good practice is to have the player touch the floor beside the feet with both hands when assuming the defensive position.

Digging Drills

1. Pepper Drill
[Corresponds to *Volleyball*, Step 10, Drill 1]

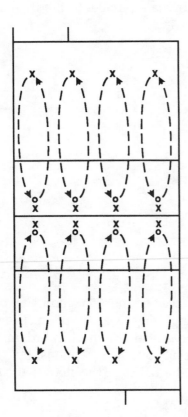

- Generally, beginners lack control with this drill. Therefore, it is extremely important that the players understand the basic safety rules.

Equipment

- 2 courts (optional)
- 2 nets (optional)
- 1 ball for every student pair

Instructions to Class

"Get a partner. Player A tosses the ball to him- or herself and spikes it toward player B. Player B digs the ball back to player A, who sets it to B. B then spikes the ball to A, who digs it back to B. This nonstop action can continue indefinitely."

- "When spiking, the goal is to hit the ball to a spot where there is no defensive player. However, in this drill the objective is to maintain a continuous rally. The spike hits must be directed to the receiver with control."
- "The objective of the digger is to place the ball high and back to the spiker."

Student Options

- "You may decide, rather than spike hitting the ball, to set it back to your partner."
- "If one partner is digging exceptionally well, the other partner may make the drill more challenging by increasing the force of the spike or changing its direction."

Student Keys to Success

- Low body posture
- Platform to target
- Consistency

Student Success Goal

- 5 digs within a nonstop sequence

Group Management and Safety Tips

- All student pairs should be arranged parallel to each other, with approximately 5 to 10 feet between pairs.
- One player can begin with the back to the net, while the other player has the back to the end line.
- Errant balls should not be retrieved before checking neighboring pairs to insure that it is safe to proceed.
- A player should not walk between a pair of players involved in a continuing rally.

To Decrease Difficulty

- Have your student reduce the force of the spike.
- Decrease the distance between the partners.
- Lower the Success Goal.

To Increase Difficulty

- Have your student increase the force of the spike.
- Increase the distance between partners.
- Have your student direct the spike to either side of the digger.
- Raise the Success Goal.

2. Digging From Three Backcourt Defensive Positions

[Corresponds to *Volleyball*, Step 10, Drills 2, 3, and 4]

Group Management and Safety Tips

- This drill is teacher-run. If you are the only teacher in the class, you may need to employ student aides to run additional student groups. These aides should be instructed in the correct methodology of the drill.
- Put no more than two groups per court.
- Preset a required number of trials for the player.
- Divide the class into the number of groups you (and any aides) can manage. Have players ready to rotate onto the court efficiently.
- Use a group of players to serve as ball retrievers, returning them to a container. Use one player to feed balls to the teacher or aide.

Equipment

- 2 courts
- 2 nets
- 4 boxes, chairs, or official's stands
- 4 containers for loose balls

Instructions to Class

''Begin on the left or right sideline approximately 20 feet from the net with your back to the sideline, or begin in the center back position on the end line. The teacher or aide stands on a box, chair, or official's stand in the left forward position on the opposite side of the net. The teacher self-tosses and spikes the ball to you. Dig the ball 2 to 3 feet higher than the top of the net and toward the center of the court.''

- ''Your beginning position should always find your back to the sideline or the end line.''
- ''The main objective of the dig is to place the ball 2 to 3 feet higher than the net and toward the center of the court; thus, the transition between defense and offense is facilitated.''

Student Options

- ''Begin the drill close to the line or 2 to 3 feet outside it.''
- ''Decide whether 'breaking' your wrists or elbows is necessary to increase the height of your dig.''

Student Keys to Success

- Back to boundary line
- Low body posture
- Platform to target
- Cushion

Student Success Goal

- 6 successful digs off of 10 spikes

To Decrease Difficulty

- Have the spiker lengthen the time between spikes.
- Have the spiker decrease the force of the spike.
- Have the spiker hit the ball directly at the digger.
- Lower the Success Goal.

To Increase Difficulty

- Have the spiker shorten the time between spikes.
- Have the spiker increase the force of the spike.
- Have the spiker direct the ball to the left, to the right, or in front of the digger.
- Raise the Success Goal.

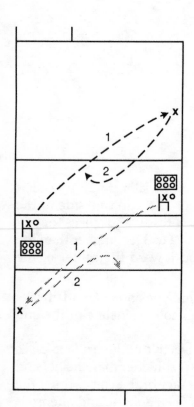

Digging from a left back defensive position

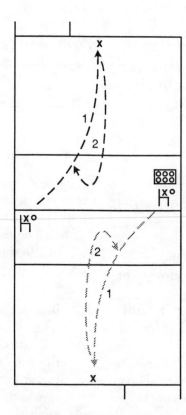

Digging from a middle back defensive position

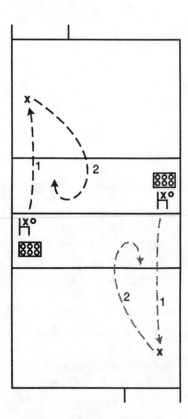

Digging from a right back defensive position

3. Two-Person Digging Drill
[Corresponds to *Volleyball*, Step 10, Drill 5]

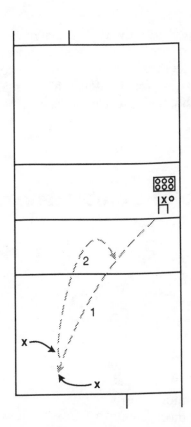

Group Management and Safety Tips

- Defensive players are positioned on the court so that when they move sideways toward a ball spiked between them, one player will be in front and the other player will be in back as they cross.
- Make sure that all players execute the drill at every back position.
- Refer to Drill 2 Safety Tips.

Equipment

- 2 courts
- 2 nets
- 4 boxes, chairs, or official's stands
- 4 containers for loose balls
- 1 ball for every player

Instructions to Class

"With a partner as another defensive player, take starting positions in either of the following combinations: left back and center back, right back and center back, or left forward and left back. A teacher or aide, on the other side of the net as in the previous drill, spikes the ball between the two defensive players. The defender closer to the net always crosses in front of the defender farther from the net as both move to dig the ball."

- "Defensive players should react by both moving toward the ball, then deciding which one should actually dig it."
- "Defensive players should not decide on the appropriate digger before moving to the ball."
- "Defensive players should continue moving after the dig so that their paths cross."

Student Options

- "Decide whether to play the ball, depending upon its predicted destination."
- "Choose in which back position to start the drill."

Student Keys to Success

- Call for ball
- Move through ball

Student Success Goal

- 5 successful digs completed by each digger off of 10 spikes

To Decrease Difficulty

- Have the spiker lengthen the time between spikes.
- Make the spiker decrease the force of the spike.
- Have the spiker hit the ball closer to one player.
- Lower the Success Goal.

To Increase Difficulty

- Have the spiker shorten the time between spikes.
- Let the spiker increase the force of the spike.
- Have the spiker direct some spikes toward the sidelines, in addition to the spikes hit between the defensive players.
- Raise the Success Goal.

Step 11   Five-Skill Combination

The combination of five skills—the serve, the forearm pass, the set, the attack, and the dig—can be best described as a combination of the attack phase of the game for one team and the transitional phase of the game for the other team. Transition is the ability to receive the opponent's attack with a sufficient amount of control to successfully counterattack. Many coaches feel that a team's ability to complete the transition from defense to offense correlates highly with the team's mastery of the opposition.

Five-Skill Combination Drills

1. *Serve, Forearm Pass, Set or Back Set, Attack and Dig Drill*
[Corresponds to *Volleyball*, Step 11, Drills 1 and 2]

Group Management and Safety Tips

- Put two groups on each court.
- Depending upon the skill level and control of the players, it may be necessary to alternate the serve between the two groups.
- Having both groups serving simultaneously permits more contacts by each player; the more contacts, the greater the individual proficiency.
- Another idea for setting up this drill is to have only one drill running on each court. Have four or five players in lines, taking turns performing the skill.
- If two groups are working simultaneously on the same court, the forearm passer of one group must be instructed to watch out for the spike coming from the attacker of the other group.
- At least one player should be used to retrieve the dug ball, returning it to the serving area.
- When two groups are on the same court, they must coordinate the direction of the serve and attack.

Equipment

- 2 or more courts
- 2 or more nets
- 3 balls for every five-player team

Instructions to Class

"In a group of five, have a server and a digger on one court and a passer, a setter, and an attacker on the opposite court. The server underhand serves the ball to the passer, who is in the left or right back position of the other court. The passer forearm passes the ball to the setter, who shouldn't have to move more than a step. The setter sets high (at least 5 to 7 feet higher than the net) and outside to the attacker, who starts positioned on the attack line at the left or right sideline. The attacker spikes the ball over the net to the left or right back area of the opponent's court. The digger plays the ball so that it is 2 to 3 feet higher than the top of the net and to the center of his or her own court."

- "This drill should be performed with as much control as possible."
- "Use the underhand serve."
- "The attacker must attack crosscourt."

Student Options

- "Work on all three types of attacks—the dink, the off-speed spike, and the hard-driven spike."
- "The receiver may choose not to play a ball if it is judged to be going out of bounds."

Student Keys to Success

- Call for ball
- Pass with control
- Accurate set
- Variety of attacks

Student Success Goals

- 12 out of 15 legal serves
- 10 good forearm passes off of 12 serves
- 8 good sets off of 10 passes
- 6 legal spikes off of 8 sets
- 4 good digs off of 6 spikes

To Decrease Difficulty

- Have the server lengthen the time between serves.
- Have the server decrease the force of the serve.
- Have the server heighten the trajectory of the serve.
- Lower the Success Goals.

To Increase Difficulty

- Have the server shorten the time between serves.
- Let the server use an overhand floater serve.
- Have the server increase the force of the serve.
- Do not let the server serve directly at the receiver.
- Raise the Success Goals.

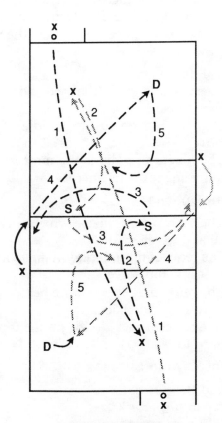

Receiver right back
Attacker left forward
Digger left back

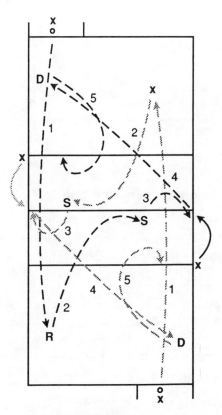

Receiver left back
Attacker right forward
Digger right back

2. One Setter Three-on-Three Drill

[Corresponds to *Volleyball*, Step 11, Drill 3]

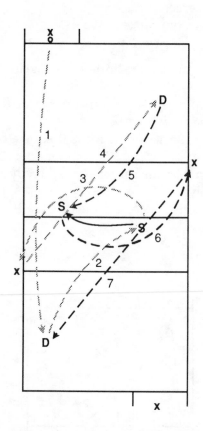

Instructions to Class

"For this drill, you need three players on each side of the court—a server, a digger, and an attacker. A seventh player acts as a setter, alternating sides of the net, depending upon the location of the ball.

"The game is initiated with a serve, and the ball is rallied generally according to regular game rules. The setter, though, always assumes a position right of center front on the side of the court where the ball is being played, changing sides of the court as the ball goes over the net. The setter sets the hitters at the attack line to increase the other side's digging opportunities. The team winning a rally scores a point. The team losing the rally makes the next serve."

- "Call for every ball."
- "Every attack over the net should be aggressive."
- "Digs should go to the middle of the court."
- "The height of a dig is the most important element for its success."

Student Options

- "The server may choose which serve to use and its direction."
- "The receiver must decide where to move to receive the serve."
- "The setter may choose whether to set to the front or the back."
- "The attacker may decide on the type of attack to use."

Student Keys to Success

- Read the position
- Prepare for attack
- Call for serve reception
- Vary the attack

Group Management and Safety Tips

- Put only one group on each court.
- With a large class, have extra groups waiting at an end line. As soon as a rally is completed, a new group quickly moves onto the court.
- Sets off the net allow for easier digging and, thus, longer rallies.
- In beginning classes, using two setters increases individual involvement.

Equipment

- 2 courts
- 2 nets
- 1 ball for every seven-player group

Student Success Goal

- Be the first team to reach a certain number of points

To Decrease Difficulty

- Allow only underhand serves.
- Use two setters instead of one.
- Play with two teams of four or five players each, the added players being attackers.

- No dinks may land in front of the attack line.
- Lower the Success Goal.

To Increase Difficulty

- Decrease the number of players per side.
- Allow a variety of serves.
- Allow attacks any distance from the net.
- Raise the Success Goal.

3. Diggers and Receivers Drill

[Corresponds to *Volleyball*, Step 11, Drill 4]

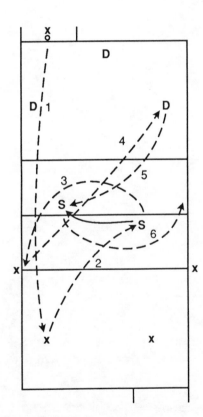

Equipment

- 2 courts
- 2 nets
- 1 ball for every five-person team

Instructions to Class

"For this drill you need two teams of five players each on opposite sides of the net. Team A has a server, three diggers, and a setter. Team B has two serve receivers, two attackers, and a setter.

"Team A serves; team B receives, setting up an attack with the set being made to the attack line. Team A digs the ball and sets at least 7 feet higher than the top of the net so that the ball lands on or within 1 foot of the left sideline (there's no further attack).

"Team A serves 5 times, and then the two teams reverse roles. The receiving team gets 1 point for a successful attack, and the digging team gets 1 point for a succesful dig and set."

- "Call for every ball."
- "All attacks should be aggressive."
- "The first priority for good digs is height, then direction."
- "Direct your digs to the center of the court."

Student Options

- "The server may choose which type of serve to use."
- "The attacker may decide on the type of attack to use and its direction."

Group Management and Safety Tips

- Two teams play together on each court.
- With a large class, have extra teams on the end lines, ready for quick changes after a given number of points (2 to 5).
- You should serve as an official for deciding points where controversy exists.
- The server should announce the score prior to serving.

- "Decide which team will begin as the diggers and which team as the attackers."

Student Keys to Success

- Read opponent's attack
- Read opponent's defense
- Call every ball
- Aggressively send ball to opponents

Student Success Goal

- Be the first team to reach a certain number of points

To Decrease Difficulty

- Let the server use only the underhand serve.
- Enlarge the target area for the set.
- Do not allow dinks in front of the attack line.
- Lower the Success Goal.

To Increase Difficulty

- Allow a variety of serves.
- Allow attacks from any distance from the net.
- Raise the Success Goal.

Step 12 **Spike**

Once the basic skills of the attack have been learned, it is necessary to distinguish between an on-hand and an off-hand attack. The basic elements of the attack—timing, heel plant, arm swing, ball contact, and so on—are the same regardless of the position of the attacker on the court. There is a difference, however, in the setter's position in relation to the attacker and the handedness of that attacker. These differences pertain to all three methods of attack—the dink, the off-speed spike, and the hard-driven spike—but are most important in the execution of the hard-driven spike.

A spiker hits on-hand when the approaching set is on the same side of the spiker's body as his or her dominant hand. A spiker hits off-hand when the approaching set is on the side of the body opposite the dominant hand. In general, a spiker finds it easier to spike on-hand and is also capable of a more powerful attack with this position. This concept is very important in your lineup considerations. A team presents the strongest attacking posture when fielding right-handed players in the left forward and center forward positions, and a left-handed player in the right forward position.

The most important aspect of spike execution is the location of the ball in relation to the spiker's hitting hand and body. When hitting an on-hand crosscourt spike, the player contacts in front of the hitting shoulder. When going down the line, though, the spiker contacts the ball at the midline of the body. The location of the ball during the execution of the off-hand spike is just the opposite, at the midline of the body for crosscourt spikes and in front of the shoulder for down-the-line spikes.

In detecting your students' errors, your only concern, besides the ones already reviewed for the three methods of attack, is the location of the ball at contact in relation to the attacker's body. Players cannot control the direction of their attack unless they pay particular attention to this concept.

During a class or a practice situation, you must be aware of the amounts of time your students spend hitting on-hand and hitting off-hand. You must realize that when both right-handers and left-handers are working a drill, some players will be hitting on-hand, while others hit off-hand. Because most players are predominantly right-handed, teachers often spend more time practicing the attack from the left forward position. This causes two problems: (a) the left-handers practice longer hitting off-hand, and (b) the right-handers do not have enough practice hitting off-hand. It is your responsibility as teacher to make sure that players have equal time practicing both on-hand and off-hand. All drills presented previously for practicing the attack are appropriate for developing both on-hand and off-hand proficiency.

1. Spiking From a Set or Back Set Drill

[Corresponds to *Volleyball*, Step 12, Drills 1 and 2]

Group Management and Safety Tips

- Place no more than two four-player teams on each court.
- Have the tosser begin by using a fairly easy toss; an underhand toss is suggested.
- The tosser needs to be aware of the direction of the other team's attack. If their attack will be down the line, the tosser should stand in the middle of the court. If their attack will be crosscourt, the attacker should stand between the attack line and the net, or as close to the right or left sideline as possible.
- The attackers on both teams should hit simultaneously from the same position on the court (left or right).

Equipment

- 2 courts
- 2 nets
- Tape for targets
- 1 ball for every player

Instructions to Class

''Get together in a team of four: a tosser on one side of the net and a receiver, a setter, and an attacker on the opposite side. Set up a 2-foot-wide target parallel to the right or left sideline.

''The tosser throws the ball hard over the net to the receiver, who is standing in the backcourt. The receiver passes the ball to the setter at the net right of center front, who sets the ball high outside to the attacker waiting at the attack line. The attacker should try spiking the ball over the net both down the line and crosscourt into the back one-third corner of the opponent's side.''

- ''Accurate passing is essential for success.''
- ''The two groups should communicate to each other their attackers' intended spike directions.''

Student Options

- ''Choose the height and force of the toss.''
- ''The attacker may decide whether to spike from the right side or the left side of the net.''
- ''The setter may decide what type of set to practice.''

Student Keys to Success

- Attacker wide offcourt in preparation for approach
- Attacker waits until set drops before beginning approach
- Heel plant
- Powerful arm swing

Student Success Goals

- 4 out of 5 accurate down-the-line spikes
- 4 out of 5 accurate crosscourt spikes

To Decrease Difficulty

- Have the tosser throw the ball with less force and more height.
- Have the tosser throw the ball directly at the receiver.
- Lower the Success Goals.

To Increase Difficulty

- Have the tosser throw the ball with more force and a lower trajectory.
- Have the tosser throw the ball 3 to 4 feet away from the receiver.
- Raise the Success Goals.

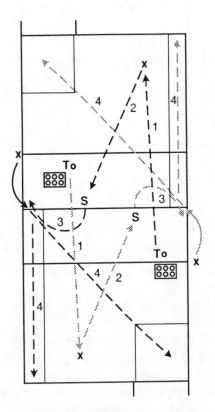

**Receiver right back
Attacker left forward**

**Receiver left back
Attacker right forward**

2. Spike Hit for Direction Drill
[Corresponds to *Volleyball*, Step 12, Drill 3]

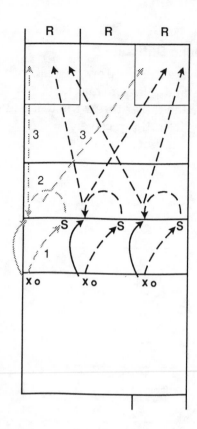

Group Management and Safety Tips

- Put no more than three pairs on each court.
- All spikers should hit in the same direction.
- A third person could be added to each pair as a retriever, getting the spiked ball and returning it to the attacker.
- Retrievers should remain outside the boundaries of the court to reduce the chance of being hit by a spike from another pair. With a large class, have lines of attackers working with a single setter. Each player spikes and returns to the end of the line.
- A game could be made from this drill: Each spiker attempts to get 10 target hits before another spiker.

Equipment

- 2 courts
- 2 nets
- 4 cloth targets
- 1 ball for every student

Instructions to Class

"Get a partner. One of you starts as a setter at the net, the other as a spiker at the attack line 8 feet to the left of the setter. Place two 10-foot target squares in the back corners of the opponent's court.

"The attacker passes the ball high to the setter. The setter sets the ball back to the spiker. Without jumping, the spiker spikes the ball over the net to either of the two large target areas."

- "The spiker should make sure that the shoulders are square to the selected target."
- "The spikers should get to the ball before attempting to hit it."

Student Options

- "The three pairs may decide where on the court to work."
- "The setter may choose whether to use a front set or a back set."
- "The spiker may choose which of the corner targets to aim at."

Student Keys to Success

- Shoulders to target
- Get to ball
- Hit at full extension
- Hand snaps over ball to impart topspin

Student Success Goals

- 5 out of 10 spike hits landing in the left back target area
- 5 out of 10 spike hits landing in the right back target area

To Decrease Difficulty

- Enlarge the target areas.
- Lower the Success Goals.

To Increase Difficulty

- Reduce the target areas.
- Raise the Success Goals.

3. Pressure Spiking Drill
[Corresponds to *Volleyball*, Step 12, Drill 4]

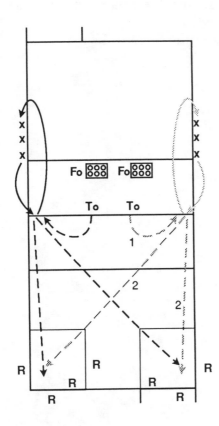

Group Management and Safety Tips

- Two groups can work on each court, one on each sideline on the *same* side of the court.
- The more volleyballs available, the better the drill will run.
- The spikers must always circle in a forward direction to prevent collisions.
- Having feeders for the tosser speeds up the drill, putting greater pressure on the spikers.
- Extra players are used as retrievers.
- Retrievers must be careful not to roll the balls under the feet of the attackers.
- Establish a signal for stopping the drill when a stray ball rolls into a position that could be dangerous.

Equipment

- 2 courts
- 2 nets
- 4 cloth targets
- As many balls as possible (30 per group would be ideal)

Instructions to Class

"Three spikers line up one behind the other at the attack line on the left or right sideline. A tosser stands at the net, and additional players are needed as ball retrievers and feeders for the tosser.

"The tosser continuously tosses balls high to the sideline. The first spiker approaches, spikes, and returns to the end of the line by circling forward within the court. The second spiker immediately follows and spikes, followed by the third spiker. The retrievers and feeders must get the balls back to the tosser as quickly as possible. Action is continuous, with the time between tosses as minimal as possible until 30 tosses have been made.

"This drill can be executed by using either a down-the-line spike or a crosscourt spike to a 10-foot-square target in the opposite corner of the court. The spikers should practice approaching from both sidelines."

- "The approach begins when the toss is halfway to the spiker."
- "The spikers must quickly move out of the way after an attack."
- "The spikers must always move in a forward direction after the attack."
- "Balls must be fed to the tosser as quickly as possible."

Student Options

- "The spikers may use either an on-hand or an off-hand attack."
- "The spikers may attack either down the line or crosscourt."

Student Keys to Success

- Ready for attack every time
- Attack with force
- Quickly recover after attack

Student Success Goal

- 10 good spikes into the designated targets off of 30 tosses

To Decrease Difficulty

- Have the tosser set the ball higher.
- Have the tosser lengthen time between sets.
- Increase the number of spikers.
- Lower the Success Goal.

To Increase Difficulty

- Have the tosser set the ball lower.
- Have the tosser shorten the time between sets.
- Raise the Success Goal.

Step 13 Block

The teaching progression for blocking consists of teaching the footwork, the jump and penetration, and the combination of the two. The ideal situation is to have the player develop the footwork so that it becomes a natural reaction when needed. The player's concentration can then be focused on the attacker and the ball.

In single blocking, the player seldom needs to move more than 1 to 3 feet along the net. In double blocking, the player runs distances up to 12 feet. The distance covered dictates the movement pattern that should be employed. The greater the distance, the quicker the player must move in order to arrive at the blocking position in time. For small distances the sliding step is efficient. However, the cross-step is quicker and more suitable for covering larger distances.

SINGLE BLOCK

In the single block, a lone blocker is wholly responsible for defending against the ball at the net. The blocker must line up one-half body width to the hitting side of the attacker, attempting to place one hand on each side of the attacker's hitting arm. The purpose of the block is to direct the opponent's attack immediately back into their court. A block is also considered successful if the ball is deflected high to one's own backcourt or merely if the presence of the blocker causes the attacker to make an error. Blocking is a difficult skill to perform but often helps a team score points in a match situation.

MULTIPLE BLOCK

In a multiple block, one player is responsible for the attacker. This player performs the same as if it were a single block. One or two other players join to make a double or triple block, adjusting their positions according to the location established by the player setting the block. The joining players should pay attention to the set blocker, rather than the attacker or the ball (Figure 13.1). These joining players take away the angle from the attacker, who might otherwise be able to hit past a single blocker's hands. The hands of all the blockers should be close enough together that the ball cannot go between them.

Figure 13.1 Joining player focuses on set blocker, not attacker or ball.

Block Rating

CRITERION	BEGINNING LEVEL	INTERMEDIATE LEVEL	ADVANCED LEVEL
Preparation	• Concentrates on ball	• Watches attacker some of time, but concentrates too heavily on ball	• Concentrates on attacker
	• Does not line up in correct position	• When watching attacker, usually gets one-half body width to attacker's hitting side	• Initial position, one-half body width to attacker's hitting side
	• Uses extended arm swing to gain height on jump	• Swings arms slightly but from bent arm position	• Raises arms from bent arm position to ball
Execution	• Starts with arms extended and low	• Hands begin at shoulder level, arms raised from starting position without extra swing	• Arms extend and reach from starting position with no swing (Figure 13.2)
	• Afraid to penetrate for fear of hitting net	• Penetrates net but does not reach for ball	• Penetrates and orients to ball
	• Jumps too soon	• Jump is timed just after attacker jumps; ready for attacks close to net, but doesn't delay enough for attacks away from net	• Jumps just after attacker's jump and delays when attacker is off the net
	• Reaches for ball, colliding with set blocker in multiple block	• Joins set blocker but reaches for ball instead of taking away angle	• In multiple block, closes block, blocks out angle (Figure 13.3)

CRITERION	BEGINNING LEVEL	INTERMEDIATE LEVEL	ADVANCED LEVEL
Follow-Through	• Frequently lands unbalanced on one foot, often causing net fouls • Forgets to withdraw hands • After landing, does not look for ball to prepare for next play	• Solid, controlled landing, but fails to bend knees for cushioning • Withdraws hands too slowly • Can push off one foot or other for movement toward ball	• Lands on both feet, cushions landing • Withdraws hands quickly after ball contact • Turns off block quickly and prepares for next play

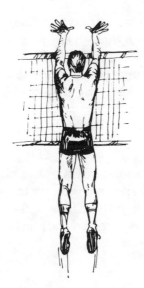

Figure 13.2 Arms raised to blocking position without swing.

Figure 13.3 Closing a double block.

Error Detection and Correction for the Block

One of the most frequent errors seen in the performance of the block is the blocker's tendency to pay too close attention to the ball rather than to the opposing attacker. Players setting the block *must* learn to pay closer attention to the attacker. As soon as the ball has left the opposing setter's hands and its direction is evident, the blocker should move his or her concentration from the ball to the attacker. When the attacker's arm swings toward the ball, the ball will again come into view anyway. At this point it is essential that the blocker see the ball, along with the arm, so that he or she can place the hands on the ball, if possible.

ERROR	CORRECTION
1. The blocker does not line up properly on the attacker.	1. The blocker must watch the attacker and not concentrate on the ball. If a blocker jumps to block a ball that an attacker does not choose to spike, this is a good indication that the blocker is watching the ball.
2. The blocker is returning to the floor as the attack is being made.	2. The blocker is too anxious to block and has jumped too soon. The blocker must concentrate on the attacker, not the ball.
3. The deflected ball falls between the block and the net.	3. This blocking error is considered to be the worst; even though the blocker has good position, timing, and contact, a negative result occurs. The blocker must penetrate the net to keep the deflected ball on the attacker's side.
4. The ball deflects off the blocker's hands and goes out of bounds.	4. When blocking outside, the player must turn the hand that is closer to the sideline so that when the ball is deflected off the hands, it is directed back into the opponent's court.
5. The blocker lands off balance or on one foot.	5. At the upper levels of play, landing on one foot after the block is considered a valuable timesaver for turning in anticipation of the next play. At the beginning level, though, it is not recommended. Landing on both feet gives the beginning player surer balance and a larger base for cushioning the landing.
6. The blocker does not bend the knees during landing.	6. Cushioning the landing by bending the knees spreads the force of impact over greater distance. This helps the player avoid injury.

ERROR

CORRECTION

7. The joining blocker moves into the player setting the block.

7. The moving blocker should not be concerned about the location of the ball and the attack, but should concentrate on the set blocker. The joining blocker must close the block while controlling body momentum so as not to collide with the set blocker.

8. The ball contacts the joining player's hands and remains on the blockers' side of the net.

8. As the joining blocker moves toward the set blocker, the shoulders are square to the sideline of the court. As the blocker closes, the outside shoulder must rotate toward the net so that the shoulders are square to the net before the blockers jump.

9. The joining blocker reaches toward the attacker's hitting hand.

9. The ball is the set blocker's responsibility. The joining blocker is only responsible for the angle. The ball contacts the joining blocker's hands only if the attacker angles the spike crosscourt.

Blocking Drills

1. Toss to Block Drill
[Corresponds to *Volleyball*, Step 13, Drill 1]

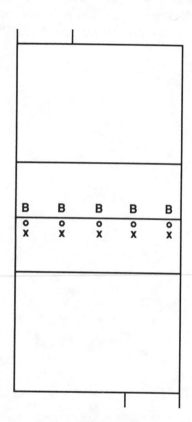

Group Management and Safety Tips

- Put no more than five student pairs on each net.
- It is essential to teach your players how to toss the ball to enhance the drill's success.
- The overhead throw must be hard, straight ahead, and in a downward direction.
- The players need to be aware of the groups next to them and of balls that might roll under their feet.

Equipment

- 2 courts
- 2 nets
- 1 ball for every student pair

Instructions to Class

"Get a partner. One of you be a tosser, and the other a blocker on the opposite side of the net.

"The tosser, using a two-handed overhead throw, jumps and throws the ball over the net in a downward motion. The blocker jumps and attempts to block the ball before it penetrates the net. The blocked ball should land within the boundaries of the opposite court."

- "If the blocker is tall enough, the hands must penetrate over the top of the net and into the opposite court."
- "If the blocker is not tall enough to penetrate, the hands should be raised and facing the ceiling, making the ball rebound upward. This is referred to as a *soft block*."
- "The blocker can direct the ball to the left or the right by turning one hand when contacting the ball."

Student Options

- "The blocker must decide when to jump in relation to the tosser's distance from the net. The farther the tosser is from the net, the longer the blocker has to wait before jumping."
- "The blocker must decide whether to penetrate the net or to make a soft block."
- "The blocker may decide whether to direct the ball to the left or the right."

Student Keys to Success

- No arm swing
- Jump just after tosser
- Fingers spread wide, thumbs point to ceiling
- Penetrate net with hands
- Withdraw hands quickly
- Bend knees to cushion landing

Student Success Goal

- 6 good blocks off of 10 throws

To Decrease Difficulty

- Have the blocker stand on a chair to experience the ball-hand contact without worrying about timing the jump.
- Lower the Success Goal.

To Increase Difficulty

- Have the tosser vary the distance of the throw from the net.
- Have the tosser throw the ball slightly to the left and to the right, in addition to straight ahead.
- Raise the Success Goal.

2. *Blind Blocking Drill*

[Corresponds to *Volleyball*, Step 13, Drill 2]

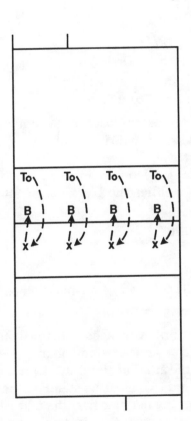

Equipment

- 2 courts
- 2 nets
- 2 balls for every three-player team

Instructions to Class

''For this drill you need a team of three. A blocker and a tosser stand on one side of the net, and a spiker on the opposite side.

''From a position behind the blocker, the tosser throws the ball over the net, high and relatively close to the net. The attacker jumps and spikes the ball, aiming at the blocker. The blocker jumps and attempts to block the ball back at the attacker; it should land in bounds.''

- ''The toss over the net must be high and within 3 feet of the net.''
- ''The attacker initially spikes the ball straight ahead into the block.''
- ''The blocker must not watch the tosser; rather, the blocker concentrates on the attacker.''
- ''The blocker's hands must penetrate the net.''

Group Management and Safety Tips

- Put no more than four three-player teams on each net; the fewer teams per net, the better.
- The ultimate safety factor here is awareness of the spikes of the adjoining teams and balls rolling underfoot.
- All spikers should be on the same side of the net.

Student Options

- ''The attacker decides whether to spike or dink if the toss is not accurate.''
- ''The attacker may spike straight ahead, to the left, or to the right.''
- ''The blocker must decide whether to penetrate the net or make a soft block.''
- ''The blocker must decide when to jump.''

Student Keys to Success

- Line up on attacker's hitting side
- Time jump by attacker's distance from net
- Jump after attacker jumps
- Penetrate over net
- Withdraw hands quickly
- Bend knees to cushion landing
- Turn from net to prepare for next play

Student Success Goal

- 4 good blocks off of 10 spikes

To Decrease Difficulty

- Have the tosser toss close to the net.
- The ball could be tossed to the same spot every time.
- Have the blocker stand on a chair.
- Lower the Success Goal.

To Increase Difficulty

- Have the tosser move the toss around, making the blocker adjust.
- Have the tosser throw lower.
- Raise the Success Goal.

3. Double Blocking Drill

[Corresponds to *Volleyball*, Step 13, Drill 3]

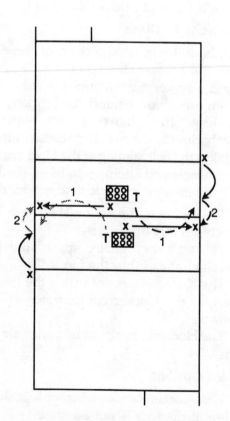

Group Management and Safety Tips

- Put no more than two groups on each court.
- Place attackers on opposite sides of the net.
- Set the tosser closer to the sideline than the blocker, who is near the middle of the court.
- Use a signal to stop drill action if a ball rolls under either the blockers' or attackers' feet.

Equipment

- 2 courts
- 2 nets
- 2 balls for every four-player team

Instructions to Class

"For this drill you need a team of four. A tosser and an attacker stand on one side of the net with the attacker at the attack line near the sideline and two blockers stand on the opposite side of the net (one near the middle of the court and one near the sideline). The tosser, positioned right of center front near the net, throws the ball high (6 to 8 feet above the top of the net) and relatively close to the net. The attacker approaches and spikes the ball over the net. The middle blocker joins the outside blocker, who has set the block, to form a double block. The blockers jump together and attempt to block the ball back at the attacker so that it lands within the boundaries of the court."

- "The outside blocker watches the attacker and sets the block."
- "The middle blocker waits for the toss then looks for the outside blocker and joins at the set position."
- "The blockers must jump at the same time."
- "The outside blocker should turn his or her outside hand in toward the center of the court."
- "The blockers' hands must penetrate the net."

Student Options

- "The attacker may spike down the line or crosscourt on the diagonal."
- "The attacker may spike or dink."
- "The blockers must decide when to jump."
- "The tosser may vary the distance of the toss off the net."

Student Keys to Success

- Outside blocker sets block
- Middle blocker joins
- Outside blocker lines up on ball
- Middle blocker takes angle
- Blockers jump after attacker jumps
- Penetrate over net
- Withdraw hands quickly
- Bend knees to cushion landing
- Turn from net to prepare for next play

Student Success Goal

- 4 of 10 spikes blocked

To Decrease Difficulty

- Have both blockers start at sideline.
- Have the tosser toss the ball to the same spot every time.
- Have attacker spike in only one direction.
- Lower the Success Goal.

To Increase Difficulty

- Have the tosser toss the ball lower.
- Have the tosser toss at different distances from the sideline.
- Raise the Success Goal.

4. *Endurance Blocking Drill*
[Corresponds to *Volleyball*, Step 13, Drill 4]

Group Management and Safety Tips

- Put no more than one group of eight on each court.
- Before overhead passing, the passer should make sure that there are no balls underfoot.
- Establish a signal to prevent the players from jumping if a dangerous situation exists.

Equipment

- 2 courts
- 2 nets
- 1 ball for every player

Instructions to Class

"This drill requires a group of eight players—two combination blockers-hitters, one setter, and one overhead passer on each side of the net. The passers should have an ample supply of balls (at least 10) readily available. On one side of the net, team A's two hitters begin on the attack line with the setter at the net. On the opposite side of the net, team B's two blockers are in a ready position, the setter in the right back position. Both passers are in their respective backcourt areas.

"The passer on the hitters' side (team A) begins the drill by passing the ball high to the setter, who sets either hitter. The blockers on team B react with a single block if it is a quick set, or a double block if it is a high, outside set or back set. The blocked ball should land in the attacker's court; the attackers don't need to return it.

"The team B passer immediately overhead passes another ball high to the penetrating setter, who sets one of the team B hitters (in the role of blocker just seconds before). The team A blockers (earlier, hitters) react to the attack with a good block. The drill continues indefinitely, the hitters and blockers constantly changing roles like this."

- "As soon as the attack is completed, the attackers must prepare to block."
- "The outside blocker sets the block on the attacker's hitting arm."
- "The middle blocker joins the outside blocker and takes away the angle."
- "As soon as the block is completed, the blockers must prepare to hit."

Student Options

- "The setter may set either attacker."
- "The attacker may select the angle of the attack."
- "The attacker may choose the appropriate method of attack."
- "Blockers may decide whether to penetrate the net or make a soft block."

Student Keys to Success

- Blocker penetrates net
- Cushion landing by bending knees
- Turn off net and look for ball immediately after landing
- Quick transition from defense to attack

Student Success Goal

- 5 successful blocks by your team

To Decrease Difficulty

- Have the passer overhead pass the ball high to the setter.
- Have the passer allow more time between passes.
- Lower the Success Goal.

To Increase Difficulty

- Have the passer send lower overhead passes to the setter.
- Have the passer allow less time between passes.
- Have the setter set low to the attacker.
- Raise the Success Goal.

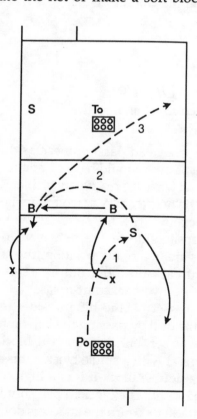

Team A attacks
Team B blocks

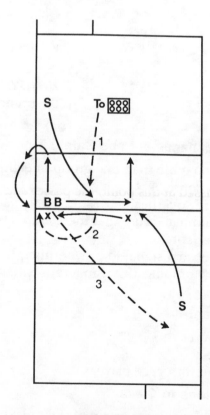

Team B attacks
Team A blocks

Step 14 Six-Skill Combination

With the combination of the serve, the forearm pass, the set, the attack, the block, and the dig, your players have been introduced to the essential skill sequence for participating in a competitive game of volleyball. Players at this stage can play a regulation game and be highly successful.

The skills and strategies that will be covered from this point on are necessary to advance to higher levels of play. The drills that are included in this step will enhance a team's ability to play using organized teamwork. Good team play can begin on a very basic level, even before complex offensive and defensive strategies are introduced.

Six-Skill Combination Drills

1. Combining Six Skills Drill
[Corresponds to *Volleyball*, Step 14, Drills 1 and 2]

Group Management and Safety Tips

- Put only one six-player group on each court.
- With a large class, to reduce the time students have to wait their turns, each group can serve six balls, then allow another group to rotate onto the court.
- Even though attack coverage has not been discussed at this point, the passer and the setter should be instructed to move toward the attacker after the set.
- In order for the blocker and the digger to have the opportunity to play the ball, the attacker must be fairly accurate with the angle of the spike.
- Setter should set in one direction four times, then switch to the opposite direction.

Equipment

- 2 courts
- 2 nets
- 1 ball for every three players

Instructions to Class

"In a group of six, have a server, a blocker, and a digger on one side of the net; and a passer, a setter, and an attacker on the other side. The server serves an underhand serve to the right or left back of the court. The passer forearm passes the ball to the setter, who sets or back sets high and outside to the attacker. The attacker spikes the ball over the net on the diagonal toward the digger.

"The blocker and the digger both attempt to play the ball. The blocker tries to keep the ball on the opponent's side. If this fails, the digger should place the ball high to the center of the digger's side of the court."

- "Even though there is only one receiver, this individual should call for the ball every time."
- "The hitter should call for the set each time so that the setter becomes used to hearing a call."
- "The blocker should block to take away the angle from the hitter."

Student Options

- ''The server may decide which type of serve to use.''
- ''The setter may determine the height of the set.''
- ''The blocker may decide whether to block the angle or the line.''

Student Keys to Success

- Call for pass
- Pass high to setter
- Attacker calls for set
- Block one-half body width to hitting side
- Always try for three-hit combination of pass, set, attack

Student Success Goals

- 10 out of 12 good serves
- 8 successful forearm pass-set-spike combinations off 10 serves
- 3 successful blocks or digs off of 8 spikes

To Decrease Difficulty

- Have the server toss the ball over the net rather than serve.
- Have the server toss or serve directly at the receiver.
- Have the blocker take the line.
- Lower the Success Goals.

To Increase Difficulty

- Let the server use a variety of serves.
- Let the server serve to any location on the court.
- Have the blocker vary his or her positioning, taking the line or taking the angle.
- Raise the Success Goals.

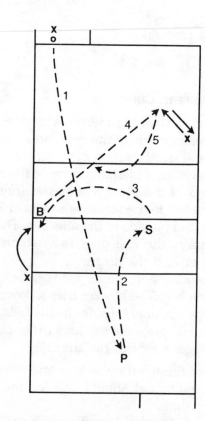

Passer right back
Attacker left forward

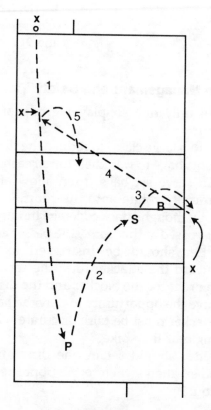

Passer left back
Attacker right forward

2. *Five-Player Reception Drill*
[Corresponds to *Volleyball*, Step 14, Drill 3]

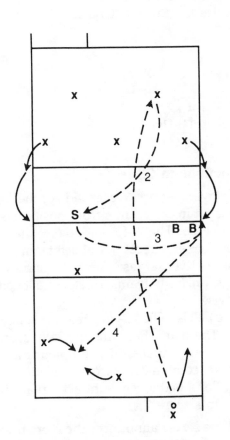

"The serving team attempts to block with a double block. Any ball not successfully blocked should be dug high to the center of the digger's side."

- "The server should vary the serve's force and direction."
- "The receiver should call for the serve before the ball crosses the net."
- "Every effort should be made to execute the three-hit combination of pass, set, and attack."
- "When double blocking, the outside blocker should concentrate on the hitter, and the middle blocker should take away the angle."

Student Options

- "The server may choose what type of serve to use and the serve's direction."
- "The receivers must decide who will receive the ball."
- "The setter may select which attacker to set."
- "The attacker may determine the angle of the attack."

Student Keys to Success

- Call for serve early
- Open up to (turn and face) receiver
- Set ball high to outside of court
- Outside blocker sets block, middle blocker joins

Student Success Goals

- 10 out of 12 good serves
- 8 accurate forearm pass-set-spike combinations off of 10 serves
- 3 successful blocks or digs off of 8 spikes

To Decrease Difficulty

- Have the server toss the ball rather than serve.
- Have the server serve directly at the receiver.
- Have the team indicate in advance which attacker will receive the set.
- Lower the Success Goals.

Group Management and Safety Tips

- Put only two six-player teams on each court.
- Alternate serving every third serve.
- After every serve, the teams play out the point to its completion.
- Rotate one position after each team serves four.

Equipment

- 2 courts
- 2 nets
- 1 ball for every three players

Instructions to Class

"Six players set up on each side of the court. The server on one side serves underhand. The receiving team, in the W-formation (refer to diagram), attempts a pass-set-spike combination, the set going alternately to the left forward and the right forward, and the spike going on the diagonal.

To Increase Difficulty

- Have the server vary the serve's force and direction.

- Have the setter vary the set direction, to the left front and the right front.
- Have the setter vary the height of the set.
- Raise the Success Goals.

3. Six-Player Modified Game

[Corresponds to *Volleyball*, Step 14, Drill 4]

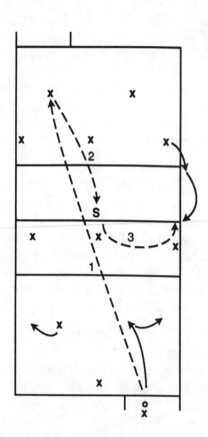

Instructions to Class

''Six players set up on each side of the court. The player in each center front position is the team's setter. The W-formation (see diagram) is used for serve reception. Each team makes 5 consecutive serves. After 10 serves the players on both teams rotate one position clockwise.

''The ball is rallied as in a regular volleyball game. The team that wins the rally scores a point. A team successfully completing a pass-set-spike combination scores an additional point. For a bad serve, subtract a point from the team's score.''

- ''The server announces the score prior to serving.''
- ''The server should vary the serve's force and direction.''
- ''The receivers call for the serve before the ball crosses the net.''
- ''Every effort should be made to execute the three-hit combination of pass, set, and spike.''
- ''When double blocking, the outside blocker should concentrate on the hitter, and the middle blocker should take away the angle.''

Student Options

- ''The server may choose what type of serve to use and its direction.''
- ''The receivers must decide who will receive the ball.''
- ''The setter may select which attacker to set.''
- ''The attackers may determine the angle of the attack.''

Group Management and Safety Tips

- Put two six-player teams on each court.
- Alternate serving every fifth serve.
- After every serve, the teams play out the point to its completion.
- Rotate one position after each team serves five.
- You should serve as an official for awarding or taking away disputed points.

Equipment

- 2 courts
- 2 nets
- 1 ball for every three players

Student Keys to Success

- Call for serve early
- Open up to receiver
- Set ball high to outside of court
- Outside blocker sets block, middle blocker joins

Student Success Goal

- Be the team earning the greater number of points after six rotations (60 total serves)

To Decrease Difficulty

- Have the server toss the ball rather than serve.

- Have the server serve directly at the receiver.
- Have the setter indicate in advance which attacker will receive the set.
- Add 3 points for every successful three-hit combination.

To Increase Difficulty

- Have the server vary the serve's force and direction.
- Have the setter vary the set direction, to the left front and to the right front.
- Have the setter vary the height of the set.
- Subtract 2 points for a bad serve.

Step 15 Advanced Serves

Once a player has mastered the overhand floater serve and the underhand serve he or she can successfully compete at any level. As players advance in skill level, though, it is advantageous that they master two advanced serves, the topspin and the roundhouse floater. The topspin serve is a forceful serve that drops quickly. The roundhouse floater serve is a slow serve that has noticeable lateral deviation in its movement. Players who have the ability to use a variety of serves during a match can effectively keep the opposition off balance.

TOPSPIN

The topspin serve is effective due to its force, its rapid speed, and its quick drop that does not permit the receiving team sufficient time to react. It is also difficult to determine whether the topspin serve will land in the court or out of bounds. Such a serve approaching the end line or sidelines may drop quickly at the last moment, showing a receiver to have misjudged the result.

The one predictable aspect of the topspin serve is its line of direction. Spin stabilizes a ball in flight; when topspin is imparted on the ball, its direction does not change from the initial line of force. Receivers should find this characteristic helpful.

Topspin Serve Rating

CRITERION	BEGINNING LEVEL	INTERMEDIATE LEVEL	ADVANCED LEVEL
Preparation	• Body begins perpendicular to net, but insufficient body rotation to keep serve in bounds • Toss in front of contacting shoulder	• Body perpendicular to net, rotates body into ball • Toss is above contacting shoulder	• Body perpendicular to net, rotates forcibly into ball • Toss is slightly behind shoulder
Execution	• Contact with bent arm • Contact point on ball too high • Wrist snaps, but body does not rotate into serve	• Contact with arm fully extended • Contact point on lower back of ball • Body rotation not strong enough	• Contact with arm fully extended • Ball contact point on lower back with heel of hand • Forceful body rotation into ball, strong wrist snap

CRITERION	BEGINNING LEVEL	INTERMEDIATE LEVEL	ADVANCED LEVEL
Follow-Through	• Does not transfer weight forward	• Weight transferred onto court	• Rotates into ball and transfers weight forward
	• Stops arm motion at contact	• Arm swings down and across body after contact	• Forceful wrist snap at contact, arm follows through forcibly to waist
	• Hips thrown backward	• Hips thrown backward	• Hips move in direction of serve

Error Detection and Correction for the Topspin Serve

As it is with most serves, the toss for the topspin serve is extremely important for successful results. Your players should practice the toss until it becomes automatic. Remind them that the toss for the topspin serve should be slightly behind the hitting shoulder. Another area of concern is hand contact on the ball: You must stress that contact be made just below the bottom back of the ball, followed by a wrist snap over the top.

ERROR

CORRECTION

1. The ball goes into the net.

2. The ball does not drop quickly but sails out of bounds over the end line.

3. The ball goes out of bounds over the opponent's left sideline.

4. The player takes two or three steps to reach the toss before serving.

1. The ball must be tossed, and contacted, behind the hitting shoulder.

2. As the ball is contacted, the wrist must be forcibly snapped, bringing the fingers over the top of the ball.

3. The body must be rotated into the contact.

4. The ball must be tossed near the body so that only a forward transfer of weight is necessary upon contact. Elimination of the extra steps improves the efficiency of the serve.

ROUNDHOUSE FLOATER

The roundhouse floater serve was originally made popular by the Japanese. It is a serve that can easily be performed by players who are weaker in arm strength, because it tends to utilize the larger muscle groups of the body. Often a player who has difficulty performing the overhand floater and topspin serves easily performs the roundhouse floater serve. The ball reacts with the same floating action as the overhand floater serve; therefore, it is difficult to receive. The roundhouse floater serve is sometimes executed from a deeper position in the service area than is normal for the other serves because of its tendency to rise.

Roundhouse Floater Serve Rating

CRITERION	BEGINNING LEVEL	INTERMEDIATE LEVEL	ADVANCED LEVEL
Preparation	• Shoulders angle to sideline, feet point too much toward net • Concentrates on target	• Position of shoulder perpendicular to net, feet parallel to net • Maintains eye contact with ball	• Shoulders perpendicular to net and feet point to sideline • Concentrates on ball
Execution	• Ball tossed too far behind body • Arm bent on contact • Wrist snaps • Not enough body rotation	• Ball tossed in front of body and closer to nonhitting shoulder • Arm fully extended • Contact made with open hand, wrist not locked • Body begins to rotate, but timing incorrect	• Ball tossed in front of hitting shoulder • Arm drops back and remains extended throughout (Figure 15.1) • Contact on heel of hand, with locked wrist • Body rotation used effectively to impart force to ball

CRITERION	BEGINNING LEVEL	INTERMEDIATE LEVEL	ADVANCED LEVEL
Follow-Through	• Weight not transferred • Arm follow-through as in tennis swing • Remains in serving area rather than moving onto court	• Weight transferred to forward foot • Follow-through too extensive • Rotates body well and quickly moves onto court	• Transfer of weight onto forward foot immediately on contact • Slight follow-through of arm • Body rotation and movement onto court, quickly preparing for next play

Figure 15.1 Serving arm remains extended throughout serve.

Error Detection and Correction for the Roundhouse Floater Serve

As in all serves, a consistent toss is imperative for success. If a player is having difficulty performing the roundhouse floater serve successfully, first check the accuracy of the toss. The errors associated with the roundhouse floater serve are usually caused by inadequate tossing. The ball is generally tossed too low, too close to the body, or too far behind the body. The player should also attempt to eliminate all extraneous movement when performing this serve.

ERROR 🚫

CORRECTION

1. The served ball goes into the net.	1. The toss must be high enough so that the arm can contact the ball at full extension. The toss must also be close to the body.
2. The serve does not reach the net.	2. The body must be rotated into the contact. The heel of the open hand must cut into the ball.
3. The ball goes out of bounds over the sidelines or the end line.	3. When correcting sideline errors, make sure that the toss is in the proper location and that the body rotates into the contact but not beyond it. When correcting end line errors, make sure that the hand contacts the ball on its center back.
4. The server runs two or three steps in an approach before the serve.	4. The server must eliminate all extraneous movements.

Advanced Serving Drills

1. Wall Serve Drill

[Corresponds to *Volleyball*, Step 15, Drill 1]

Group Management and Safety Tips

- Have the players stand at least 5 feet apart.
- The players should be aware of balls other than their own rebounding off the wall.
- The players can serve at their own rates of speed.

Equipment

- Line marked on the wall
- 1 ball for every player

Instructions to Class

"Stand in a serving position approximately 20 feet from the wall, on which is marked a line at the proper net height. Toss the ball and serve it into the wall. Try both topspin and roundhouse floater serves."

- "Try to have the ball contact the wall as close to the 'net' line as possible."
- "Pick out an imaginary point on the wall and use that spot as a target."
- "Take time to concentrate before serving."

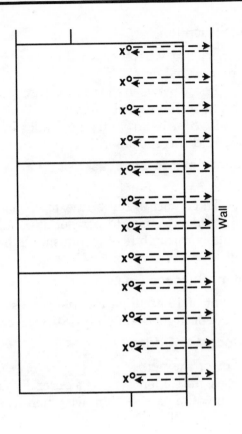

Student Options

- "Practice either the topspin serve or the roundhouse floater serve."
- "Increase your distance from the wall until you are farther than 30 feet away."

Student Keys to Success

- Concentrate on ball
- Make accurate toss
- Eliminate excessive movement
- Contact with heel of open hand
- Limit follow-through on roundhouse floater serve

Student Success Goals

- 9 out of 10 good topspin serves
- 9 out of 10 good roundhouse floater serves

To Decrease Difficulty

- Have the server move closer to the wall, up to 10 feet away.
- Lower the Success Goals.

To Increase Difficulty

- Have the server move farther away from the wall.
- Place targets on the wall.
- Raise the Success Goals.

2. *Partner Serve at the Net Drill*

[Corresponds to *Volleyball*, Step 15, Drill 2]

Group Management and Safety Tips

- Students on the same side of the net should stand at least 5 feet apart, preferably farther if space allows.
- The players must be aware of others around them.
- If the balls are being served without control, it may be necessary to have all the students on a side serve together.

Equipment

- 2 courts
- 2 nets
- 1 ball for every student pair

Instructions to Class

"At a distance of 20 feet from the net, serve the ball over the net, without its touching the net, to a partner standing 20 feet on the other side. The partner must be able to catch the ball without moving more than one step in any direction."

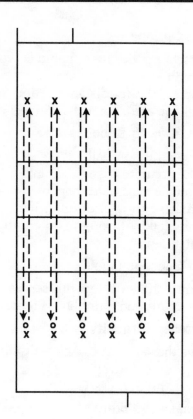

Student Options

- "Serve to wherever on the court your partner moves."
- "Choose between the roundhouse floater serve or the topspin serve."
- "Move farther from the net until you are behind the end line."

Student Keys to Success

- Toss ball accurately
- Make contact at full arm extension
- Shoulders square to partner at contact
- Follow-through for topspin should be in direction of serve

Student Success Goals

- 7 out of 10 accurate topspin serves
- 7 out of 10 good roundhouse floater serves

To Decrease Difficulty

- Lower the net.
- Have the student serve at a closer distance.
- Allow the partner to move when receiving the ball, depending upon the amount of room available.
- Lower the Success Goals.

To Increase Difficulty

- Have the student serve from a greater distance from the net.
- Have the partner change locations on the court.
- Raise the Success Goals.

- "Your hitting hand should be directed toward your receiving partner."
- "The position of your shoulders is very important in directing the ball to a selected point."

3. End Line Serve Drill

[Corresponds to *Volleyball*, Step 15, Drill 3]

Group Management and Safety Tips

- Every player may serve at his or her own rate of speed.
- The players must be aware of other served balls, particularly those that are long and high.
- If the players lack control, have everyone on one side of the net serve at the same time.

- A player low in skill should remain outside the boundaries of the court whether serving or receiving.

Equipment

- 2 courts
- 2 nets
- 1 ball for every student pair

Instructions to Class

"Two partners stand on opposite end lines and serve back and forth. Try both types of advanced serves. Serves may land anywhere within the boundaries of the partner's side of the court."

- "Take time before serving."
- "Take a breath."
- "Concentrate."
- "Do not rush the serve."

Student Options

- "Choose which serve to execute."
- "You may decide to practice serving to a particular direction or spot on the court."

Student Keys to Success

- Choose direction and position body accordingly
- Good toss essential
- Heel of hand must contact ball
- Follow through in direction of serve

Student Success Goals

- 9 out of 10 good topspin serves
- 9 out of 10 good roundhouse floater serves

To Decrease Difficulty

- Lower the net.
- Let the student serve to any spot on the court.
- Lower the Success Goals.

To Increase Difficulty

- Make the student serve to a particular spot on the court.
- Penalize missed serves by subtracting them from the running total.
- Raise the Success Goals.

4. *Consistency Drill*
[Corresponds to *Volleyball*, Step 15, Drill 4]

Group Management and Safety Tips

- Every player may serve at his or her own rate of speed.
- The player must be aware of other served balls, particularly those that are long and high.
- If the players lack control, have everyone on one side serve at the same time.
- A player low in skill should remain outside the boundaries of the court whether serving or receiving.

Equipment

- 2 courts
- 2 nets
- 1 ball for every student pair

Instructions to Class

"This is the same as the End Line Serve Drill, but with different Success Goals."

- "Take time before serving."
- "Take a breath."
- "Concentrate."
- "Do not rush the serve."

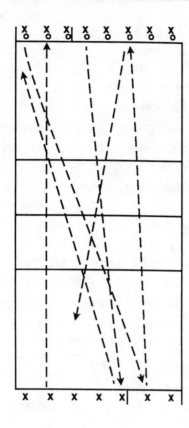

Student Options

- "Choose which serve to execute."
- "You may decide to practice serving to a particular direction or spot on the court."

Student Keys to Success

- Choose direction and position body accordingly
- Good toss essential
- Heel of hand must contact ball
- Follow through in direction of serve

Student Success Goals

- 25 consecutive good topspin serves
- 25 consecutive good roundhouse floater serves

To Decrease Difficulty

- Allow the student to serve closer to the net.
- Lower the Success Goals.

To Increase Difficulty

- Have the student serve to only one half of the court (the court can be divided either side to side or front to back).
- Raise the Success Goals.

5. Serve for Accuracy Drill

[Corresponds to *Volleyball*, Step 15, Drill 5]

Group Management and Safety Tips

- The servers should all remain behind their respective end lines.
- Servers on both sides of the court may serve at the same time.
- Make sure that there are an equal number of servers on both sides of the net.
- This drill can be made competitive, with each team (all servers on one side of the net) attempting to get one serve into every target area before the opposing team.

Equipment

- 2 courts
- 2 nets
- 4 targets or tape for target lines
- 1 ball for every two players

Instructions to Class

"Place a target sheet approximately 10-feet square in one of the six rotational positions. On the opposite side of the court, stand in the serving area (right one third of the court) and serve, attempting to hit the target. This drill should be attempted with the target in each of the six areas."

- "Your initial position when serving the ball is the key to successfully directing the ball to the target."
- "All serves should be made from the legal serving area."
- "Three or four servers may serve at one time."

Student Options

- "Choose which serve you want to use."
- "You may move left or right within the serving area."
- "You may select which target you would like to serve to first."

Student Keys to Success

- Accurate toss
- Contact at full arm extension
- Heel of hand cuts into ball
- Quick wrist snap when serving topspin
- Arm directed toward target

Student Success Goals

- 20 or less topspin serves needed to hit the target 5 times, repeating for each target position
- 20 or less roundhouse floater serves needed to hit the target 5 times, repeating for each target position

To Decrease Difficulty

- Use a larger target.
- Let the student serve from anywhere behind the end line.
- Lower the Success Goals.

To Increase Difficulty

- Use a smaller target.
- Raise the Success Goals.

6. Team Serving Drill

[Corresponds to *Volleyball*, Step 15, Drill 6]

Group Management and Safety Tips

- Both teams should be serving at targets in the same rotational position.
- Both teams should begin with the same number of volleyballs.
- Up to three servers can serve at the same time from a service area.
- Everyone should be aware of serves coming from the opposite group, especially when the target is immediately in front of the serving area.

- Two students or instructors should be used to count the good serves; counting should be done out loud.

Equipment

- 2 courts
- 2 nets
- 4 targets or tape for target lines
- 1 ball for every person

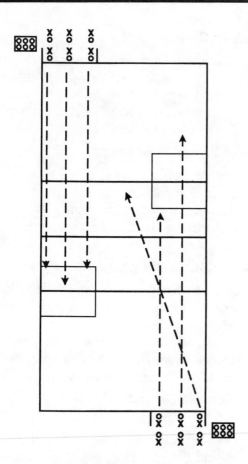

bers of the team step forward to serve. Servers continuously switch places after each repetition.''

- ''Although you are attempting to serve as quickly as possible, you should still concentrate and take your time before serving.''
- ''Good beginning position is essential for successful serve direction.''
- ''Concentration is more important for success than speed.''

Student Options

- ''Choose which target area you want to serve to first.''
- ''Decide which serve to execute.''

Student Keys to Success

- Accurate toss
- Concentration
- Arm swings to target
- Heel of hand cuts into ball

Student Success Goal

- 20 serves hitting the target prior to your opponents for each of the six target positions

To Decrease Difficulty

- Enlarge the target.
- Let the student serve from anywhere behind the end line.
- Lower the Success Goal.

To Increase Difficulty

- Decrease the size of the target.
- Stipulate a time restriction for trying to hit each target.
- Raise the Success Goal.

Instructions to Class

''With two teams of six players each, one team groups in each service area of the court. Ten-foot-square targets are set up in the same rotational position on both sides of the court (see diagram). Have plenty of volleyballs at each service area, an equal number at each.

''Two or three servers on each team begin serving at the target all at the same time. After serving, each player retrieves a ball and prepares to serve again. Meanwhile, other mem-

7. Minus Two Drill

[Corresponds to *Volleyball*, Step 15, Drill 7]

Group Management and Safety Tips

- Each player should begin with a volleyball, serve, quickly retrieve a ball, and go to the end of the line to wait his or her turn to serve again.

- The players should be aware of serves coming from the opposite group.
- With a large class, have two or three teams serving from the same serving area. If this is done, each team should have its own scorekeeper.

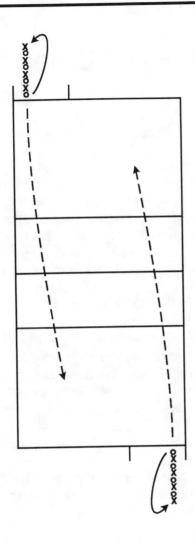

Instructions to Class

"This is almost the same as the previous drill. Here the serve needs only to land within the boundaries of the opposite court. Only one person serves at a time on each side. Divide into teams of no more than 6 players and form a line in the service area. Each person serves only once before the next person immediately serves once. Retrieve a ball after serving.

"For each legal serve, your team scores 1 point. For every bad serve, the team is penalized 2 points. The first team to reach 20 points wins."

- "Although you are attempting to get more serves into the court before the opposing team, you should still take your time to concentrate before each serve."
- "The time for rushing is in retrieving the ball and returning to the end of the line."
- "This drill tends to create pressure that can be very gamelike."

Student Options

- "Choose which serve you want to use."
- "Decide your team's order of service."

Student Keys to Success

- Concentrate
- Take your time
- Aim
- Excellent ball toss
- Arm swing to target

Student Success Goal

- 20 team points

To Decrease Difficulty

- Lower the Success Goal.

To Increase Difficulty

- Have the team try to reach the Success Goal in a stipulated amount of time.
- Let the students serve to only one half of the opposing court, divided front to back or side to side.
- Raise the Success Goal.

- The fewer the players on a team, the more the opportunities to serve per player.
- If teams are finding it difficult to keep their point totals positive, the penalty for a bad serve can be halved.

Equipment

- 2 courts
- 2 nets
- 1 ball for every player

Step 16 Individual Defensive Skills

Although the individual defensive skills of rolling and sprawling are essential for higher levels of play, your players' first defensive priority is to learn good movement patterns. At the beginner level, the ball is seldom spiked hard enough to necessitate the sprawl or the roll; players should move to the ball so that rolling and sprawling are rarely needed.

These individual defensive skills are exciting to watch, and players use them when not necessary. However, when executing these two skills, players find it difficult to recover and get ready for the next play, and there is a chance of injury. Therefore, these skills should be used as little as possible.

When performing either defensive skill, players should position their bodies as close to the floor as possible before executing the skill. This means that when the body contacts the floor, the impact is relatively small.

ROLL

The roll extends the distance a player is capable of covering to receive a ball. The roll is preferred to the sprawl because it allows the player to return quickly to the feet in a smooth, uninterrupted movement. Although many instructors teach a particular movement pattern for performing the roll, the most recent thought is that the method of the roll is not of great importance.

The most important aspect of the roll is that it be executed with the body very low to the floor. Players should perform the roll so that the first body parts contacting the floor are the most naturally padded areas. Things for your players to keep in mind when executing a roll are moving quickly to the ball, lowering the body to the floor by executing a long, striding step, playing the ball prior to the body's contacting the floor, and quickly returning to the feet to be ready for the next play.

Roll Rating

CRITERION	BEGINNING LEVEL	INTERMEDIATE LEVEL	ADVANCED LEVEL
Preparation	• Keeps feet together or moves to ball in high position with hands together • Body posture high throughout movement	• Moves to ball with hands separated, gets to correct spot for execution • Body posture still too high when ready to execute	• Arrives at spot to play ball, using a long stride for last step • Body low to floor before execution

CRITERION	BEGINNING LEVEL	INTERMEDIATE LEVEL	ADVANCED LEVEL
Execution	• Hits floor with too much force • Plays ball after contacting floor • Does not control body so that padded parts hit first, does not roll naturally • Does not control dig	• Body fairly low to floor • Contacts ball before hitting floor most of time • Rolls naturally, padded body parts usually contact floor first • Dig result low	• Body almost touching floor • Plays ball before floor contact • Naturally moves into roll after playing ball, rolling motion quick and smooth and padded parts contact floor first (Figure 16.1) • Dig high to center of court
Follow-Through	• Has difficulty returning to feet • Difficulty locating ball once on feet	• Returns to feet quickly • Locates ball most of time	• Returns to feet quickly, gets in position and ready • Has good feeling for ball location and finds it with ease

Figure 16.1   Contact floor first with padded body parts.

Error Detection and Correction
for the Roll

Due to the floor contact that occurs in the roll, it is recommended that the initial instruction take place on mats. As soon as the players have mastered the ability to stride toward the ball, lowering the body close to the floor, the roll can be safely performed on the floor without mats.

ERROR    **CORRECTION**

1. The player experiences discomfort when contacting the floor.

1. Place emphasis on the player's last stride toward the ball. This stride automatically results in the player's lowering the body close to the floor. The wider the stride, the closer to the floor.

2. The player contacts the floor prior to hitting the ball.

2. In the roll, the ball must be contacted while the player is in a "falling" posture, but before actual contact with the floor. The roll, in fact, should be looked at as a method of recovery, not as a method of playing the ball.

3. The player is not able to return to the feet, but remains on the floor.

3. Once the roll begins, it is a movement whose momentum should naturally bring the player to the feet. The player must be relaxed for this to happen.

4. The player does not let the ball drop low enough before playing it.

4. If the ball is in a high position and the player is able to play it in that position, there should be no need for a roll. The lower the player lets the ball drop, though, the more time there is to play it and complete the roll.

ERROR 	CORRECTION
5. The dug ball lacks sufficient height to be played by another player with ease.	5. The goal of the digging player is to hit the ball 5 to 10 feet higher than the top of the net and so that it remains on his or her side of the court.

SPRAWL

The sprawl has developed from another skill known as the dive. Many players found the dive difficult to execute because of insufficient arm strength with which to catch their falling body weight. This ability is essential to dive without injury. In the sprawl, though, it is not necessary for a player to catch the body weight on the arms. In the sprawl the force of the falling body is spread over more body area.

As previously discussed, the roll is used to retrieve a ball that is too far away in any direction to allow for a normal dig. However, the sprawl is generally used to receive a ball that is falling in front of the player. The sprawl does not allow the player to return to the feet as quickly as the roll does. The roll, therefore, is the preferred method of playing the ball when there is a choice.

Sprawl Rating

CRITERION	BEGINNING LEVEL	INTERMEDIATE LEVEL	ADVANCED LEVEL
Preparation	• Does not take long enough stride toward ball • Does not correctly judge location of ball	• Strides toward ball but stops motion before execution • Correctly judges position of ball	• Continuous motion into sprawl • Correctly judges ball, and moves to execution point

Sprawl Rating

CRITERION	BEGINNING LEVEL	INTERMEDIATE LEVEL	ADVANCED LEVEL
Execution	• Plays ball with body too high, tries to catch weight with hands • Hits floor before contacting ball • Body hits floor hard, with no attempt to slide • Does not place one knee out to side	• Low position, waits for ball • Plays ball before it drops low enough but before body contacts the floor • Begins to slide body on floor after playing ball • Puts one knee to side	• Position low to floor in forward stride • Digs ball high with body low to floor and keeps ball on own side of court (Figure 16.2) • Pushes forward with rear foot to enhance good slide onto chest • Extends back leg
Follow-Through	• Hits floor and does not slide • Does not return to feet • Not ready for next play	• Contacts floor sliding, but not smoothly • Returns to feet slowly • Attempts to be ready for next play, but is late	• Slide extended over sufficient distance to dissipate force (Figure 16.3) • Returns to feet quickly • Ready for next play

Figure 16.2 Low body position for digging.

Figure 16.3 Slide to dissipate force of dig.

Error Detection and Correction for the Sprawl

Sprawl errors are generally easy to detect. A player not getting to a low body position contacts the floor with a great deal of force, and injury may occur. If a player attempts to play the ball after contacting the floor, this will cause a break in the movement and the sprawl will not be smooth. Also, a dig is not acceptable if the ball is not high enough to allow a teammate to play it with relative ease.

ERROR

CORRECTION

1. The player does not allow the ball to drop low enough to the floor prior to playing it.

1. The ball should be played at a height of no more than 2 feet above the floor.

2. The player contacts the floor before contacting the ball.

2. As soon as the player contacts the floor, the possible range that he or she can cover is limited. If the player contacts the floor early and is not in the correct location, he or she will not be able to play the ball. Player must judge ahead of time the correct location for playing the ball.

3. The player does not return to the feet.

3. The player must be prepared to return to the feet quickly.

Individual Defense Drills

1. Roll Without Ball Drill
[Corresponds to *Volleyball*, Step 16, Drill 1]

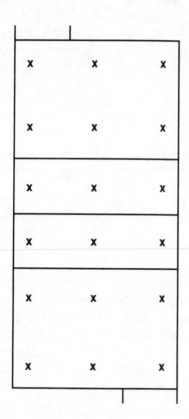

Equipment
- Mats (optional)

Instructions to Class
"Working individually without a ball, practice the rolling skill. Get into a low position, make sure that your padded body parts contact the floor first, and return to your feet as quickly as possible."

- "Check every time to make sure you have enough space before you begin the roll."
- "You are reminded that the lower you get to the floor before executing the skill, the easier and safer it is."

Student Options
- "Choose whether to roll to the right or to the left."
- "Choose which type of roll is most comfortable."

Student Keys to Success
- Long, striding step
- Low body position
- Padded body parts contact floor
- Roll and quickly return to feet

Student Success Goal
- 10 rolls to either side

To Decrease Difficulty
- Have a partner aid the student in the performance of the skill.
- Let the student begin already in a low position.
- Lower the Success Goal.

To Increase Difficulty
- Increase the distance the student must cover before rolling.
- Raise the Success Goal.

Group Management and Safety Tips
- Every student should have 10 feet of clearance all around him or her. If space prevents this, you should control the roll practice so that everyone rolls at the same time and in the same direction.
- Initial practice can be done on mats to eliminate the fear factor, but the mats should be removed as soon as possible.
- Students should be encouraged to wear knee pads.

2. *Dig to Roll Drill*

[Corresponds to *Volleyball*, Step 16, Drill 2]

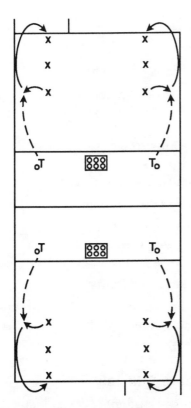

Group Management and Safety Tips

- Have groups of three or more defensive players working with each tosser.
- Students execute a roll and go to the end of the line.
- Students are encouraged to wear knee pads.
- Two groups work on each side of the net, the defensive players moving to opposite sidelines.
- Tosses should be underhand and relatively easy. The prime objective of the tosser is to make the receiver cover some distance, rather than to be concerned with the force of the toss.

Equipment

- 1 ball for every two players

Instructions to Class

"Divide into teams of four players each. A tosser stands near the net, facing the end line. Three defensive players stand in a line in the backcourt.

"The tosser throws a low, easy ball to the outside (that is, closer to the nearest sideline) of the first defensive player in line. The defensive player should let the ball drop low, dig the ball, and roll quickly, returning to the feet."

- "The toss should be far enough away to require a roll and present a challenge to the receiver."
- "The distance of the toss should be determined by the ability of the receiver."
- "As the defensive player moves to the ball, he or she judges where to be to play the ball."

Student Options

- "Decide which direction to practice first."
- "Decide whether a roll is actually needed."

Student Keys to Success

- Long, striding step
- Low body position
- Play ball before contact with floor
- Ball drops as low as possible before contact
- Hit ball higher than top of net
- Direct ball back toward tosser

Student Success Goals

- 5 successful dig-roll combinations off of 10 tosses to the right side
- 5 successful dig-roll combinations off of 10 tosses to the left side

To Decrease Difficulty

- Have the tosser throw the ball closer to the digger.
- Let the tosser throw the ball higher.
- Lower the Success Goal.

To Increase Difficulty

- Have the tosser throw the ball farther from the digger.
- Have the tosser throw the ball lower.
- Raise the Success Goal.

3. Sprawl Without Ball Drill

[Corresponds to *Volleyball*, Step 16, Drill 3]

Group Management and Safety Tips

- Have all players sprawling in the same direction (see setup for Drill 16.1).
- A hardwood floor is the best surface for learning and practicing the sprawl.
- Your students should be aware of others sprawling, to avoid collisions.

Equipment

- None

Instructions to Class

"Working individually, practice the sprawling skill without a ball. Take a large step forward, slide forward as your body contacts the floor, and return to your feet as quickly as possible."

- "Push off with your rear foot to increase the sliding distance."
- "Arch your back and remember to keep your head up."
- "Always make sure the area in front of you is clear prior to sprawling."

Student Option

- None

Student Keys to Success

- Long, striding step forward
- Body as low to floor as possible
- Push off rear foot
- Slide on stomach and chest
- Bend one knee
- Reach forward with arm

Student Success Goals

- 5 sprawls forward
- 5 sprawls to the right
- 5 sprawls to the left

To Decrease Difficulty

- Let the student begin on one knee.
- Conduct practice on a smooth, nonstick surface.
- Lower the Success Goals.

To Increase Difficulty

- Make the student cover a greater distance before sprawling.
- Raise the Success Goals.

4. Dig to Sprawl Drill

[Corresponds to *Volleyball*, Step 16, Drill 4]

Group Management and Safety Tips

- Two or three groups can work on the same half of the court, as long as all the groups are sprawling in the same direction at the same time.
- The players must be careful of stray balls on the court. Use players waiting in line as retrievers.
- Although not needed, nets may be set up so that the players can judge the height of their digs.

Equipment

- 1 or more balls for every two players

Instructions to Class

"Defensive players stand in lines of three or more, beginning 20 feet from the net. A tosser stands near the net, facing them.

"The tosser tosses a low ball so that it would drop 3 or 4 feet in front of the defensive player. The defensive player steps forward, reaches, and plays the ball in a low position, digging it high to the center of the court and sprawling."

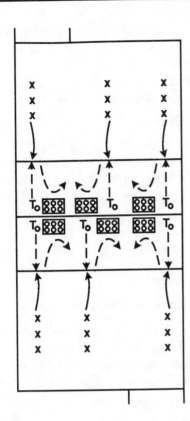

- "The tosser may decide what direction to toss the ball."
- "The defensive player may hit the ball with the forearms or the back of the hands."

Student Keys to Success

- Long, striding step toward ball
- Long slide to dissipate force
- Ball drops as low as possible
- Dig ball high
- "Break" wrists to improve dig height

Student Success Goal

- 5 successful dig-sprawl combinations off of 10 tosses

To Decrease Difficulty

- Have the tosser throw the ball closer to the defensive player.
- Let the defensive player start from a position on one knee.
- Lower the Success Goal.

To Increase Difficulty

- Have the tosser make the defensive player move a greater distance.
- Have the tosser throw the ball with more force.
- Require the defensive player to dig the ball to a specified height in order for it to be counted toward the Success Goal.
- Raise the Success Goal.

- "Play the ball either with both hands or one hand."
- "Dig the ball 10 to 12 feet high."
- "If you experience difficulties, begin from a position with one knee on the floor."

Student Options

- "Decide on what direction in which to sprawl first."

5. Roll or Sprawl Decision Drill

[Corresponds to *Volleyball*, Step 16, Drill 5]

Group Management and Safety Tips

- Two student pairs can work on the same side of the court as long as they divide the area in half.
- The players must always be aware of stray volleyballs.

Equipment

- 1 ball for every student pair

Instructions to Class

"Get a partner. One of you stands in any one of the defensive positions on the court. A tosser stands at the net, facing the other.

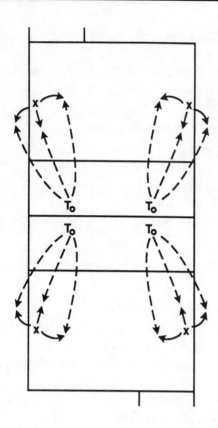

"The tosser throws the ball to either side or in front of the defensive player. The defensive player must decide which defensive skill to use in digging the ball and recovering correctly—the roll, or the sprawl."

- "The tosser should throw the ball an appropriate distance from the defensive player; that is, the toss should present a challenge."
- "The defensive players must react to the ball and its location to decide which skill to use."

- "If the defensive player can get to the ball and play it without rolling or sprawling, he or she should do so."
- "The defensive player should use the tosser as a target for the dig."

Student Options

- "The defensive player needs to decide whether to sprawl or to roll."
- "The defensive player determines whether one of these individual defensive skills is even needed."
- "The defensive player may decide which hand method—two hands, one hand, or the back of the hand—is best in a given situation."

Student Keys to Success

- Quick movement and decision making
- Ball drops low before contact
- Contact ball before hitting floor
- Dig ball high and toward center of court

Student Success Goal

- 5 correct defensive plays off of 10 tosses

To Decrease Difficulty

- Have the tosser throw the ball closer to the defensive player.
- Have the tosser throw the ball with less force.
- Have the tosser indicate the direction of the throw before tossing.
- Lower the Success Goal.

To Increase Difficulty

- Have the tosser throw the ball with more force.
- Have the tosser throw the ball farther from the defensive player.
- Raise the Success Goal.

6. Spike Hit, Dig, Sprawl, or Roll Drill

[Corresponds to *Volleyball*, Step 16, Drill 6]

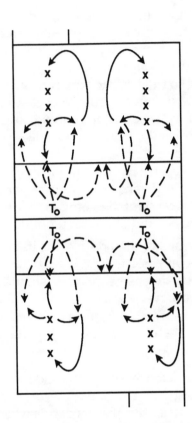

Group Management and Safety Tips

- With a large class, have three or four defensive players rotating.
- Two pairs or groups can work on each half of the court, as long as each limits their movement.
- Your students should always be aware of neighboring groups and stray balls.

Equipment

- 2 courts
- 2 nets
- 1 ball for every student pair

Instructions to Class

"Set up in pairs as in the Roll or Sprawl Decision Drill. Now the partner at the net tosses the ball to him- or herself and spike hits it at the defensive player. The defensive player digs the ball higher than the net and to the center of the court, using a roll or a sprawl when needed. The spike hitter catches the ball."

- "The spiker begins with fairly easy spike hits."
- "The spike hit should be adapted to the ability of the receiver."
- "The receiver should roll or sprawl only when appropriate."

Student Options

- "The receiver may decide whether a sprawl or a roll is even needed."
- "The receiver decides on which hand position to use on the ball."

Student Keys to Success

- Read motion of spiker's arm
- Anticipate direction of ball and react
- Let ball drop low
- Dig ball high
- Recover quickly for next play

Student Success Goal

- 7 successful digs off of 10 spike hits

To Decrease Difficulty

- Have the spiker indicate the direction of the ball before spiking.
- Have the spiker hit the ball with less force.
- Have the spiker hit the ball higher.
- Lower the Success Goal.

To Increase Difficulty

- Have the spiker hit the ball lower.
- Have the spiker hit the ball farther from the receiver.
- Have the spiker hit the ball with greater force.
- Raise the Success Goal.

7. Spike, Dig, Roll or Sprawl Drill

[Corresponds to *Volleyball*, Step 16, Drill 7]

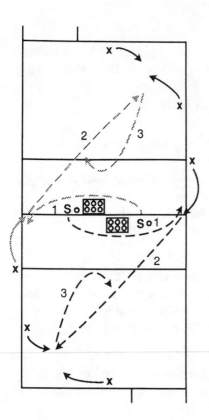

Group Management and Safety Tips

- Two teams can work either on the same side of the court, going in the same direction, or on opposite sides of the court working on a diagonal.
- Everyone needs to be aware of stray volleyballs and uncontrolled spikes from the other group.

Equipment

- 2 courts
- 2 nets
- 1 ball for every two players

Instructions to Class

''Get together a team of four players, two of you on offense and two on defense. On one side of the net, a setter stands close to the net, and a spiker starts at the attack line in the left front position. On the other side, one defensive player is positioned in the center back on the end line, and the other defender stands on the left sideline about 20 feet from the net.

''On the offensive side, the setter gets the ball to the spiker, who spikes the ball on the diagonal to the left back quarter of the other side. The defenders both move toward the ball, quickly deciding who should play it. One of them digs the ball, using a roll or sprawl, if necessary.

''The attackers receive a point for each spike not dug. The defensive players receive a point for each successful dig going higher than the top of the net and to the center of the court.''

- ''The spiker should spike the ball between the two receivers.''
- ''Both defensive players should move toward every spike.''
- ''The center back player should always move behind the left back player.''

Student Options

- ''The defensive players decide which one should play the ball.''
- ''The defensive players decide whether an individual defensive skill is necessary.''
- ''The defenders decide which individual defensive skill is appropriate.''
- ''Decide whether you want to be an offensive or defensive player first.''

Student Keys to Success

- Watch arm of spiker to determine direction of spike
- Move toward ball and react according to its location
- Defensive player should not make early decision as to who will play ball
- Call for ball if time allows

Student Success Goal

- Be the first team to reach a certain number of points

To Decrease Difficulty

- Have the spiker indicate the intended direction of the spike.

- Have the players practice one direction for a number of trials before changing the direction.
- Have the spiker hit with less force.
- Have the spiker hit the ball directly at one of the defensive players.
- Lower the Success Goal.

To Increase Difficulty

- Have the spiker hit with greater force.
- Have the spiker hit the ball in any direction.
- Raise the Success Goal.

Step 17   4-2 Offense

When you introduce your players to offensive or defensive systems, it is extremely important that you realize that for every rotation, every player moves into a new and completely different position. Due to this aspect of volleyball, every court alignment must be practiced for all six rotations. This can be rather time consuming, but it is essential for student understanding and success. It is highly recommended that when practicing team formations, a team concentrate on one rotation at a time until perfected.

The 4-2 offense is the simplest offensive system to use. It is recommended that this be the first system you introduce to your players. This offense is simple because the setting is handled by one of the front row players. The setter must think of him- or herself as a setter-attacker because he or she will set as well as attack. The attack option of the setter in this offense needs to be developed in order to keep the opposing defense honest; if the setter does not use the option, the opposing blockers do not have to be prepared to block in this position and can better cover the remaining two attackers.

Error Detection and Correction for the 4-2 Offense

Even players with excellent skills can become confused when it comes time to combine skills with team formations and court movement. Correct court positioning for each play depends upon (a) anticipation by the players and their ability to read and react to the plays, (b) their ability to get to the correct positions before the ball is contacted, and (c) their ability to execute the appropriate skills.

ERROR ⃠

CORRECTION

ERROR	CORRECTION
1. The setter receives the serve.	1. If the setter is in the proper position—hiding at the net—the temptation to receive the serve is eliminated. In any circumstance, the setter should be encouraged never to receive the serve.

ERROR

CORRECTION

2. A free ball falls between a front row player and a back row player.

2. The forward line often thinks in terms of being only spikers and placing that as their top priority. The forwards must realize, however, that their first responsibility is to receive a free ball. The forwards must time their free ball movement off the net so they are stopped and ready to play the ball before the third hit is contacted by the opponent.

3. The attackers do not cover a ball that rebounds off the opponent's block.

3. This error usually occurs for one of two reasons: Either the attacking team does not get its players in the correct position for coverage, or the players who do move into position do not get close enough to the attacker or low enough. The player who generally has the greatest problem in assuming the correct coverage position is the nonattacking blocker. The person closest to the sideline must put the outside foot on the sideline and not react to any ball beyond that point.

4. The receiver makes a poor pass that hits the back of another player.

4. All six players must be actively involved in the serve reception. Anyone not receiving serve must open up to the receiver and be ready to help cover in case the receiver makes a poor pass.

5. The receiving team is indecisive over who should receive the ball.

5. Instruct your players that they must determine who will receive serve and call for it before the serve crosses the plane of the net. Generally speaking, each player is capable of covering a great deal of court space. When a ball falls between two players, it is usually due to indecision rather than a lack of time to move into position.

6. The spiker reaches back, attempting to play the ball after it rebounds off the block.

6. The only ball that the attacker should play off the block is one that remains between the attacker and the net. The attacker should allow balls bouncing behind him or her to drop to the other players covering.

4-2 Offense Drills

1. Wing Out Drill
[Corresponds to *Volleyball*, Step 17, Drill 1]

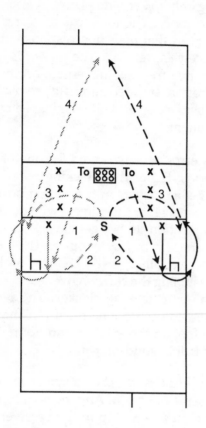

Instructions to the Class

''Divide into teams of three. Place a chair at the attack line at the left sideline. One player is a setter positioned at the net in the middle of the court. A left forward is in a blocking position. A tosser stands on the opposite side of the net.

''The tosser yells 'Free!' and tosses the ball high and easy to the attack line. The left forward moves straight back to the attack line, and overhead passes the ball to the setter, who sets a high, outside set. The forward 'wings out' around the chair and approaches to complete an attack. Repeat this drill on the right side of the court.''

- ''The tosser should toss the ball at varying heights so that the receiver must choose the appropriate passing skill, such as a forearm or overhead pass.''
- ''The forward should not move off the net until the tosser yells 'Free!' ''
- ''The forward's initial movement off the net should be straight back to the attack line.''
- ''The attacker must move to the outside of the chair as quickly as possible after passing the ball to the setter.''

Student Options

- ''The attacker may choose the appropriate method of receiving the tossed ball.''
- ''The attacker may choose the direction of the attack.''
- ''The attacker may decide whether to hit on-hand or off-hand first.''

Student Keys to Success

- Move to attack line quickly
- Set position before passing ball
- Pass ball and wing out
- Pass ball high
- Begin approach when set reaches highest point

Group Management and Safety Tips

- Two lines of attackers may work on each court, each attacker rotating to the end of the opposite line after the spike.
- Players in line must be aware of the spiked ball coming from the opposite attacking line.
- Remember to include the tosser in the rotating process or to replace the tosser after five or six tosses.

Equipment

- 2 courts
- 2 nets
- 4 chairs
- 1 ball for every player

Student Success Goals

- 8 successful attacks from the left forward position off of 10 tosses
- 7 successful attacks from the right forward position off of 10 tosses

To Decrease Difficulty

- Place the chair closer to the net.
- Have the tosser throw the ball at only one height.
- Have the tosser throw the ball to the same spot every time.

- The setter could set the ball high.
- Lower the Success Goals.

To Increase Difficulty

- Place the chair farther from the net, as far as the attack line.
- Have the tosser throw the ball lower.
- Have the tosser throw the ball to a variety of locations.
- Have the setter make lower sets.
- Raise the Success Goals.

2. *Serve Receive Drill*
[Corresponds to *Volleyball*, Step 17, Drill 2]

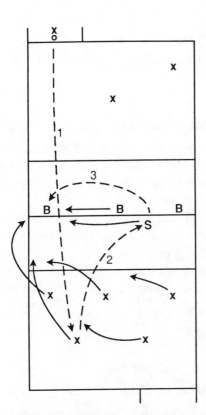

Group Management and Safety Tips

- Put one or two groups on each court. If two groups are used, the serve should alternate, first from one side, then the other. When the server on one side is serving, forward players on the same side of the net should be ready to block.

- Extra players can be used as servers.
- If the serving team is having difficulty receiving the attack, the drill may be changed so that the attacker only catches the set, rather than hitting it over the net.

Equipment

- 2 courts
- 2 nets
- 5 to 10 balls per court

Instructions to Class

''A team of six lines up on one side of the court, with a server on the opposite side. The server serves the ball underhand to the receiving team. The team is in a W-formation with the setter in the center forward position. The team receives the serve, executes an attack either forward or back, and covers the attacker correctly. The team receives 5 good serves, then rotates one position. Continue this until you have rotated all the way around to your original starting positions.''

- ''All attacking-team players should be in their coverage positions when the attacker contacts the ball.''
- ''Players covering can make sure they get low enough by touching their hands to the floor when they reach their coverage positions.''

Student Options

- "The receiving team must decide who will receive the serve."
- "The setter may set either forward or back."
- "The attacker has the choice of directing the spike in any direction."

Student Keys to Success

- Loudly call for ball
- Pass high to setter
- Nonreceivers open up
- Others to cover positions before contact by attacker
- Covering players low and ready

Student Success Goal

- 24 successful attacks with correct coverage off of 30 serves

To Decrease Difficulty

- Have the server serve to a designated person.
- Have the team decide in advance who will spike.
- Lower the Success Goal.

To Increase Difficulty

- Have the server use a variety of serves.
- Let the server serve the ball anywhere on the court.
- The setter could set either front or back.
- Raise the Success Goal.

3. Free Ball Drill
[Corresponds to *Volleyball*, Step 17, Drill 3]

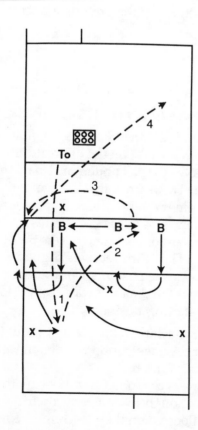

Group Management and Safety Tips

- Put one or two teams on each court. If using two teams, the tossers need to stand off the court to toss the ball. The teams need to alternate.
- If there are two teams, forwards of the nonreceiving side should begin in the blocking position.
- The tosser needs to remember to delay the toss a few seconds after yelling "Free!"

Equipment

- 2 courts
- 2 nets
- 5 or 6 balls per court

Instructions to Class

"A team of six lines up on one side of the court, with the three forwards at the net in blocking position. The center back is in the center of the court, and the left and right backs are on their respective sidelines 20 feet from the net. A tosser is on the opposite side of the net.

"The tosser yells 'Free,' delays a couple of seconds, then tosses the ball over the net high and easy. The team of six quickly moves into the W-formation. They receive the ball, set an attack, and cover the attacker.

"The team receives 5 balls, then rotates one position. Continue this drill until you have rotated to your original starting positions."

- "Outside forwards should move straight back to the attack line and set their positions before the ball is tossed."
- "The receiver must square the shoulders in the direction of the pass."
- "After the pass, forwards need to wing out and prepare to attack."
- "Coverage must be in place before contact by the attacker."

Student Options

- "The receiver must decide the appropriate method for receiving the toss."
- "The setter may decide whether to set forward or back."
- "The attacker may select the direction of the attack."

Student Keys to Success

- Move to attack line quickly
- Set position before playing ball
- Square shoulders in direction of pass
- Low position on coverage

Student Success Goal

- 24 successful attacks with proper coverage off of 30 tosses

To Decrease Difficulty

- Start the players in free ball position.
- Have the toss go to a consistent height.
- Have the toss go to a designated receiver.
- Lower the Success Goal.

To Increase Difficulty

- The ball could be tossed to a variety of heights and locations.
- The tosser could throw the ball quicker after yelling "Free!"
- Raise the Success Goal.

4. *Cover and Dig Drill*
[Corresponds to *Volleyball*, Step 17, Drill 4]

Group Management and Safety Tips

- Put only one group on each court.
- For this drill to be effective, the blockers must be able to successfully block the attack.
- If the blockers are not blocking the ball well, you may have to introduce a different method of blocking. The block-it is a teaching aid designed specifically for this type of drill. The pitch-back is a teaching aid used in basketball that can be used successfully in this drill. Both effectively simulate a good block.

Equipment

- 2 courts
- 2 nets
- 4 boxes for blockers to stand on
- Block-it or pitch-back, if needed
- 5 to 10 balls per court

Instructions to Class

"A team of six stands on one side of the court in the same starting positions (W-formation) as in the Serve Receive Drill (Drill 2). Two blockers stand on boxes on the right side of the court on the opposite side of the net.

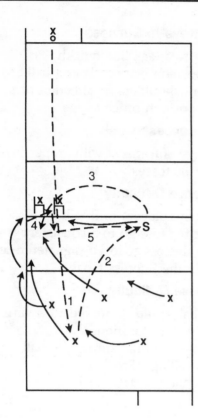

- "The set should be high to the outside."
- "The attackers should hit into the blockers' hands, because this is a drill to practice digging by the coverage."
- "The dig by the coverage should be high."

Student Options

- "The tosser may decide the direction of the toss."
- "The setter may choose the direction of the set when completing the attack off the coverage."
- "The attacker may choose the direction of the attack."

Student Keys to Success

- Cover in low position
- Dig ball high
- Cover second attack

Student Success Goal

- 18 out of 30 successful digs off the opposing block

To Decrease Difficulty

- The tosses could go high, easy, and directly at the receiver.
- Have the tosser lengthen the time between calling "Free!" and tossing.
- Have the setter set high.
- The attacker should hit the ball directly into the blockers' hands.
- Lower the Success Goal.

To Increase Difficulty

- Have the tosser vary the height and direction of the tosses.
- Have the tosser shorten the time between calling "Free!" and tossing.
- Raise the Success Goal.

"A tosser on the same side as the blockers yells 'Free!' and throws a ball high over the net. The team receives the free ball, sets the attack to the left forward, and covers. The blockers block the ball. The attacking coverage attempts to set up with a successful dig—a dig that initiates a second completed attack.

"The team receives 5 tosses, then rotates one position. Continue the drill until the players have returned to their original positions."

5. Serve and Free Ball Drill

[Corresponds to *Volleyball*, Step 17, Drill 5]

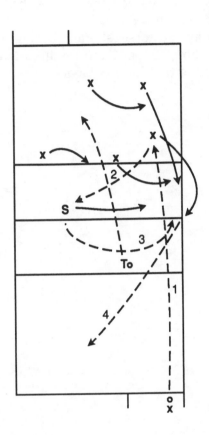

Group Management and Safety Tips

- Set up two teams on each court.
- When using two teams on a court, the free ball tosser must be outside the court boundaries.
- Extra players can be used as tossers and servers.
- One team receives serve and sets the attack five consecutive times; then the opposite team does the same.
- When one team is attacking, the other team can work on defense, beginning always with the three forwards at the net and ready to block.

Equipment

- 2 courts
- 2 nets
- 3 balls for every six-player team

Instructions to Class

"Have a team of six on one side of the net, and a tosser and a server each with a ball on the opposite side. The server serves. The receiving team, positioned in the W-formation, receives serve, sets the attack, and covers. Then the team immediately assumes starting positions as in the Free Ball Drill (Drill 3): three forwards at the net in blocking position, center back in the center of the court, and left and right backs on their respective sidelines 20 feet from the net. The opposing tosser calls 'Free!' and tosses a ball high over the net. The receiving team passes the free ball, sets an attack, and covers.

"Play immediately continues with another serve and attack, immediately followed by another free ball. The team receives 5 good serves, then rotates one position. The drill continues until all the players have returned to their starting positions."

- "Move to the free ball position quickly, getting there even before the attacker contacts the ball."
- "Even though the tosser yells 'Free,' the receiving team should also yell 'Free!'"
- "You must make a good pass on the free ball."

Student Options

- "The server may choose which method of serve to use and the serve's direction."
- "The receiver must determine whether it would be more advantageous to receive the ball with a forearm pass or an overhead pass."
- "The setter has a choice of which attack player to set."
- "The tosser determines the direction of the free ball he or she tosses."

Student Keys to Success

- Quick movement off net
- Cover entire court

- Set before attacker contacts ball
- Call ball as soon as possible
- Make every pass a good one

Student Success Goals

- 24 successful attacks off of 30 serves
- 24 successful attacks off of 30 free balls

To Decrease Difficulty

- Make the server serve the ball underhand.
- The serve or tossed free ball could go directly to the receiver.
- The tosser should wait a longer time between yelling "Free!" and tossing the ball.
- Lower the Success Goal.

To Increase Difficulty

- Let the server use any method of serving.
- Have the server serve the seams between potential receivers.
- Let the tosser vary the free ball toss in height and force.
- Have the tosser shorten the time between yelling "Free!" and tossing the ball.
- Raise the Success Goal.

Step 18 2-1-3 Defense

The 2-1-3 defense is the easiest defense to learn in volleyball. Each player on the court is responsible for receiving only one type of attack, either an off-speed or a hard-driven spike. It is a very effective defense against beginning-level teams that generally lack power in their attack. This formation covers the court area well and adapts quickly to a surprise attack.

When receiving a ball, most teams attempt to complete the three-hit combination of pass, set, and attack. At beginning levels, though, teams often are not skilled enough to consistently accomplish this desired result. Defending against such teams is complicated by their irregular style of play. In many cases, teams return the ball over the net on any of the three contacts. The defenders are put into a position where they don't know what to expect; thus, it is difficult to be in the correct positions. The 2-1-3 defensive alignment seems to serve a team well when defending against unorthodox attacks.

Error Detection and Correction for the 2-1-3 Defense

A team's success on defense is largely dependent upon reading the attack of the opponents. Defending players need to be alert for any clues that the opponents display that will help them accurately guess the opponent's intention. Examples of such clues include (a) the position of the set ball in relation to the net and the sidelines, (b) the location of the attacker in relation to the set and the sidelines, (c) the angle of the attacker's shoulders when the arm swings for the attack, and (d) the height of the set.

For example, let's look at one of these clues more closely. If the set is made outside of the antenna, it would be impossible for the attacker to hit the ball down the line and still send the ball over the legal portion of the net. The line defender observing this knows that he or she does not have to protect the line and should adjust the position accordingly.

ERROR 🚫

CORRECTION

1. The ball goes through the block.

1. This can be corrected by either having the middle close the block or by not allowing the outside to adjust the set position after the middle closes.

ERROR 🚫   **CORRECTION**

2. The attacker successfully hits down the line.

2. The line behind the block must be protected by the back on that side. This back must be aware of the block location. If the block leaves the line open for the attack, the back must stay on the line and approximately 20 feet from the net. If the block protects the line from the attack, the back may move toward the center of the court or in for dink coverage.

3. The attacker successfully dinks over the block.

3. The center back is responsible for the majority of dinks. It is helpful if the blockers are trained to read the attack and yell when they know the attacker's intention is to dink. The center back and the back on the line should move in toward the block upon hearing the signal.

4. The ball rebounds off the player in the power alley and continues out of bounds.

4. The power alley player must be positioned outside of the center blocker's inside shoulder so as to see the attacker and the ball. This player should begin in a position with the back to the sideline so that the spike will always be in front of him or her. A good principle of defense is to be positioned to always play the ball from the outside of the court into the center.

5. The ball goes off the blockers' hands and out of bounds.

5. The blocker closest to the sideline of the court should always turn the outside hand of the block so that a deflected ball will be directed back into the center of the court.

2-1-3 Defense Drills

1. Digging a Dink: Left or Right Forward Attacker Drill

[Corresponds to *Volleyball*, Step 18, Drills 1 and 2]

Group Management and Safety Tips

- Put one group on each court, with a second group waiting to rotate into the drill.
- Groups rotate after every five drill attempts.
- Extra players may be used as additional attackers.
- When executing the drill with a right forward attacker, it is easier to use a tosser to toss the ball to the setter.

Equipment

- 2 courts
- 2 nets
- 1 ball for every three players

Instructions to Class

"On one side of the net, there is a setter and an attacker in the left or right forward position. On the opposite side, there are three blockers and a center back. The attacker tosses the ball to the setter, who sets the ball to the attacker. The attacker dinks the ball over the block, either down the line or to the center of the court. The center back covers dinks down the line, and the off blocker covers dinks to the center of the court."

- "The attacker should vary the selection of attack direction."
- "The attacker should disguise the attack by making it appear to be a spike."
- "The blockers should yell 'Dink' every time."
- "The defensive player should dig the dink high."

Student Options

- "The setter may vary the height of the set."
- "The attacker has the choice of dinking toward the center of the court or down the line."

Student Keys to Success

- Attacker approaches as if to spike
- Blockers yell "Dink" every time
- Diggers read attacker to determine dink direction
- Defensive players move quickly to ball and dig it high

Student Success Goals

- On offense, 10 successful dinks off of 12 sets
- On defense, 8 successful digs off of 10 dinks

To Decrease Difficulty

- Do not let the attacker vary the direction of the dink.
- Lower the Success Goals.

To Increase Difficulty

- Have the setter vary the height of the set.
- Have the attacker spike a hard-driven ball occasionally to keep the defensive players honest.
- Raise the Success Goals.

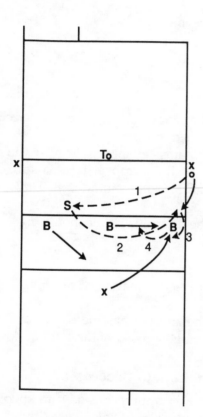

Left forward dinks down the line

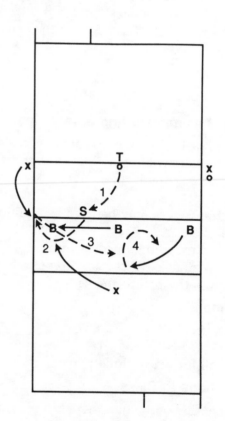

Right forward dinks to the center of the court

2. Digging Down-the-Line Spikes: Right or Left Back Drill

[Corresponds to *Volleyball*, Step 18, Drills 3 and 4]

Group Management and Safety Tips

- Put one group on each court.
- The two original drills can be combined on one court (right and left backs simultaneously) by using two attackers (in the left forward and right forward positions) and two defenders (in the left back and right back).
- The setter should then set both positions alternately.
- The players should rotate to every position.
- Another player should toss the ball to the setter when the setter is back setting to the attacker.

Equipment

- 2 courts
- 2 nets
- 1 ball for every three players

Instructions to Class

"On one side of the net, there are three blockers and a right or left back defending the line. On the opposite side, there are a left or right forward and a setter.

"The attacker tosses the ball to the setter, who sets high and outside. The blockers give the attacker the line (they line up to block only the angle). The attacker spikes the ball down the line. The right or left back digs the ball high to the center of the court, and the center forward sets an attack."

- "Blockers must give the attacker the line by blocking the angle."
- "Defending players must hold their positions on the line in anticipation of digging."

Student Options

- "Decide in which position to begin drill."
- "If there are two attackers, the setter can decide in which direction to set—front or back."

Student Keys to Success

- Anticipate and read attack
- Move to position
- Be low and ready
- Dig ball high

Student Success Goals

- 10 down-the-line spikes off of 12 sets
- 6 successful digs by the right or left back off of 10 spikes
- 4 completed attacks on the transition off of 6 digs

To Decrease Difficulty

- Let the setter set the ball a greater distance from the net.
- Have the blockers attempt to take the line away from the attacker.
- Lower the Success Goals.

To Increase Difficulty

- Do not use a block.
- Have the setter vary the height of the set.
- Raise the Success Goals.

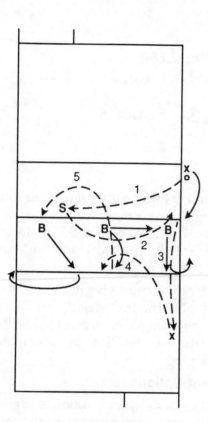

Left forward attacks down the line

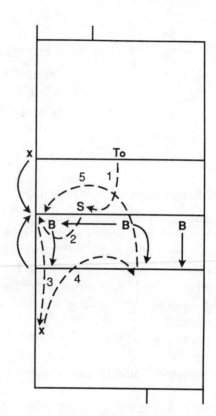

Right forward attacks crosscourt

3. *Digging Crosscourt: Left or Right Back Drill*

[Corresponds to *Volleyball*, Step 18, Drills 5 and 6]

Group Management and Safety Tips

- These two drills can be worked together, using two attackers and two defensive players.
- The setter can then receive the ball from either attacker and set that attacker.
- The blockers should take the line away from the attacker.
- An additional player is needed to toss the ball to the setter when back setting to the attacker.

Equipment

- 2 courts
- 2 nets
- 1 ball for every three players

Instructions to Class

"On one side of the net, there are three blockers and a left or right back defensive player. On the opposite court, there are a setter and an attacker in the left or right forward position.

"The attacker or additional player tosses the ball to the setter, who sets high and outside. The left or right back or the off blocker digs the ball, and the forwards attempt to complete an attack on transition."

- "The back in the power alley must take position outside of the middle blocker's inside shoulder so that the attacker and the ball can be seen."

- "Either the defensive player in the power alley or the off blocker may receive the spike."
- "The attacker should always attempt to complete the attack even if the set is not perfect."

Student Options

- "The setter may set either front or back."
- "The attacker may direct the spike to the power alley or with a sharp angle closer to the net."

Student Keys to Success

- Backcourt defensive players and off blocker start with backs to sideline
- Power alley player lines up outside middle blocker's inside shoulder to see attacker and ball
- Low position, with weight forward
- Once forward movement begins, move through ball

Student Success Goals

- 10 crosscourt spikes off of 12 sets
- 6 successful digs off of 10 spikes
- 4 completed attacks on the transition off of 6 digs

To Decrease Difficulty

- Let the setter set the ball farther off the net.
- Do not make the setter alternate sets to each side.

- Have the attacker spike directly at a defensive player.
- Lower the Success Goals.

To Increase Difficulty

- Make the setter set the ball close to the net.

- Have the setter vary the height of the set.
- Have the attacker vary the direction of the crosscourt spike.
- Have the attacker direct the spike between the defensive players.
- Raise the Success Goals.

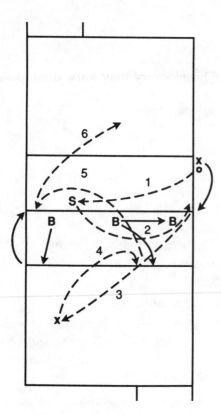

Left forward attacks crosscourt

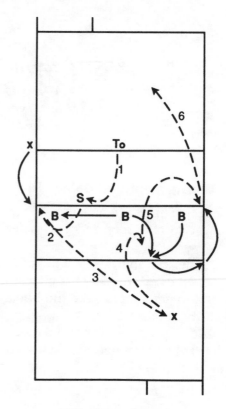

Right forward attacks crosscourt

4. Attack and Counterattack Drill

[Corresponds to *Volleyball*, Step 18, Drill 7]

Group Management and Safety Tips

- With a larger class, the extra players can be used as additional attackers.
- When additional attackers are used, they must be aware of the counterattack so as not to be hit by the ball.
- All players need to participate in the drill at all defensive positions.

Equipment

- 2 courts
- 2 nets
- 1 ball for every four players

Instructions to Class

"A team of six on one side of the court sets up in base defensive position. A tosser, setter, and two attackers are on the opposite side.

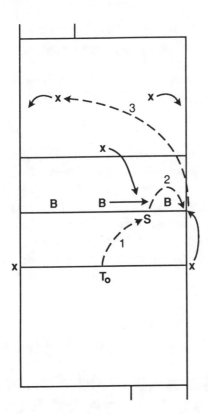

"The tosser overhand tosses the ball to the setter, who sets either attacker, permitting him or her to spike over the net. The defending team must block the spike, or receive it and attempt to execute a counterattack. If the attacking players are unable to spike, the defending team should move to a free ball position to receive the third hit over. When the team executes the attack, they must cover the attacker.

"The defending team should complete 6 successful counterattacks, then rotate one position. Continue this drill until the players have rotated back to their original positions."

- "The defensive backcourt players should always react to the direction of the set, adjusting their positions in relation to its location and the position of the blockers."

- "The attacker should vary the attack as much as possible both in method and in direction."
- "The ball should be dug high to the center of the court to facilitate the counterattack."

Student Options

- "The setter may set either attacker."
- "The setter may vary the height of the set and the set's distance from the net."
- "The blockers may vary their position, either giving or taking the line away from the attacker."

Student Keys to Success

- Read attack
- Assume correct defensive position
- Be low and ready
- React to ball
- Dig high to center of court
- Play through ball

Student Success Goals

- 10 spikes off of 12 sets
- 6 successful digs and transition attack completions out of 10 spikes received

To Decrease Difficulty

- Have the setter set the ball off the net.
- Have one team select one type and direction of attack and practice it for six attempts.
- Lower the Success Goals.

To Increase Difficulty

- Have the tosser occasionally toss the ball over the net instead of to the setter.
- Let the attacker vary the type of the attack as much as possible.
- Have the attacker always direct the attack between two defensive players.
- Have the setter play the ball over the net.
- Raise the Success Goals.

Step 19   International 4-2 Offense

Although the International 4-2 offense is similar to the regular 4-2, using it allows a team certain advantages. First, the location of the setter in the right forward position means that the two attackers, if right-handed, are both hitting on-hand. This makes the overall attack stronger. Also, from the right forward position, it is much easier for the setter to attack the ball on the second hit when there is a good pass. Third, using this offense permits a middle attack, which prepares a team for introduction to a multiple offense. The only disadvantage to the International 4-2 comes when a team has a short setter, because this is the position blocking the opponent's strong-side hitter.

Error Detection and Correction for the International 4-2

The errors made in the International 4-2 are similar to those made in the regular 4-2. The primary differences are usually centered around the right back position. In both the serve reception and free ball formations, the setter remains at the net ready to play the second ball. The right back must adjust his or her position by covering the right forward area vacated by the setter. In these two formations, the right back almost appears to be a forward.

If the right back does not adjust there will be a vulnerable area on the court. Sometimes the setter forgets that the right back is not an eligible attacker and sets this player. Both the setter and the right back must remember that there are only two eligible attackers in this offense. The left and center backs must remember to shift to the right, becoming the two points of the W when the right back moves toward the net.

ERROR

CORRECTION

1. The setter receives the serve.	1. If the setter is correctly positioned at the net, there should be no temptation to receive the serve. The setter must switch to the right side quickly and close to the net.

ERROR 🚫	**CORRECTION**
2. A free ball drops to the floor without anyone receiving it.	2. This occurs in two specific areas. If the ball drops between the forwards and the backs and is near the attack line, it is generally the fault of the two forwards or the right back. The two forwards must quickly move back to the attack line while the right back moves forward to the attack line. All players must be in position and ready before the ball is contacted by the attacker. If the ball falls in the right back corner of the court, the center back has not adjusted to cover that position after it is vacated by the right back.
3. The ball rebounds off the opponent's block and drops to the floor on the attacker's side.	3. The three-person coverage must position close to the attacker and in a low posture ready to react to the ball off the opposing block. The person closest to the sideline must make sure that the outside foot is on the line, so as not to play any ball that is going out of bounds.
4. The attacker attempts to play a ball that rebounds off the block.	4. The attacker should play only balls that rebound off the opponent's block and remain between him or her and the net.
5. The serve falls to the court between two players.	5. Early decision making is essential. The receivers should call for the ball before it crosses the net into their court. The left-side players should always be more aggressive in playing a ball between them and players to their right.
6. A player in the W-formation gets hit in the back by a passed ball.	6. Every player must be actively involved in serve reception. If not playing the ball, the player must open up to the receiver by turning and facing the receiver.
7. The setter attempts to back set.	7. The two eligible attackers are in the center forward and left forward positions. The right-side player is a back row player; if set, he or she must not jump and spike, but may still return the ball over the net.

International 4-2 Offense Drills

1. Wing Out Drill

[Corresponds to *Volleyball*, Step 19, Drill 1]

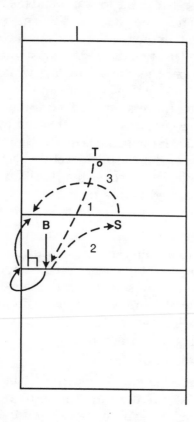

Instructions to Class

''Divide into teams of three. Place a chair at the attack line at the left sideline. Have a partner be a setter at the net on the right side of the court. A left forward is in blocking position on the same side of the court as the chair. The other player is a tosser on the opposite side of the net.

''The tosser yells 'Free!' and tosses the ball high and easy to the attack line. The left forward moves straight back to the attack line, overhead passes the ball to the setter, wings out around the chair, and approaches for an attack. The setter sets a high, outside set. The forward attacks. The drill is repeated with a center forward in the center of the court instead of a left forward.''

- ''The tosser should toss the ball at varying heights so that the receiver must choose the appropriate passing skill—forearm or overhead pass.''
- ''The forward should not move off the net until the tosser yells 'Free!'''
- ''Initial movement off the net should be straight back to the attack line.''
- ''The attacker must move around the chair as quickly as possible after passing the ball to the setter.''

Student Options

- ''The attacker may choose the direction of the attack.''
- ''The attacker may choose the appropriate method of receiving the tossed ball.''
- ''The attacker may decide whether to hit on-hand or off-hand first.''

Student Keys to Success

- Move to attack line quickly
- Set position before passing ball
- Pass ball and wing out
- Pass ball high
- Begin approach when set reaches highest point

Group Management and Safety Tips

- Two lines of attackers can work on each court, with each attacker rotating to the end of the opposite line after spiking.
- Players in line must be aware of the spiked ball coming from the opposite attacking line.
- Remember to include the tosser and the setter in the rotating process, or replace them after five or six plays.
- This drill can be run from either the left or center of the court.

Equipment

- 2 courts
- 2 nets
- 4 chairs
- 1 ball for every player

Student Success Goals

- 8 successful attacks from the left forward position off of 10 tosses
- 8 successful attacks from the center forward position off of 10 tosses

To Decrease Difficulty

- Place the chair closer to the net.
- Allow the tosser to throw the ball at only one height.
- Make the tosser throw the ball to the same spot every time.
- The setter could set the ball high.
- Lower the Success Goals.

To Increase Difficulty

- Place the chair farther from the net, as far as to the attack line.
- Have the tosser throw the ball lower.
- Let the tosser throw the ball to a variety of locations.
- The setter should use lower sets.
- Raise the Success Goals.

2. *Serve Receive Drill*
[Corresponds to *Volleyball*, Step 19, Drill 2]

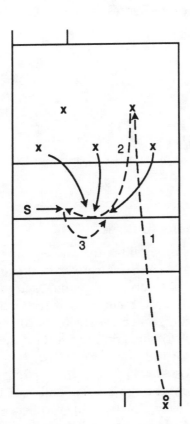

Group Management and Safety Tips

- Put either one or two teams on each court. If two groups are used, the serve should alternate, first from one side, then the other. When one side is serving, the forward players on that side should be at the net ready to block.
- Extra players may be used as servers.
- If the serving team is having difficulty receiving the attack, the drill may be changed so that the attacker only catches the set rather than hitting it over the net.

Equipment

- 2 courts
- 2 nets
- 5 to 10 balls per court

Instructions to Class

"A team of six lines up on one side of the court, with a server on the opposite side of the court. The server serves the ball underhand to the receiving team. Using the W-formation with the setter in the right forward position, the team receives the serve, executes an attack by either the left or center forward, and covers the attacker.

''The team receives 5 good serves, then rotates one position. Continue this drill until you have rotated around to your original starting positions.''

- ''Other offensive players should be in their coverage positions when the attacker contacts the ball.''
- ''Covering players can make sure they get low enough by touching their hands to the floor when they reach their coverage positions.''

Student Options

- ''The receiving team must decide who will receive the serve.''
- ''The setter may set either the left forward or the center forward attacker.''
- ''The attacker has the choice of directing the spike in any direction.''

Student Keys to Success

- Loudly call for ball
- Pass high to setter
- Nonreceivers open up
- Get to cover position before contact by attacker
- Be low and ready

Student Success Goal

- 24 successful attacks with the correct coverage off of 30 serves

To Decrease Difficulty

- Make the server serve to a designated person.
- Let the team decide in advance who will spike.
- Lower the Success Goal.

To Increase Difficulty

- Let the server use a variety of serves
- Let the server serve the ball anywhere on the court.
- Raise the Success Goal.

3. Free Ball Drill

[Corresponds to *Volleyball*, Step 19, Drill 3]

Group Management and Safety Tips

- Put one or two teams on each court. If using two teams, the tossers need to stand off the court to toss the ball. Tossers need to alternate so only one team is working at a time.
- The forwards of the nonreceiving side should begin in the blocking position.
- The tossers need to remember to delay the toss a few seconds after yelling ''Free!''

Equipment

- 2 courts
- 2 nets
- 5 to 6 balls per court

Instructions to Class

''A team of six lines up on one side of the court, with the three forwards at the net in blocking position. The center back is in the center of the court, and the left and right backs are on their respective sidelines 20 feet from the net. A tosser is on the court on the opposite side of the net.

''The tosser yells 'Free,' delays for a couple of seconds, then tosses the ball over the net high and easy. The team of six quickly moves into the W-formation, receives the ball, sets an attack, and covers the attacker. The right back must move forward to fill the position not filled by the setter, who must remain at

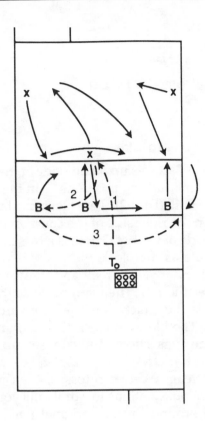

• "The outside forward should move straight back to the attack line and not wing out until *after* the ball has been passed."
• "Coverage must be in place before contact by the attacker."

Student Options

• "The attacker must decide on the appropriate method for receiving the toss."
• "The setter may decide whether to set the left forward or the center forward attacker."
• "The attacker may select the direction of the attack."

Student Keys to Success

• Move to attack line quickly
• Set position before playing ball
• Square shoulders to direction of pass
• Low position on coverage

Student Success Goal

• 24 successful attacks with the proper coverage off of 30 tosses

To Decrease Difficulty

• Start the players in free ball position.
• Make the tosser throw the ball to a designated receiver.
• Have the tosser throw at a consistent height.
• Lower the Success Goal.

To Increase Difficulty

• Have the tosser throw the ball quicker after yelling "Free!"
• Let the tosser throw the ball to a variety of heights and locations.
• Raise the Success Goal.

the net. The center back adjusts to the right back area of the court.

"The team receives 5 balls, then rotates one position. Continue this drill until you have rotated around to your original starting positions."

• "The forwards need to set their positions before the ball is tossed."
• "The receiver must square his or her shoulders to the direction of the pass."

4. Cover and Dig Drill

[Corresponds to *Volleyball*, Step 19, Drill 4]

Instructions to Class

"A team of six sets up on one side of the court in the same starting positions as in the Serve Receive Drill (Drill 2). Two blockers stand on a box on the right side of the court on the opposite side of the net. There is a tosser on the same side as the blockers.

"The tosser yells 'Free!' and throws a high ball over the net. The team receives the free ball, sets the attack to the left forward, and covers. The blockers block the ball, and the coverage digs successfully to set up for a second attack.

"The team receives 5 tosses, then rotates one position. Continue this drill until you have rotated around to your original positions."

- "Sets should be high to the outside."
- "The attacker should hit into the blockers' hands because this is a drill to practice digging by the coverage."
- "The dig by the coverage should be high."
- "A successful dig is one that initiates a second attack."

Student Options

- "The tosser may decide the direction of the toss."
- "The attacker may choose the direction of the attack."
- "The setter may choose the direction of the set when completing an attack off the coverage."

Student Keys to Success

- Cover in low position
- Dig ball high
- Cover second attack
- Blockers keep ball in play

Student Success Goal

- 18 successful digs off of 30 opposing blocks

Group Management and Safety Tips

- Put only one group on each court.
- For this drill to be effective, the blockers must be able to block the attack successfully.
- If the blockers are not blocking the ball well, you may have to introduce a different method of blocking, such as a block-it or a pitch-back.

Equipment

- 2 courts
- 2 nets
- Boxes for blockers to stand on
- 5 to 10 balls per court
- Block-it or pitch-back, if needed

To Decrease Difficulty

- Have the tosser make the tosses high, easy, and directly at the receiving player.
- Make the tosser allow more time between calling "Free!" and tossing.
- The setter could make high sets.
- The attacker should hit ball directly into the blockers' hands.
- Lower the Success Goal.

To Increase Difficulty

- Let the tosser throw the ball to varying heights and directions.
- Have the tosser shorten the time between the free ball call and the toss.
- Raise the Success Goal.

5. Serve and Free Ball Drill
[Corresponds to *Volleyball*, Step 19, Drill 5]

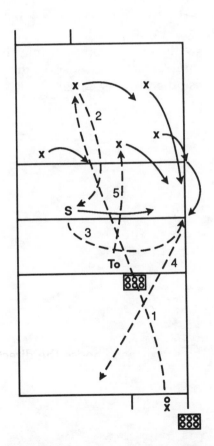

- One of the teams on the court may receive serve and set their attack five consecutive times; then the opposite team may do the same.
- When one team is attacking, the other team can work on defense, always beginning with the three forwards at the net, ready to block.

Equipment

- 2 courts
- 2 nets
- 3 balls for every six-player team

Instructions to Class

"A team of six set up in the W-formation. A tosser and a server are on the opposite side of the net, each with a volleyball.

"The server serves. The receiving team sets, attacks, and covers. The team immediately assumes the starting positions as in the Free Ball Drill (Drill 3). The tosser calls 'Free!' and tosses the ball high over the net. The receiving team passes the free ball, sets an attack, and covers.

"Play continues with another serve, immediately followed by another free ball, and so on. The team receives 5 good serve-free ball sequences and rotates one position. Continue this drill until you rotate around to your starting positions."

Group Management and Safety Tips

- Put two teams on each court.
- When using two teams on a court, the free ball tosser must be outside the court boundaries.
- Extra players may be used as the tossers and the servers.

- "Move to the free ball position quickly, getting there before the attacker contacts the ball before the toss."
- "Even though the tosser yells 'Free,' the receiving team should also yell 'Free!'"
- "The receiver must make a good pass on the free ball."

Student Options

- "The server may choose the method and direction of the serve."
- "The receivers must determine whether it would be more advantageous to receive the ball with a forearm pass or an overhead pass."
- "The setter has a choice of which attack player to set."
- "The tosser may determine the direction of the free ball."

Student Keys to Success

- Quick movement off net
- Cover entire court
- Coverage sets before attacker contacts ball
- Call ball as soon as possible
- Every pass must be good

Student Success Goals

- 24 successful attacks with the correct coverage off of 30 serves
- 24 successful attacks with the correct coverage off of 30 free balls

To Decrease Difficulty

- Make the server serve the ball underhand.
- The serve or tossed free ball could go directly to the receiver.
- Make the tosser wait a longer time between yelling "Free!" and tossing the ball.
- Lower the Success Goals.

To Increase Difficulty

- Let the server use any method of serving.
- Have the server serve the seams.
- Let the tosser vary the free ball toss's height and force.
- Have the tosser shorten the time between yelling "Free!" and tossing the ball.
- Raise the Success Goals.

Step 20 6-2 Offense

There are technically three multiple offenses in volleyball: the 6-2, the 5-1, and the 6-0. Rarely is the 6-0 offense used; therefore, it will not be covered in this text. These three offenses are categorized as multiple offenses because they are characterized by a setter penetrating from the back row to the net to perform setting responsibilities. This allows a team to employ a much more powerful attack, because all three forward line players are eligible to spike.

This type of offense lends itself well to the development of attack systems, including quick middle hits and combination plays. A combination play is a prearranged movement with two or three attackers anticipating the set. The setter makes the decision as to which attacker receives the ball. The purpose of a combination play is to disguise the attack in order to confuse the opposing blockers. (Combination plays, however, are beyond the scope of this book.)

The 6-2 offense is more popular than the 4-2 at advanced levels of play, but not as popular as the 5-1 offense. The main reason for its lesser popularity is that it employs two setters. Many coaches feel that a two-setter system is more difficult because the attackers must adapt to two differing styles of setting. Other coaches see this as an advantage because it allows them to utilize a small, quick, highly talented setter who may not have the ability to play the front row. In the National Federation of State High School Associations and NAGWS (National Association for Girls and Women in Sport) rules, where substituting is more liberal, a coach can use this small player for back row setting duties. When this setter rotates to the front row, he or she can be substituted for by a player specializing as an attacker and blocker.

Error Detection and Correction for the 6-2 Offense

In a multiple offense the setter must be in excellent physical condition. A setter's movement is typically to penetrate to the net, set the attack, cover the attack, and return to the right back position. This movement by the setter continues throughout the game every time his or her team receives the ball from the opponents. Most errors committed in the 6-2 offense are centered around either the setter not moving to the correct position soon enough or the rest of the team not adjusting to the setter's movement.

Other errors are often caused by the attackers not anticipating every set. Each attacker must believe that he or she will receive the set every time and should not begin movement toward coverage until knowing where the set will in fact be directed.

ERROR 🚫	CORRECTION
1. A pass or a dig reaches the net before the setter.	1. The opponents usually attempt to attack the right back area of the court. The setter must move to the net as quickly as possible, allowing time to set the position before playing the ball. However, on defense the setter must not move until it is evident that the attack will not be to the right back area. This is best described by the key words "defense first."
2. The attack or the third ball over lands in the right back position with no one to receive it.	2. The setter must stay in the defensive position until determining the direction of the oncoming attack. Once deciding to penetrate, the setter must communicate this intention to teammates by yelling "Free!" The center back must then adjust to the area vacated by the right back position.
3. The setter and the center forward collide when trying to cover an attacker.	3. The movement of the center forward and the setter to the covering position should come after the initial movement of the center forward to the net for a possible quick attack.
4. A free ball falls between the front row players and the back row players.	4. The three forwards must move to the attack line as quickly as possible after the free ball has been called. This allows them to be in position at the time the ball is contacted by the opponents on the third hit, and to be ready to react to the play.
5. The serve falls to the ground between the two back row players in the W.	5. The players on the left side of the court are always more aggressive in receiving any ball between them and other players.
6. One player blocks after a free ball has been called.	6. On defense it is extremely important that all players on a team follow the same formation. If one player decides to make an individual decision, differing from the setter's call, vulnerable areas of the court will exist.

6-2 Offense Drills

1. *Serve Reception and Attack*
[Corresponds to *Volleyball*, Step 20, Drill 1]

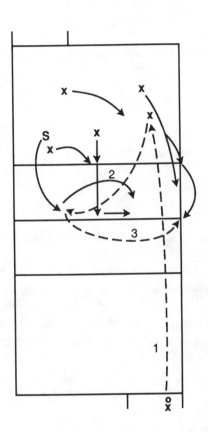

Instructions to Class

"A team of six lines up on one side of the court, with a server on the opposite side of the court. The server serves underhand to the receiving team. Using a W-formation with the setter in the right back position, the team receives the serve, executes an attack with any of the three front row attackers, and covers the attacker. The ball must land within the boundaries of the opposite court for the attack to be considered successful.

"The team receives 5 good serves, then rotates one position. The drill continues until you have rotated around to your original starting positions."

- "Call for the ball before it crosses the net."
- "Every team member should be involved either mentally or physically during serve reception."
- "The pass must be accurate."
- "If the setter cannot play the pass, the right forward should assume the setting role."

Student Options

- "The server may determine the direction of the serve."
- "The setter may determine which attacker to set."
- "The setter may determine the speed of the attack by varying the height of the set."
- "The attacker may determine the direction of the attack."

Student Keys to Success

- Call ball early
- Set position before playing ball
- Setter should indicate location to which receiver should pass ball

Group Management and Safety Tips

- Two groups can be on one court, one group playing defense while the other group is attacking. The serve alternates after every five attempts.
- Extra players can be used as servers.
- Make sure that there are no stray balls on or around the immediate court area.

Equipment

- 2 courts
- 2 nets
- 3 balls for every six-player team

Student Success Goal

- 24 completed attacks off of 30 successful receptions of serve

To Decrease Difficulty

- The serve could go directly to the receiver.
- Have the server make the serve high and easy.
- Have the setter set to only one position for all 5 serves in rotation.
- Lower the Success Goal.

To Increase Difficulty

- Let the server use more force and a lower trajectory.
- Let the server use a variety of serves.
- Have the server serve the seams.
- Tell the setter who to set as he or she receives the pass.
- Raise the Success Goal.

2. *Free Ball and Attack Drill*
[Corresponds to *Volleyball*, Step 20, Drill 2]

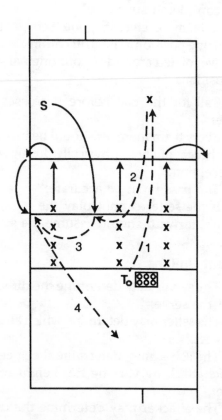

Group Management and Safety Tips

- Put only one group on each court.
- Additional players could position themselves in line on the opposite side of the net.

- After each attack, the hitter rotates to the end of the line.
- Due to the attackers' moving off the net, the remaining attackers should be in line on the opposite side of the net, ready to move to a base defensive blocking position as soon as the player ahead of them has attacked.
- Everyone should watch for stray balls on the court, especially in the area of the attack.

Equipment

- 2 courts
- 2 nets
- 3 balls for every six-player group

Instructions to Class

''Three attackers, a setter, and a passer set up on one side of the net; a tosser stands on the opposite side. The three attackers begin in the three front row positions in the base defensive formation. The setter begins in the right back of the court. The passer begins in the left back position.

''The tosser yells 'Free!' and tosses the ball to the passer. The passer passes to the setter, who has penetrated to the net. At the free ball call, the attackers drop back to the attack line and prepare to hit. The setter sets to one of the three attackers, who make a successful attack. All players should cover as appropriate. The team receives 15 free balls.''

- ''The setter must penetrate to the net as soon as the free ball is called.''
- ''The setter should repeat the free ball call.''
- ''The attackers must move to the attack line quickly, arriving there prior to the toss.''
- ''The attackers must move straight back from the net, not winging out until after the ball has been passed.''
- ''When passing the free ball, the attacker must angle the shoulders in the direction of the pass.''
- ''All players should be in their coverage positions by the time the ball is attacked.''

Student Options

- ''The tosser may toss to any of the three receivers.''
- ''The setter may set any of the three attackers.''

Student Keys to Success

- Quick movement to attack line
- Angle shoulders toward direction of pass
- Wing out after pass is completed
- Setter moves to net as soon as free ball is called

Student Success Goal

- 12 completed attacks off of 15 tosses

To Decrease Difficulty

- Have the tosser increase the time between the free ball signal and the toss.
- The tosser could toss high, easy balls to the receivers.
- The tosser could indicate in advance whom the toss will be toward.
- Lower the Success Goal.

To Increase Difficulty

- The toss could be low and hard.
- Have the tosser shorten the time between the free ball signal and the toss.
- Have the tosser indicate the attacker when the ball is being passed to the setter.
- Raise the Success Goal.

3. Setter Penetration and Right Back Covering Drill

[Corresponds to *Volleyball*, Step 20, Drill 3]

Group Management and Safety Tips

- Have two groups per court alternating attacks.
- Forwards on the nonreceiving side may practice blocking.

Equipment

- 2 courts
- 2 nets
- 3 balls for every four-player team

Instructions to Class

''A middle attacker, an outside attacker, a setter, and a center back player set up on one side of the net. A tosser stands on the opposite side of the net.

''The tosser yells 'Free!' and tosses the ball to the right back corner of the opposite court. At the 'Free!' signal, the setter penetrates to the net, and the center back must quickly move to cover the right back area of the court. The center back passes to the setter, who sets to the middle or outside hitters to complete the successful attack. The team receives 15 free balls.''

- ''The setter repeats the free ball signal before penetrating.''

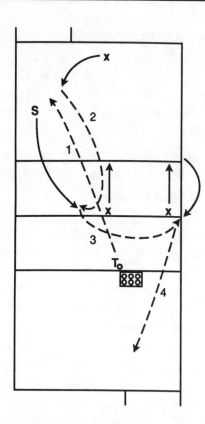

- "The center back adjusts to the right on the setter's free ball call."
- "The center back should be in the right back position before playing the ball."
- "The attackers move straight back and wing out after the pass is made."

Student Options

- "The tosser may decide on the force and direction of the toss."

- "The setter may decide to set center or outside."
- "The attackers may decide on the type and direction of attack."

Student Keys to Success

- Setter's free ball signal essential
- Center back's quick response and position
- Accurate passing and setting

Student Success Goals

- 12 out of 15 free balls passed by the center back to the setter
- 10 group attacks completed off of 12 tosses

To Decrease Difficulty

- Have the tosser lengthen the time between the free ball signal and the toss.
- Make the tosser throw the ball with a high trajectory and little force.
- Have the tosser throw the ball to the same spot every time.
- Lower the Success Goals.

To Increase Difficulty

- Have the tosser vary the direction and location of the toss within the right back area of the court.
- Let the tosser throw the ball hard.
- Have the tosser shorten the time between the free ball signal and the toss.
- Raise the Success Goals.

4. Set, Cover, and Recover Drill

[Corresponds to *Volleyball*, Step 20, Drill 4]

Group Management and Safety Tips

- Have two groups per court alternating attempts.
- Extra players may line up as either setters or attackers, so there may be more than three in each group.
- Everyone should be careful of stray balls rolling underfoot.

- If attackers direct the spikes only down the line, both groups may work simultaneously.

Equipment

- 2 courts
- 2 nets
- 3 balls for every six players

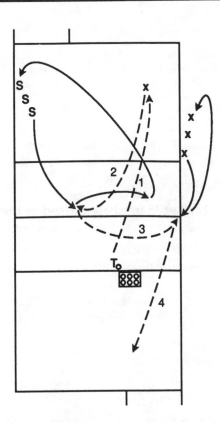

Instructions to Class

"Have three setters lined up in the right back position, a passer in the left back position, and three hitters lined up in the left front position on one side of the court. A tosser stands on the opposite side of the net.

"The tosser throws the ball over the net to the passer. The passer passes the ball to a setter, who has penetrated to the setter's position at the net. The setter sets the ball high outside to the attacker. The setter must follow the set by moving to the coverage position, arriving there before the attacker contacts the ball. As always, the ball must land within the boundaries of the other side of the court. After the ball is attacked, the setter quickly returns to the end of the setting line in the right back position, and the attacker goes to the end of the attack line.

"The tosser immediately tosses the next ball to the passer, and the play is repeated with the second setter and second attacker. The team receives 15 tosses."

* "The setter must set and follow to the coverage position."
* "The setter should touch the floor with the hands to ensure a low coverage posture."
* "The coverage floor touch must occur before the ball is contacted by the attacker."
* "The setters should return to the right back position after coverage by backpedaling."

Student Options

* "The tosser may vary the force and direction of the toss."
* "The setter may vary the height of the set to the outside position."
* "The attacker may decide on the direction of the attack."

Student Keys to Success

* Call for reception
* Pass high to setter
* Follow pass to coverage
* Touch floor with hands
* Backpedal to right back position

Student Success Goals

* 12 good sets and coverages off of 15 tosses
* 10 successful attacks off of 12 sets

To Decrease Difficulty

* The tosser should toss the ball directly at the passer.
* The setter's starting position can be at the net.
* The setter could send higher sets to the attacker.
* Lower the Success Goals.

To Increase Difficulty

* Let the tosser vary the direction and force of the toss.
* Have the setter set the ball lower to the outside hitter.
* Raise the Success Goals.

Step 21 2-4 Defense

When you compete against an opponent that has a powerful attack the 2-1-3 defense is not adequate for defensive coverage if you have weak blockers. The 2-4 defense provides better court coverage against this type of opponent. In the 2-4 defense, the perimeter of the court is covered extremely well, whereas the middle of the court is vulnerable. In order to successfully use the 2-4 defense, all players must have the capability of reading the opposing attack.

Another difference between the 2-1-3 and the 2-4 is that in the 2-1-3 defense, every player must be prepared to play both hard and soft attacks. At higher levels of play, the 2-4 defense is used almost exclusively. More advanced teams may be capable of employing either defense as needed, depending on the opponent. It is suggested that at the beginning level, a team will be more efficient defensively if they concentrate on executing one defensive system well. Adjustments can be made when using the 2-4 defense, allowing a team to successfully cover the entire court even when confronted with a highly successful off-speed attack.

Error Detection and Correction for the 2-4 Defense

When not even one player of a defending team attempts to play an opposing attack, it is usually because the players are thinking first rather than just reacting to the play. On almost every defensive play, two players should be moving toward the ball. The players are originally positioned on the court so that if movement occurs in a side-to-side direction, one player will naturally cross in front of the other. Players do not have time to think about their actions. They must concentrate on achieving a correct beginning position before the ball is attacked and on simply reacting after the attack.

ERROR 🚫

CORRECTION

ERROR	CORRECTION
1. The center back and the left back collide in the middle of the court when attempting to receive an off-speed attack.	1. The movement of the center back should be more in a side-to-side direction than forward. Even if the off-speed attack is directed toward the center of the court, defending against it is not the center back's responsibility. The two outside backs, left and right, must move in to play this ball.

ERROR 🚫	CORRECTION
2. When the setter is a right back and digs the attack, no one plays the second ball.	2. The setter must communicate that he or she has played the first ball and is not eligible to set. The person in the right forward position is the first choice for setting this ball.
3. A dink over the block drops to the floor without being dug.	3. The player on the sideline behind the block must prepare to dig either a hard-driven spike or a dink over the block. Reading the intention of the attacker greatly enhances the ability to dig the dink successfully.
4. The line player does not attempt to play a ball spiked straight at him or her when it is at chest height or higher.	4. This is a very difficult play for the line player behind the block. The player must react by blocking the ball in any method possible because if he or she doesn't play it, there is no one to cover behind him or her.
5. A deep dink or a high ball falls to either back corner of the court.	5. The center back is responsible to move to the corner to play this ball. The setter should immediately penetrate to the net and not attempt to cover the corner.
6. A spiked ball goes through the block and hits the floor.	6. The middle of the court is extremely vulnerable in this situation. The center back must learn to move forward into the center of the court whenever the center forward does not close the block.

2-4 Defense Drills

1. Six-Player Defensive Drill

[Corresponds to *Volleyball*, Step 21, Drill 1]

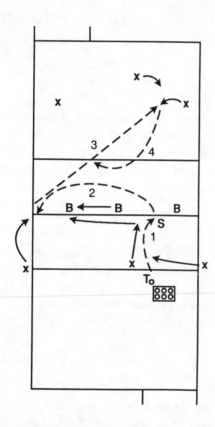

"The tosser overhand tosses the ball to the setter, who sets any of the attackers. The setter should disguise which attacker will be set, so that the defense must react to the attack as though in a game. The attacker spikes over the net. The defending team must either block the spike, or receive it and attempt to execute a counterattack. If the attacking players are unable to spike, the defending team should move to a free ball position to receive the third hit over. When the defenders successfully make the transition and execute the attack, they must cover the attacker.

"The defending team should receive 5 attacks, then rotate one position. Continue until you are back in your original positions."

- "The toss to the setter should be high and easy."
- "The setter should try to disguise the direction of the set."
- "The setter should hit the second ball over occasionally to keep the defense honest."

Student Options

- "The tosser may vary the direction and force of the toss."
- "The setter may set any of the three attackers."
- "The attacker may select the direction of the attack."

Student Keys to Success

- Watch for direction of set
- Move to appropriate beginning defensive positions
- Read attack
- React to ball
- Prepare for attack on transition

Student Success Goal

- 20 successful blocks or digs and counterattacks off of 30 spikes

Group Management and Safety Tips

- Put only one group on each court.
- Extra players may be placed in hitting lines, each moving to the end of the line after an attack attempt.
- Everyone must be aware of extra balls rolling underfoot, signaling to stop the drill when this occurs.

Equipment

- 2 courts
- 2 nets
- 3 balls for every six players

Instructions to Class

"A team of six sets up on one side of the court in base defensive position. A tosser, a setter, and three attackers set up on the opposite side.

To Decrease Difficulty

- Make the tosser throw the ball high, easy, and directly at the setter.
- The attackers could tell the defensive team which attacker will spike.
- The defenders could tell the attackers in which direction to spike.
- Lower the Success Goal.

To Increase Difficulty

- Let the tosser vary the height and location of the toss.
- The setter could set the ball lower to the attacker.
- Raise the Success Goal.

2. *Digging the Power Attack Drill*

[Corresponds to *Volleyball*, Step 21, Drill 2]

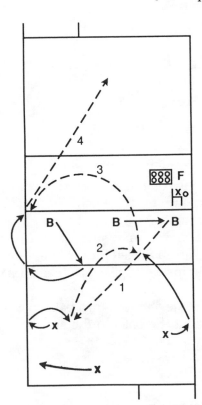

- Use retrievers to return balls to a person handing the balls to the spiker.
- This drill can also be run with a spiker in the right forward position.

Equipment

- 2 courts
- 2 nets
- 2 boxes
- 10 balls for each court

Instructions to Class

"A team of six sets up on one side of the court. On the other side, a spiker in the left forward position stands on a box with a feeder alongside.

"The spiker self-tosses the ball high enough to allow the middle blocker to join the outside blocker, then attacks crosscourt. The team attempts to dig the spike and complete an attack in transition. The ball must land in bounds on the attack. As usual, the drill is run with 5 spikes followed by the team rotating one position."

- "The power alley player must line up properly every time."
- "The attacker must have the control to place the ball in a variety of directions within the power alley."

Student Options

- "The team has the option to set any player to complete the transition."
- "The attacker should vary the direction of the spike within the power alley."

Group Management and Safety Tips

- Put only one group on each court.
- Everyone should watch for stray balls underfoot.
- Extra players can line up and rotate as attackers in the left forward position. Each player will make 5 spike hits, then go to the end of the line.

Student Keys to Success

- Watch block form
- Position outside block
- Keep ball and opposing attacker's arm in view
- Back to sideline
- Read attack
- React to ball
- Continue moving forward

Student Success Goals

- 20 good digs off of 30 spikes
- 15 completed attacks off of 20 digs

To Decrease Difficulty

- Have the spiker indicate the direction of the intended attack.
- Have the spiker self-toss the ball higher.
- Have the middle blocker begin in a joined position.
- Lower the Success Goals.

To Increase Difficulty

- Have the spiker self-toss the ball lower.
- Have the spiker vary the direction and speed of the spike.
- Raise the Success Goals.

3. Setter Digs and Right Forward Sets Drill

[Corresponds to *Volleyball*, Step 21, Drill 3]

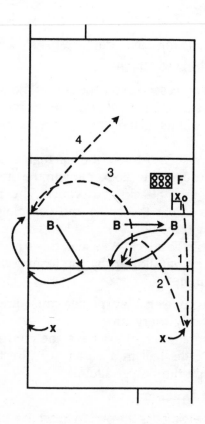

Group Management and Safety Tips

- Put only one group on each court.
- Everyone must watch for stray balls underfoot.
- Extra players may line up and rotate as attackers in the left forward position. Each player makes 5 spike hits, then goes to the end of the line.
- Use retrievers to return balls to a person handing the balls to the spiker.

Equipment

- 2 courts
- 2 nets
- 2 boxes
- 10 balls per court

Instructions to Class

"This drill uses the same formation as the previous drill. Here, though, the left forward on the box spikes down the line. This forces the right back, the regular setter, to dig the ball, which means that another player must set. It is preferable that the right forward set in this situation. This drill is run with 5 spikes before the team rotates one position."

- "The setter should signal on every play that someone else is needed to play the second ball."
- "The right forward should play the second ball, if possible."
- "The right forward should execute a high, easy set in this situation."
- "All players should listen for the setter's call and quickly react if it is obvious that the right forward cannot play the ball."

Student Options

- "The spiker has the option of attacking soft or hard."
- "The spiker may vary the attack but should always make a hit that will be dug by the right back."
- "All players must decide which player is most appropriate to handle the second ball."
- "The right forward can set either the center or the left forward."
- "The attackers should vary the direction of the attacks on transition."

Student Keys to Success

- Setter digs ball high
- Setter signals he or she has played first ball
- Right forward or closest player calls for ball
- High, easy sets used in transition
- Complete transition attack by covering

Student Success Goals

- 20 successful digs off of 30 spikes
- 15 completed attacks off of 20 digs

To Decrease Difficulty

- Make the spiker tell the setter what type of attack will be executed.
- Have the spiker indicate the direction in which the attack will be executed.
- The spiker should use a higher self-toss.
- Lower the Success Goals.

To Increase Difficulty

- The spiker should use a lower self-toss to force receivers to react more quickly.
- Let the spiker vary the direction and force of the attack.
- Raise the Success Goals.

4. Covering Crosscourt Dinks Drill

[Corresponds to *Volleyball*, Step 21, Drill 4]

Group Management and Safety Tips

- Put two groups on each court. One group receives 5 dinks; then the second group receives 5 dinks.
- The ball should be rallied to completion every time.
- Due to the individual on the box, the setter must be careful not to set the ball to the high outside area of the court. The outside person can be used as an attacker, but the ball must be set in from the sideline.
- If the ball is set to the outside attacker and it appears that it will be dangerous for the outside attacker to attack, there should be a signal to stop play.

Equipment

- 2 courts
- 2 nets
- 4 boxes
- 10 balls for every six players

Instructions to Class

"This drill uses the same formation as the previous two drills. Now, though, the left forward on the box dinks the ball toward the center of the court and close to the net. The left forward of the opposing team should dig this dink. This drill runs with 5 dinks, followed by the team rotating."

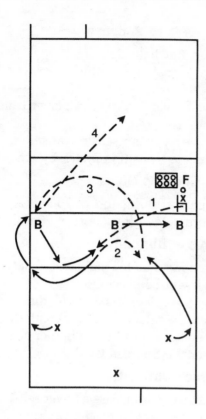

Student Options

- "The left forward may vary the direction of the dink."
- "The defending left forward and left back must decide who should play the ball, depending on its location."
- "The setter may choose who to set the ball to upon transition."

Student Keys to Success

- Quickly move to ball
- Get into low position
- Dig ball high and to center of court
- Cover every time

Student Success Goals

- 20 successful digs off of 30 dinks
- 15 completed attacks off of 20 digs

To Decrease Difficulty

- Make the attacker dink the ball with more height and distance.
- Have the attacker self-toss the ball higher to allow the blockers more time to assume a blocking position.
- Have the attacker lengthen the time between dinks.
- Lower the Success Goals.

To Increase Difficulty

- Have the attacker shorten the time between dinks.
- Let the attacker dink the ball with less height and distance.
- Raise the Success Goals.

- "Blockers should jump to block every time."
- "The left forward should vary the direction of the dink so that either the left forward or the left back of the opposing team should dig it."
- "The defenders should dig the ball high and to the center of the court."

5. *Digging Deep Dinks to the Right Back Corner Drill*

[Corresponds to *Volleyball*, Step 21, Drill 5]

Group Management and Safety Tips

- One side of the court digs 5 dinks; then the other side digs 5 dinks.
- Rally the ball to completion every time.
- Due to the player on the box, the setter must be careful not to set the ball to the high outside area of the court. The outside person can be used as an attacker, but the ball must be set in from the sideline.

- If the ball is set to the outside attacker and it appears that it will be dangerous for the outside attacker to attack, there should be a signal to stop play.
- If the defending players are moving too soon in anticipation of the play, the attackers may spike on occasion to keep them honest.

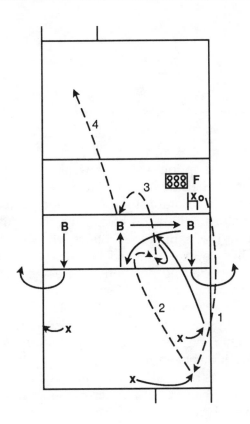

Equipment

- 2 courts
- 2 nets
- 4 boxes
- 10 balls for every six players

Instructions to Class

"This drill uses the same formation as the three previous drills. However, the left forward dinks deep or passes the ball high to the right back corner of the opposing court. The center back defensive player should dig this ball as the setter penetrates to the net. Drill is run with 5 dinks or passes; then the team rotates."

- "The center back player must begin in the correct position in the center of the court and must not move toward the right sideline before the ball is hit."

- "Blockers should jump to block every attack."
- "The setter should yell 'Free!' while penetrating to the net."
- "The center back player must move to the corner and dig the ball."

Student Options

- "The left forward may decide the height and the direction of the dink toward the right back corner of the court."
- "The setter must decide whether to play the ball or penetrate to the net."
- "The setter may decide which attacker to set in transition."

Student Keys to Success

- Quick decision making
- Move to ball
- Set position
- Dig ball high toward center of court
- Follow set to cover

Student Success Goals

- 20 successful digs off of 30 dinks or passes
- 15 completed attacks off of 20 digs

To Decrease Difficulty

- The attacker should dink the ball with more height.
- Have the attacker lengthen the time between dinks.
- Lower the Success Goals.

To Increase Difficulty

- Have the attacker dink the ball so low that it just clears the block.
- The attacker should shorten the time between dinks.
- The attacker could mix in hard-driven spikes more frequently.
- Raise the Success Goals.

Step 22   5-1 Offense

In the 5-1 offense, the biggest advantage to the attackers is that they only have to get used to the playing characteristics of one setter. This makes good timing between the setter and the hitters much easier to develop.

In order for a 5-1 offense to have more hitting power in all six rotations, the setter needs to always consider the option of attacking on the second hit. This attack can be either a hard-driven spike or a dink. When the setter dinks the second ball it is often referred to as a *dump*. This option can be very effective because the opposing team is usually expecting a hard-driven spike. Even though a 5-1 offense is considered to be less powerful when the setter is a front row player, if the setter uses the second-hit option well, this weakness is not apparent. Left-handed setters are even more effective in accomplishing this option because their attack will be on-hand from their position on the right side of the court.

When you are using a 5-1 offense, an additional specialized position is necessary. The player opposite the setter in the rotation is referred to as the *off setter*. This player covers the right side of the court in a way similar to the setter, but sets the ball only in situations where it has been necessary for the setter to receive the first ball. It is to the advantage of a team to have a left-hander in this position, as well.

Error Detection and Correction for the 5-1 Offense

When discussing the errors that are prevalent in the 5-1 offense, it is necessary to group them into two categories depending on the location of the setter. When the setter is in the front row, the errors would be identical to those found in the International 4-2 offense. If the setter is penetrating from the back row, errors would be similar to those found in the 6-2 offense. Many of the errors are associated with players' not assuming their correct positions, leaving the team unable to cover the court completely.

ERROR ⊘	CORRECTION

Setter in Front Row

1. The setter receives the serve.

1. The setter should hide at the net and not receive the serve under any circumstances.

2. A free ball falls between a front row player and a back row player.

2. The two forwards must move off the net to the attack line as quickly as possible and assume a ready position prior to the opponent's making contact with the ball to send it over the net.

3. The ball rebounds off the opponent's block and falls to the floor on the attacker's side.

3. Three players must assume a coverage position around the attacker.

4. A player in the W-formation gets hit on the back by a passed ball.

4. Every player must open up to the receiver by turning and facing the receiver.

5. The serve falls to the court between two players.

5. Receivers must call for the serve prior to the ball's crossing the net.

6. The ball rebounds off the block and falls to the court between the coverage and the sideline.

6. The player covering closest to the line should have the outside foot on the sideline and should not play a ball that rebounds off the block beyond the sideline side of the body.

7. The attacker prevents the coverage from playing the ball.

7. The attacker should not play a ball that rebounds off the block unless it stays between the attacker and the net.

8. A free ball falls to the court in the right forward position.

8. The setter is the right forward and remains at the net; therefore, the right back must adjust to cover the right forward area of the court.

9. The setter attempts to back set.

9. The two eligible attackers are in the center forward and left forward positions; there is no right forward attacker to back set to.

Setter in Back Row

1. A pass or dig reaches the net before the setter.

1. The setter must move to the net on serve reception as soon as the serve is contacted. On defense the setter must move to the net as soon as it is evident that the attack will not be to the right back area.

ERROR 🚫

CORRECTION

2. The attack lands in the right back position with no one to receive it.

2. The setter must realize that the primary responsibility is defense and that the secondary responsibility is to direct the attack.

3. The setter and the center forward collide when trying to cover an attacker.

3. The center forward must charge to the net for a quick attack on each offensive series.

4. A free ball falls between the front row players and the back row players.

4. All three forwards must move quickly to the attack line, set themselves, and be prepared to play a free ball.

5. A third ball over the net lands in the right back position with no one to play it.

5. The setter must communicate the free ball call to all teammates. The center back must adjust to cover the vacated area when the setter penetrates to the net.

6. The serve falls to the ground between the two back row players in the W.

6. The left back player should be the more aggressive player on serve receive when the serve is between the two back players.

5-1 Offense Drills

1. Set, Cover, and Recover Drill

[Corresponds to *Volleyball*, Step 22, Drill 1]

Group Management and Safety Tips

- Two groups may work on one court as long as the attackers direct their spikes crosscourt.
- Always have a signal to stop activity if a stray ball rolls into an area where it could be dangerous.
- Tosses to the setters may be made fairly quickly, one right after another.
- Retrievers should keep a good supply of balls available for the tosser.
- Blockers may be employed to make the drill more gamelike.

Equipment

- 2 courts
- 2 nets
- 10 balls for every six players

Instructions to Class

''Three setters line up in the right back position; a passer starts in the left back position; and three hitters line up in the left front position on one side of the court. A tosser stands on the opposite side of the court.

''The tosser tosses the ball over the net to the passer. The passer passes the ball to a set-

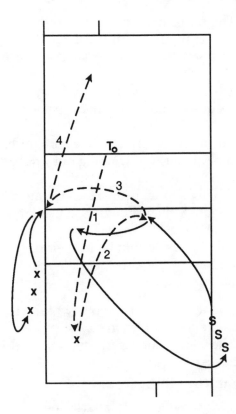

• "The setter should move to the cover position quickly and assume a low body posture."
• "The setter may check the low body posture by touching the hands to the floor."
• "The higher the set made to the attacker, the more time the setter has to move into the coverage position."

Student Option

• "The attacker may choose any type of attack and direction."

Student Keys to Success

• Set ball high
• Continue forward movement to coverage position
• Low and ready before attack is made
• Return to starting position

Student Success Goals

• Setters making 12 good sets followed by correct coverage out of 15 balls
• Group completing 12 good attacks out of 15 attempts

To Decrease Difficulty

• The higher the set, the easier it is for the setter to reach the coverage position.
• Lower the Success Goals.

To Increase Difficulty

• Have the setter set the ball lower to outside attackers.
• Have the setter set at a variety of heights.
• Use an additional tosser to force the players covering to quickly play the ball.
• Raise the Success Goals.

ter, who has penetrated to the setter's position at the net. The setter sets the ball high and outside to the attacker. The setter must follow the set to the coverage position, arriving there before the attacker contacts the ball. The attack must be in bounds.

"After the ball is attacked, the setter quickly returns to the end of the setting line in the right back position, and the attacker goes to the end of the attack line. The tosser immediately tosses the next ball to the passer, and the play is repeated with the second setter and attacker. The team receives 15 tosses."

2. *Free Ball Attack Drill*
[Corresponds to *Volleyball*, Step 22, Drill 2]

Group Management and Safety Tips

• Put only one group in each court.
• Additional players may position themselves in line behind any of the three attackers.
• After each attack, the hitter rotates to the end of the line.

• Due to the attackers' moving off the net, the remaining attackers should be in line on the opposite side of the net ready to move to a base defensive blocking position as soon as the player ahead of them has attacked.

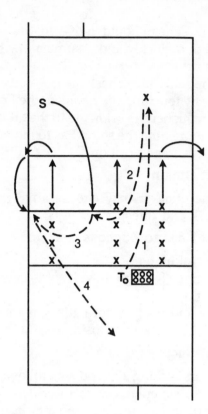

• "The setter must penetrate to the net as soon as the free ball is called."
• "The setter should repeat the free ball call."
• "The attackers must move to the attack line quickly, arriving there prior to the toss."
• "The attackers must move straight back from the net, not winging out until after the ball has been passed."
• "When passing the free ball, the attackers must angle their shoulders in the direction of the pass."
• "All players should be in their coverage positions by the time the ball is attacked."

Student Options

• "The tosser may toss to any of the three attackers, in addition to the passer."
• "The setter may set any of the three attackers."

Student Keys to Success

• Quick movement to attack line
• Angle shoulders toward direction of pass
• Wing out after pass is completed
• Setter moves to net as soon as free ball is called

Student Success Goal

• 12 good attacks off of 15 free balls

To Decrease Difficulty

• Make the tosser lengthen the time between the free ball signal and the toss.
• Have the tosser throw high, easy balls to the receivers.
• The tosser could indicate in advance whom the toss will be made toward by squaring his or her shoulders to the direction of the toss.
• Lower the Success Goal.

To Increase Difficulty

• Have the tosser throw the ball low and hard.
• Have the tosser shorten the time between the free ball signal and the toss.
• Have the tosser indicate the attacker while the ball is being passed.
• Raise the Success Goal.

• Everyone should watch for stray balls on the court, especially in the area of the attack.

Equipment

• 2 courts
• 2 nets
• 3 balls for every six players

Instructions to Class

"Three attackers, a setter, and a passer set up on one side of the net. The three attackers begin in the three front row positions in the base defensive formation. The setter begins in the right back of the court. The passer begins in the left back position. A tosser is on the other side of the net.

"The tosser yells 'Free!' and tosses the volleyball to the passer. The passer passes to the setter, who has penetrated to the net. At the free ball call, the attackers drop back to the attack line and prepare to hit. The setter sets to one of the three attackers. All players should cover as appropriate. The team receives 15 free balls."

3. Setter Penetration and Right Back Covering Drill
[Corresponds to *Volleyball*, Step 22, Drill 3]

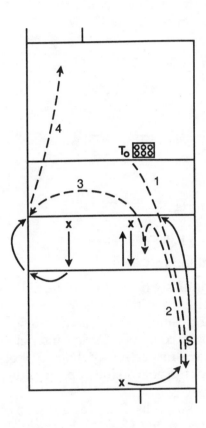

side of the net. A tosser on the opposite side of the net yells 'Free!' and tosses the ball to the right back corner of the opposite court. At the 'Free!' signal, the setter penetrates to the net, and the center back must quickly move to cover the right back area of the court. The center back passes to the setter, who sets to the middle or outside hitter to complete the attack. The team receives 15 free balls."

- "The setter repeats the free ball signal before penetrating."
- "The center back adjusts to the right on the setter's free ball call."
- "The center back should be in the right back position before playing the ball."
- "The attackers move straight back and wing out after the pass is made."

Student Options

- "The tosser may decide on the force and the direction of the toss."
- "The setter may decide whether to set center or outside."
- "The attackers may decide on the type and direction of attack."

Student Keys to Success

- Setter penetrates to net as soon as free ball is called
- Setter repeats free ball call
- Center back quickly moves to cover right back area of court
- Attackers move straight back from the net, not winging out until after ball has been passed

Student Success Goals

- Center back making 12 good passes to the setter off of 15 free balls
- 10 good attacks out of 12 attempts

Group Management and Safety Tips

- Put two groups alternating play on each court.
- Forwards on the nonreceiving side may practice blocking.

Equipment

- 2 courts
- 2 nets
- 3 balls for every four players

Instructions to Class

"A middle attacker, an outside attacker, a setter, and a center back player set up on one

To Decrease Difficulty

- Have the tosser lengthen the time between the free ball signal and the toss.
- Make the tosser throw the ball with a high trajectory and little force.
- Have the tosser throw the ball to the same spot every time.
- Lower the Success Goals.

To Increase Difficulty

- Let the tosser vary the direction and location of the toss within the right back area of the court.
- The tosser could throw the ball with more force.
- Have the tosser shorten the time between the free ball signal and the toss.
- Raise the Success Goals.

4. Free Ball Drill

[Corresponds to *Volleyball*, Step 22, Drill 4]

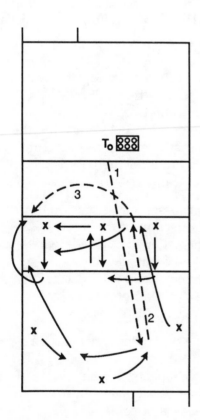

Group Management and Safety Tips

- Put one or two teams on each court. If using two teams, the tossers need to stand off the court to toss the ball. The teams need to alternate play.
- The forwards of the nonreceiving side should begin in the blocking position.
- The tossers need to remember to delay the toss a few seconds after yelling "Free!"

Equipment

- 2 courts
- 2 nets
- 5 to 6 balls per court

Instructions to Class

"A team of six lines up on one side of the court. The three forwards are at the net in blocking position. The center back is in the center of the court, and the left and right backs are on their respective sidelines 20 feet from the net. A tosser is on the opposite side of the net.

"The tosser yells 'Free,' delays for a couple of seconds, then tosses the ball over the net high and easy. The team of six quickly moves into the W-formation, receives the ball, sets an attack, and covers the attacker.

"The team receives 5 balls, then rotates one position. Continue this drill until you have rotated around to your original starting positions."

- "The forwards need to set their positions before the ball is tossed."
- "The outside forward should move straight back to the attack line and not wing out until after the ball has been passed."
- "The receiver must square the shoulders to the direction of the pass."
- "The coverage must be in place before the attacker contacts the ball."

Student Options

- "The attacker must decide on the appropriate method of receiving the toss."
- "The setter may decide whether to set the left forward attacker or the center forward attacker."
- "The attacker may select the direction of the attack."

Student Keys to Success

- Move to attack line quickly
- Set position before playing ball
- Square shoulders to direction of pass
- Low posture on coverage

Student Success Goal

- 24 successful attacks with the proper coverage off of 30 free balls

To Decrease Difficulty

- Start the players in the free ball position.
- Make the tosser throw the ball to a designated receiver.
- Have the tosser throw at a consistent height.
- Lower the Success Goal.

To Increase Difficulty

- Have the tosser throw the ball to a variety of heights and locations.
- Have the tosser throw the ball quicker after yelling "Free!"
- Raise the Success Goal.

5. *Cover and Dig Drill*
[Corresponds to *Volleyball*, Step 22, Drill 5]

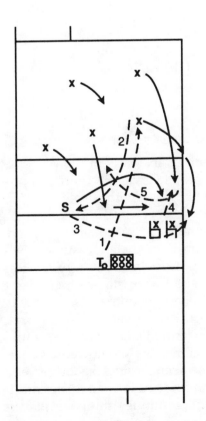

Group Management and Safety Tips

- Put only one group on each court.
- For this drill to be effective, the blockers must be able to successfully block the attack.
- If the blockers are not blocking the ball, you may have to introduce a different method of blocking, such as a block-it or a pitch-back.

Equipment

- 2 courts
- 2 nets
- Boxes for blockers
- 5 to 10 balls per court
- Block-it or pitch-back, if needed

Instructions to Class

"A team of six sets up on one side of the court in the W-formation, with the setter in the right of center front position. On the opposite side of the net, two blockers stand on a box on the right side of the court.

"A tosser on the same side as the blockers yells 'Free!' and throws the ball high over the net. The team receives the free ball, sets an attack to their left forward, and covers. The blockers block the ball, the coverage attempts to dig successfully, which means being able to set up for a second attack.

"The team receives 5 tosses, then rotates one position. This drill continues until the players have returned to their original positions."

- "The set should be high to the outside."
- "The attacker should hit into the blockers' hands because this is a drill to practice digging by the coverage."
- "The dig by the coverage should be high."

Student Options

- "The tosser may decide the direction of the toss."
- "The setter may choose the direction of the set when completing the attack off the coverage."
- "The attacker may choose the direction of the attack."

Student Keys to Success

- Cover in low position
- Dig ball high
- Cover second attack
- Blockers must keep ball in play

Student Success Goal

- 18 successful digs off of 20 opposing blocks

To Decrease Difficulty

- Have the tosser throw high, easy, and directly at the player.
- Have the tosser lengthen the time between calling "Free!" and tossing.
- The setter could set high.
- Lower the Success Goal.

To Increase Difficulty

- Let the tosser throw the ball with varying heights and directions.
- Have the tosser shorten the time between the free ball call and the toss.
- Raise the Success Goal.

6. Serve and Free Ball Drill

[Corresponds to *Volleyball*, Step 22, Drill 6]

Group Management and Safety Tips

- Put two teams on each court.
- Extra players can be used as tossers and servers.
- One team receives serve and sets their attack 5 consecutive times; then the opposite team does the same.
- When one team is attacking, the other team can work on defense, always beginning the drill with the three forwards at the net ready to block.

Equipment

- 2 courts
- 2 nets
- 3 balls for every six players

Instructions to Class

"A team of six starts in the W-formation. A tosser and a server are on the opposite side of the net, each with a ball.

"The server serves. The receiving team passes the serve, sets their attack, and covers. The team immediately assumes the starting positions as for base defense. The tosser calls 'Free!' and tosses the ball high over the net. The receiving team passes the free ball, sets an attack, and covers.

"Play immediately continues with another serve, immediately followed by another free ball. The team receives 5 good serves alternating with 5 free balls, then rotates one position. The drill continues until the players rotate around to their starting positions."

- "Move to the free ball position quickly, getting there before the attacker contacts the ball."
- "Even though the tosser yells 'Free,' the receiving team should also yell 'Free!'"
- "The receiver must make a good pass on the free ball."

Student Options

- "The server may choose the method and direction of the serve."
- "The receiver must determine whether it would be more advantageous to receive the ball with a forearm pass or an overhead pass."
- "The setter has a choice of which attack player to set."
- "The tosser may determine the direction to toss the free ball."

Student Keys to Success

- Quick movement to net
- Cover entire court
- Set coverage before attacker contacts ball
- Call ball as soon as possible
- Every pass must be good one

Student Success Goals

- 24 successful attacks with the correct coverage off of 30 serves
- 24 successful attacks with the correct coverage off of 30 free balls

To Decrease Difficulty

- Make the server serve the ball underhand.
- The serve or tossed free ball could go directly to the receiver.
- The tosser could wait a longer time between yelling "Free!" and tossing the ball.
- Lower the Success Goal.

To Increase Difficulty

- Let the server use any method of serving.
- Have the server serve the seams.
- The tosser could vary the free ball toss's height and force.
- Have the tosser shorten the time between yelling "Free!" and tossing the ball.
- Raise the Success Goal.

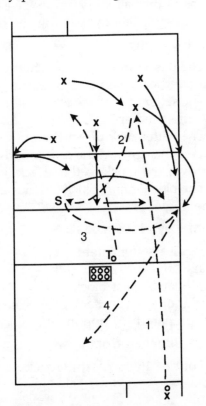

Serve reception to attack with coverage

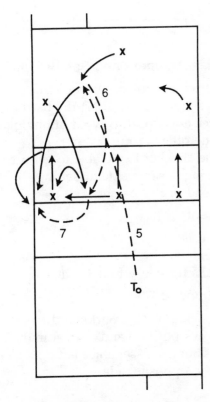

Free ball to attack with coverage

7. Setter Attacks Second Ball Drill

[Corresponds to *Volleyball*, Step 22, Drill 7]

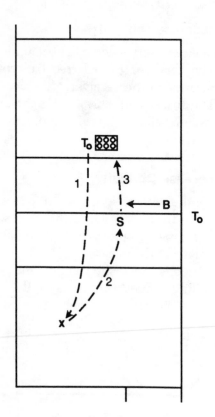

"The tosser throws the ball over the net to the passer. The passer passes the ball to the setter, who attacks the ball using either an off-speed spike, a hard-driven spike, or a dink. Off-speed hits should be directed past the blockers and toward the center of the opponent's court, dinks toward the center of the court or to the sideline behind the left front blocker."

- "The pass must be high and close to the net, within 1 or 2 feet."
- "The setter should try to disguise the fact that he or she is going to attack until the last moment."
- "When the setter attacks off-speed, he or she should concentrate on directing the ball to strategic locations on the opposite court."
- "The blocker must make an honest effort to block the ball every time to give the setter a better feel for passing the block."

Student Options

- "The passer must choose whether to use an overhead pass or a forearm pass."
- "The setter may attack with a hard-driven or off-speed spike."
- "The setter may direct the off-speed attack either toward the center of the court or over the block to the attack line."
- "The blocker may block either the line or the angle."

Student Keys to Success

- Disguise setter intent
- Vary attack
- Go over or past block
- Make off-speed attack drop quickly
- Be prepared for opponent's blocking

Student Success Goal

- 10 out of 15 successful attacks

Group Management and Safety Tips

- Put two groups on each court.
- The setter should direct the hard-driven attack crosscourt to avoid hitting players in the other group.
- If the attacker is not able to get accurate passing, a same-side tosser may be used instead of the passer.

Equipment

- 2 courts
- 2 nets
- 6 balls for every four players

Instructions to Class

"On one side of the court stand a passer in the left back position and a setter in the right front position. A tosser and a left front blocker are on the opposite side.

To Decrease Difficulty

- Make the tosser throw the ball high and easy to the passer.
- Have the tosser allow sufficient time between tosses.
- The passer could pass the ball high to the setter.
- Lower the Success Goal.

To Increase Difficulty

- Let the tosser vary the throw's force and height.
- The passer could pass the ball with varying heights to the setter.
- Raise the Success Goal.

Step 23 Game Situations

Now that your players have mastered the basic skills and have learned several options for offensive and defensive strategies, they are ready to learn how to react to an opponent in a six-on-six formation. It is suggested that a simple offense (the 4-2 or the International 4-2) and the 2-1-3 defense be used. These offensive and defensive strategies are the easiest to learn. Initially in the learning process, it is best for all teams to use the same offense and defense, allowing you to point out certain errors to the entire group.

PROGRESSION FOR INTRODUCING GAME PLAY

The players are trying to develop the ability to read the opponent's play and react by assuming the correct court formation in response. It is strongly recommended that the following progressive sequence be used to enhance the learning process:

1. Walk Through Without Ball: In this exercise, you call out court formations for one team to assume. The opposing team must react correctly. For example, if you call out a spike by the left forward, the opposing team should react with the 2-1-3 defense using a block on the right side. It is important that you call out the formations in the order they would occur in a game situation. This order is as follows:

a. serve receive
b. attack and cover
c. base defense   → attack and cover
d. free ball or block
          ↓   ↘ base defense
  attack and cover

The order will continue to repeat itself from attack and cover.

2. Toss and Catch: One team begins with an underhand serve to the opponents. After the serve, the players catch and throw the ball in the same pattern desired in regular hitting play. For example, they pass, set, and attack (on the attack the player jumps and tosses the ball over the net). The opposing team responds by using the correct formation, catching the attack, and initiating their own attack on transition.

In order for the teams to have ample time to respond properly, the tosses representing the pass and the set should be at a height desired in the performance of these skills. The toss over the net can simulate a hard-driven spike, an off-speed spike, or a dink. This exercise can be very fast-paced, eliciting the same quick movements as a regular game. It is recommended that the teams score and exchange serve as in a regular game.

3. Teacher Toss: In this exercise, the teams play a regular volleyball game initiated by a toss from you instead of by a serve. It is recommended that you toss the ball high and easy to make the three-hit combination achievable. Tosses can be alternated from one side to the other after a series of 5 to 10 tosses are made to one team.

4. Underhand Serve: In this exercise a regular game is played. The underhand serve is always used, enhancing serve reception so that rallies may occur.

This progressive sequence may be employed in the teaching of all offensive and defensive strategies in any combination. After your players have mastered one offensive and one defensive system, they are capable of competing in regular games—and it is suggested that they be given this opportunity. Class tournaments using the round-robin format are highly recommended. You should put together the teams while attempting to equalize ability as much as possible. Close competition can be exciting and keeps the interest high.

When your players have advanced to a point where they are skilled in the execution of several offenses and defenses, they will be capable of making several decisions as to what are the best strategies for their teams, such as

- What offensive system are they going to use?
- What defensive system will they try?
- Who will be their setters?
- Who are their strongest attackers, servers, and defensive players?
- What are the strengths of their opponents?
- Who will be their court leader to call and direct play?
- What will be the starting positions best utilizing each player's individual strengths?

SPECIALIZATION

There are two major concerns that you must have in presenting the concept of specialization. First, you must give the player the opportunity to practice in the specialized role as much as possible. Second, you must be concerned with the switching that is necessary to move the player to the specialized position during serve and serve reception.

Many of the drills presented in the various steps of this text can be used to help the player learn the peculiarities of the specialized position. The best way for all the players to learn the switching patterns is for the team to practice serving and serve reception in the same rotational positions for several trials in a row. It is necessary during this practice for two teams to be used; then the rally can continue beyond the initial switches made during the serve.

SIGNALING FOR SUCCESS

Every team must develop a method of communication for its players. The main form of game communication is verbal, and it is for four basic purposes: (a) to signal the intent of a player to play a ball, (b) for one player to aid another player in deciding whether or not to play a ball or how to play it, (c) to communicate the desired formation for the entire team, and (d) to communicate knowledge of the opponent's intent.

Once the signals to be used are established, the players need to practice using them. You must encourage your players to use these signals during all drills and game play.

MODIFIED GAMES

Seldom in a practice setting will you find it necessary to have your teams play a regulation game. During a scrimmage, the game is modified in such a way that a certain aspect of the game is emphasized. Generally, two teams are used, with one team practicing the point of emphasis and the opposing team reacting to continue the rally.

An example of this would be the practice of movement into the free ball formation. Both teams begin in a base defensive formation. You call ''Free!'' and toss the ball to the team practicing the reception of a free ball. This team attempts to set an attack. The opponents react by defending the attack, and play continues until the ball is dead. Both teams immediately return to base defensive position in preparation for the next free ball. After a given number of tosses, you may toss to the opposite side. If a team is not using specialization, this free ball practice would have to be completed for all six rotations. If specialization is used, this free ball practice would only have to be done in two positions.

This example shows how teams can practice in a scrimmage situation while concentrating their efforts on one aspect of game strategy. Other possibilities exist; their discovery and use are limited only by your creativity.

Step 24   Game Play Choices

By this time, your players have learned and practiced basic skills and offensive and defensive strategies. It is now necessary for them to use this knowledge in competitive game situations. The game of volleyball consists of all open skills, that is, skills that are performed in a constantly changing environment.

Each of the drills presented, on the other hand, has been executed in a fairly controlled setting where each trial is similar. The repetitive nature of these drills rarely occurs during a competitive situation. Each play during a game can be very different from the preceding or following plays. The players, therefore, must constantly be thinking about what is happening and the options available for their responses. The ability to read the opponent's play and respond correctly must be developed through practice and experience.

Through observation as coaches and teachers, we have found that regular competition develops this mental aspect of the player's game. However, regular game play is often slow at the beginning level, and the desired outcomes do not occur immediately. This is partially because students' have not completely mastered the physical skills, do not have ability to read the opponent's play, and lack understanding of offensive and defensive formations. An example of this is a coach's desiring to practice a serve receive formation and asking some players to serve at the receiving team, only to discover that those players are unable to serve consistently. It is obvious that the receiving team cannot practice serve reception when the serve does not go over the net.

Players are capable of working on offensive and defensive strategies from a mental point of view before they have attained the physical skills to successfully complete the desired pattern of play. This is one of the reasons why in many of the drills presented in this text, we have indicated that the serve should be underhand. For example, if a drill's purpose is to practice serve reception but the serve is hit with such force that the players cannot successfully pass it, the object of the drill is lost.

Rotation on a side out tends to take time and is really not essential for learning on-court decision making. Two teams competing against each other need not rotate until 5 to 10 serves have been completed. Keeping players in the same rotational positions during a certain number of serves allows individuals to understand particular positions well before moving on to new locations. This method is superior to playing a regular game, in which a player may play a position for only 1 or 2 points. The constant changing of court positions indicated by rotation often causes confusion in young players.

It is recommended that during practice all scrimmaging be accomplished in a controlled setting. The following ideas indicate ways you can control play:

- A certain number of serves are made before the team rotates.
- Serves are underhand and easy.
- You yourself serve from outside the court and close to the net.
- You stand on a platform and attack the ball toward one team. The team attempts to receive the ball and return it in transition.
- You toss the ball a certain number of times to each side before they rotate.
- Emphasize one aspect of the game at a time, such as reception of a free ball.
- Have one team work on a particular offensive strategy while the opposing team is working on a defense against that strategy.

In each of the above situations, a selected action is used to initiate play, and during the ensuing rally, the teams are working on all aspects of their games. Much time is saved with the elimination of side outs and rotations, resulting in the players' experiencing the most performance opportunities possible.

In this section we present several methods of evaluation. We feel that a teacher must determine the best method or combination of methods based on the length of the unit, the grading requirements of the institution, the level of the students, and the evaluation time available. Students should be evaluated in two basic areas, skill performance (quantitative and/or qualitative) and game knowledge, and the grade should be a combination of the results. You decide the emphasis given to each, making this known to students at the beginning of the unit.

QUANTITATIVE AND QUALITATIVE EVALUATION

Teachers must be aware of the difference between quantitative evaluation (how many times a skill can be done) and qualitative evaluation (how well a skill is performed). In the methods of evaluation we describe, especially in the American Alliance for Health, Physical Education, Recreation and Dance (AAHPERD) Skills Tests and the competency-based evaluation, it is possible for students to score well even when the quality of their performance is not high. For the AAHPERD Skills Tests it is important that you be the evaluator, because beginning students are not experienced enough to evaluate qualitative performance accurately. For example, in the skills test for the overhead volley a student may be able to volley the ball against the wall 20 times in the 30 seconds allowed, but all hits may not be considered legal. And when using the competency-based evaluation, you may find it necessary to randomly check the overall quality of performance. Due to the extensive number of items in this evaluation process, you cannot observe every student during every test.

We suggest that you do use both objective (quantitative) and subjective (qualitative) evaluations to measure student progress. For students at beginning levels of play, qualitative evaluation should carry more weight than quantitative. At this stage of learning you should be more concerned with the form than the result of performance. Once players have mastered basic skills, quantitative methods of measurement successfully discriminate performance levels. The better a player's form, the easier it is for him or her to score well on quantitative tests—thus quality of performance correlates with quantitative success.

We describe here several methods you can use to evaluate students. The student self-evaluation and the subjective teacher evaluation are used primarily for qualitative assessment of player performance, and the AAHPERD Skills Test items and the competency-based evaluation for quantitative assessment. However, both types of assessment can be achieved with any method depending on how it is administered. For qualitative assessment, you must be the administrator and the evaluator.

1. Student Self-Evaluation

This self-evaluation exercise is explained in *Volleyball: Steps to Success* (see "Rating Your Game Success"). This exercise is valuable because it encourages players to combine thinking skills with physical skills. You may choose to use this exercise not for grading, but to allow students to determine their progress.

2. AAHPERD Skills Test

The AAHPERD Skills Test for volleyball evaluates students in four areas: overhead passing, serving, forearm passing, and setting. These test items include norms for various age groups that can be used successfully at all skill levels. A test booklet may be obtained from the American Alliance for Health, Physical Education, Recreation and Dance, 1900 Association Dr., Reston, VA 22091.

3. Subjective Teacher Evaluation: Game Scoresheet

With this method you evaluate students in an actual competitive situation. We suggest that you observe only six students at a time in order to make a fair evaluation of each. Using the Game Scoresheet (see sample form), you tally each skill attempted by the player and indicate the level of success. Success can be evaluated either by the result of the skill attempt or by the player's form; you decide which is more important. If you feel that form is the priority, then you will grade students on physical form rather than result. But if you choose accuracy as the priority, you should grade on the result only. We feel that both priorities are appropriate and that the choice depends upon the emphasis you make during the learning process. You will note on the sample Game Scoresheet that the items listed are individual skills only. You may also evaluate students on their game choices by using the same checklist the players use in their self-evaluations.

Game Scoresheet

Name _____

    Place a tally mark by the skill that you observe the student performing within a game situation. Add a slash mark across the tally mark if the student was accurate, also. In the last column, total the scores for all three dates.

    For example, say the player serves six times in a game. If four of those serves land in the opponent's court, then the tally marks would look like this: + + + + − −.

Skill	Date	Date	Date	Total ___ of ___
Serve				
Pass				
Set				
Attack				
a. Dink				
b. Off-Speed				
c. Hard-Driven Spike				
Block				
Dig				
Individual Defense				
a. Roll				
b. Sprawl				

4. Competency-Based Evaluation

Another way to evaluate students is to use competency-based standards for each grade level. This method is more appropriate for advanced levels of play where performance quality is less in question. Included here are samples of suggested competencies for high school and college beginning classes. This program is a self-paced evaluation system in which students are allowed as many attempts as they can make during the unit to complete or improve their scores on any competency item. For example, a student who first completes a competency at the B level, but later completes it at the A level would receive an A. Students must be made aware that these competencies are minimum levels of achievement for each grade. In order to achieve a particular grade, every competency at that level must be reached. The competencies given here are suggested levels; any competency can be adjusted to meet student needs. You may need to experiment before deciding on the most appropriate competencies for your particular situation.

Volleyball Competencies for High School Players

These are typical competencies that could be used for a high school physical education course in beginning volleyball.

For an A

---

1. Score an average of 85 on the two written tests.
2. Attend at least 19 class periods (based on a class that meets 20 times).
3. Volley the ball 15 consecutive times against the wall to a height greater than 8 feet using the forearm pass.
4. Serve 10 consecutive good serves.
5. Score at least 27 (male) or 18 (female) on the serving skill test (AAHPERD Skills Test).
6. Set the ball with a partner 50 consecutive times.
7. Forearm pass the ball to yourself, turn, and pass it over your head to a partner at least 9 consecutive times.
8. Set the ball to yourself, touch the floor, and set again at least 8 consecutive times.
9. Score at least 36 (male) or 16 (female) on the setting skills test (AAHPERD).
10. Back set 10 consecutive times while working in the middle of the 3-player back set drill.
11. Make a total of 25 consecutive forearm passes with 2 partners in the 3-player shuttle drill.
12. Continuously set the ball to yourself for 10 consecutive sets.
13. Spike hit the ball against the wall 10 consecutive times.
14. Dink the ball 3 out of 5 times over the block so that it lands in front of the attack line.
15. Alternately forearm pass and set the ball to yourself 20 consecutive times.

For a B

---

1. Average 78 on the two written tests.
2. Attend 18 class periods.
3. 12 underhand hits against the wall.

4. 8 consecutive good serves.
5. Score 20 (male) or 14 (female) on the serving skill test (AAHPERD).
6. Set with your partner 40 consecutive times.
7. Forearm pass to yourself and set to your partner 7 consecutive times.
8. Set, touch the floor, and set 6 consecutive times.
9. Score 30 (male) or 14 (female) on the overhead pass test (AAHPERD).
10. Back set drill 8 consecutive times.
11. 20 consecutive forearm passes in the 3-player shuttle.
12. Set to yourself 8 consecutive times.
13. Spike hits against the wall 6 consecutive times.
14. Dink 2 out of 5 over a block to the attack line.
15. Forearm pass and set to yourself 16 consecutive times.

For a C

1. Average 70 on the two written tests.
2. Attend 17 class periods.
3. 10 consecutive forearm passes against the wall.
4. 6 consecutive good serves.
5. Score 16 (male) or 10 (female) on the serving skill test (AAHPERD).
6. Set with your partner 30 consecutive times.
7. Forearm pass to yourself and overhead pass to your partner 5 consecutive times.
8. Set, touch floor, and set 5 consecutive times.
9. Score 25 (male) or 10 (female) on the overhead pass test (AAHPERD).
10. Back set drill 6 consecutive times.
11. 15 consecutive forearm passes in the 3-player shuttle.
12. Set to yourself 6 consecutive times.
13. Spike hits against the wall 5 consecutive times.
14. Dink 1 out of 6 over a block to the attack line.
15. Forearm pass and set to yourself 12 consecutive times.

For a D

1. Average 60 on the two written tests.
2. Attend at least 15 class periods.
3. 8 consecutive forearm passes against the wall.
4. 5 consecutive good serves.
5. Score 12 (male) or 8 (female) on the serving skill test (AAHPERD).
6. Set with your partner 20 consecutive times.
7. Forearm pass to yourself and pass overhead to your partner 4 consecutive times.
8. Set, touch floor, and set 4 consecutive times.
9. Score 20 (male) or 8 (female) on the overhead pass test (AAHPERD).
10. Back set drill 4 consecutive times.
11. 10 consecutive forearm passes in the 3-player shuttle drill.
12. Set to yourself 5 consecutive times.
13. Spike hits against the wall 4 consecutive times.
14. Dink 1 out of 6 over a block to the attack line.
15. Forearm pass and set to yourself 10 consecutive times.

Volleyball Competencies for College Players

These are typical competencies that could be used for a college beginning volleyball class.

For an A

1. Score an average of 85 on the two written tests.
2. Attend at least 22 class periods (based on a class that meets 24 times).
3. Volley the ball 25 consecutive times against the wall to a height greater than 8 feet using the forearm pass.
4. Serve 15 consecutive good serves.
5. Score at least 28 (male) or 24 (female) on the serving skill test (AAHPERD Skills Test).
6. Set the ball with a partner 100 consecutive times.
7. Forearm pass the ball to yourself, turn, and pass it over your head to your partner at least 12 consecutive times.
8. Set the ball to yourself, touch the floor, and set again at least 12 consecutive times.
9. Score at least 40 (male) or 36 (female) on the setting skills test (AAHPERD Skills Test).
10. Back set 15 consecutive times while working in the middle of the 3-player shuttle drill.
11. Make a total of 40 consecutive forearm passes with 2 partners in the 3-player shuttle drill.
12. Continuously set the ball to yourself for 15 consecutive sets.
13. Spike hit the ball against the wall 10 consecutive times.
14. Dink 3 out of 5 times over a block so that it lands in front of the attack line.
15. Complete the volleyball lesson on PLATO, a computer program on volleyball strategies.

For a B

1. Average 78 on the two written tests.
2. Attend 21 class periods.
3. 18 forearm passes against the wall.
4. 12 consecutive good serves.
5. Score 22 (male) or 20 (female) on the serving skill test (AAHPERD).
6. Set with your partner 75 consecutive times.
7. Forearm pass to yourself and overhead to your partner 9 consecutive times.
8. Set, touch the floor, and set 10 consecutive times.
9. Score 37 (male) or 23 (female) on the overhead pass test (AAHPERD).
10. Back set drill 12 consecutive times.
11. 30 consecutive forearm passes in the 3-player shuttle.
12. Set to yourself 12 consecutive times.
13. Spike hits against the wall 8 consecutive times.
14. Dink 2 out of 5 over a block to the attack line.
15. Complete the volleyball lesson on PLATO.

For a C

---

1. Average 70 on the two written tests.
2. Attend 20 class periods.
3. 13 consecutive forearm passes against the wall.
4. 8 consecutive good serves.
5. Score 17 (male) or 15 (female) on the serving skill test (AAHPERD).
6. Set with your partner 50 consecutive times.
7. Forearm pass to yourself and overhead to your partner 7 consecutive times.
8. Set, touch the floor, and set 8 consecutive times.
9. Score 34 (male) or 16 (female) on the overhead pass test (AAHPERD).
10. Back set drill 10 consecutive times.
11. 25 consecutive forearm passes in the 3-player shuttle.
12. Set to yourself 10 consecutive times.
13. Spike hits against the wall 6 consecutive times.
14. Dink 2 out of 6 over a block to the attack line.
15. Complete the volleyball lesson on PLATO.

For a D

---

1. Average 60 on the two written tests.
2. Attend at least 19 class periods.
3. 11 consecutive forearm passes against the wall.
4. 7 consecutive good serves.
5. Score 12 (male) or 10 (female) on the serving skill test (AAHPERD).
6. Set with your partner 40 consecutive times.
7. Forearm pass to yourself and pass overhead to your partner 5 consecutive times.
8. Set, touch the floor, and set 6 consecutive times.
9. Score 30 (male) or 10 (female) on the overhead pass test (AAHPERD).
10. Back set drill 8 consecutive times.
11. 15 consecutive forearm passes in the 3-player shuttle drill.
12. Set to yourself 8 consecutive times.
13. Spike hits against the wall 5 consecutive times.
14. Dink 1 out of 6 over a block to the attack line.
15. Complete the volleyball lesson on PLATO.

5. Knowledge Test

The "Test Bank" section contains 100 test questions appropriate for testing students' knowledge of the game as presented in the text. You may select questions from this bank or formulate your own according to your needs. We recommend that you include some form of written evaluation in determining grades.

AN INDIVIDUAL PROGRAM

The sample Individual Program (see Appendix C.1) illustrates evaluation by both qualitative (technique objectives) and quantitative (performance objectives) assessments. There is also a blank form in Appendix C.2 for your use in assessing student performance. As we stated previously, the combination of methods you choose to evaluate your students will depend on the available time, the level of the students, and the type of grading your institution requires. You must decide what skills need to be emphasized for the different levels of your students. For example, with beginning students, forearm pass, overhead pass, and serve may be most important in the grading scheme. For advanced students, however, you'll probably want to place greater emphasis on the attack, the block, and game strategies.

Class size must be considered when you decide how students will be evaluated. The larger the class, the more time is needed to evaluate, and some evaluation methods are much more time-consuming than others. For example, the wall volley portion of the AAHPERD Skills Test can be administered to a large class fairly rapidly. By comparison, the serving portion is very time-consuming and requires a volleyball court. We suggest that while one group of students is being tested the remainder of the class be involved in game competition.

Following are some suggestions for skill testing with a large group:

1. For qualitative testing, the teacher must administer the test.
2. Keep students as active as possible while they wait to be tested.
3. Incorporate testing into several class periods to allow students continual practice of skills and game strategies.

4. When you use the competency-based method, set definite standards for skill performance and communicate them to students. For example, when you test the forearm pass against the wall, set a standard for the height of the ball contact on the wall (e.g., higher than net height).
5. Give students time to practice a test item before actually being evaluated on it.
6. On skill test and competency items give students more than one opportunity to complete the test. Higher scores should replace lower ones.
7. Give clear directions to students so that they understand the expectations of the skill test or competency.

The most important part of evaluation is that you tell students on the first day of class exactly how they will be evaluated. Students should know which skills will be emphasized and how grades will be determined (for example, what will be given as the percentage of their grade for qualitative versus quantitative and theoretical versus practical). We recommend that you not limit how many times students can attempt physical skills.

Test Bank

This section includes 100 questions that students should be able to answer after completing a course using the textbook *Volleyball: Steps to Success*. Understanding that teachers will and should vary in the points they emphasize, we recommend that you select from this Test Bank those questions that you feel are most important in testing the knowledge of your students. You may also feel that creating questions of your own will better indicate this level of knowledge. We believe that whether you select items from the Test Bank, create your own test items, or use some combination of the two, you are the best person to decide what is appropriate for your situation.

WRITTEN EXAMINATION QUESTIONS

Multiple Choice Directions: Write the letter of the choice that best completes the statement. Give only *one* answer.

_____ 1. In a 4-2 offense, one player tries not to receive the serve. That player is the

　　a. CF
　　b. setter in the front row

　　c. setter in the back row
　　d. CB

_____ 2. Over 90 percent of all serves should be received by

　　a. a spike
　　b. a set

　　c. an overhead pass
　　d. a forearm pass

_____ 3. When a team is receiving a serve, the forwards stand 15 feet back from the net. If a ball comes to them at shoulder level, they should

　　a. use an overhead pass
　　b. let it go by to be played by a back

　　c. use a forearm pass
　　d. use a set

_____ 4. A student is practicing her forearm pass but constantly hits it low and into the net. She is probably

　　a. hitting the ball too soon
　　b. hitting the ball with her feet parallel

　　c. hitting the ball too close to her body
　　d. hitting the ball with straight legs and while bending from the hips

_____ 5. When performing an overhead pass, the ball is contacted

　　a. 10 to 12 inches from the forehead
　　b. with the palms of the hands

　　c. 6 to 8 inches from the forehead
　　d. on the forearms

_____ 6. When setting the ball for a spike, the setter's foot closer to the net should be

　　a. in the forward position of the stride
　　b. in the rear position of the stride

　　c. pointing toward the net
　　d. pointing away from the net

_____ 7. When executing an overhead pass, a player is not getting any power into the hit. You should look for

　　a. one hand's leading the other
　　b. passing on the run

　　c. receiving the ball too close to the body
　　d. extended elbows and knees at contact

_____ 8. An underhand serve is not as effective offensively as an overhand serve because

　　a. it is highly accurate
　　b. it floats

　　c. it cannot be directed as easily
　　d. it has a high trajectory and lack of force

_____ 9. The main difference in execution between the floater serve and the topspin serve is

a. how you stand in relation to the net in the ready position

b. where you contact the ball and how you follow through

c. in how you swing your hitting arm

d. how high you release the ball on the toss

_____ 10. The most common reason for a player's being unsuccessful in serving accurately with an overhand serve is

a. no weight shift

b. poor ball toss

c. no backswing

d. no arm extension

_____ 11. An on-hand spike is

a. always performed by the right forward

b. hit on the opposite side of your body as the approaching set

c. hit without an approach

d. hit on the same side of your body as the approaching set

_____ 12. The spiker is not getting enough height on his jump. One possible error is

a. a poor set

b. failure to use his arms and legs adequately

c. a stride close approach

d. the takeoff's being too far from the net

_____ 13. The best reason for selecting a 4-2 offensive system is

a. players don't all have to be skilled in all areas; they can be specialists

b. you always have 3 spikers in the front line

c. the setter always comes to the net from the back row

d. the back row players are allowed to spike

_____ 14. Once the serve is passed to the setter, the setter should make every effort to play the ball using

a. an overhead pass or set

b. an underhand pass

c. a block

d. a spike

_____ 15. A ball that is served to the opponents and hits the court in bounds without anyone hitting it is called

a. kill

b. perfect serve

c. ace

d. spike

_____ 16. A ball not spiked by your opponents but returned to you high and easy is called

a. a block

b. a free ball

c. cake

d. base defense

_____ 17. When your opponents are playing the ball and you are waiting to see what they will do, you should be in

a. serve reception formation

b. free ball formation

c. base defensive formation

d. block + 2-1-3 defensive formation

_____ 18. The ball is contacted on the spike with

a. the heel of an open hand

b. the fingertips

c. the side of a closed fist

d. the front of a closed fist

_____ 19. The most accurate method of playing the ball is

a. the block

b. the overhead pass

c. the spike

d. the forearm pass

_____ 20. The reason why the floater serve moves during its flight is because
   a. the ball has no spin on it
   b. the ball has topspin
   c. the ball has backspin
   d. the ball is hit with a closed fist

_____ 21. When performing a forearm pass, the arms generally
   a. swing upward with force
   b. make contact at shoulder level
   c. remain almost stationary
   d. follow through above the shoulders

_____ 22. The term used to describe one team's losing the serve is
   a. hand out
   b. side out
   c. point
   d. rotation

_____ 23. When the right back has called for the ball, indicating to his teammates that he will receive the serve, all of his teammates should
   a. open up to the right back
   b. run toward the right back to help out
   c. get ready for the 2-1-3 formation
   d. call the lines for him

_____ 24. The serve is approaching the left back of the receiving team. The person who has the prime responsibility of calling the ball out over the end line is the
   a. LF
   b. LB
   c. RB
   d. CB

_____ 25. The following are all defensive plays, except for
   a. spike
   b. block
   c. dig
   d. save

_____ 26. All the following terms are associated with the spike, except
   a. off-hand
   b. cushioning
   c. off-speed
   d. step-close takeoff

_____ 27. The primary responsibility of the center back in the 2-1-3 defensive alignment is
   a. to dig the spike
   b. to block the spike
   c. to pick up all dinks that come over the block
   d. not to play the ball, if at all possible

_____ 28. The purpose of the heel plant in the spike is to
   a. avoid too much force on the toes
   b. change forward momentum into upward momentum
   c. prevent wear and tear on the soles of your sneakers
   d. to help you get greater arm swing

Note: 29 through 34. Your team is using a 4-2 offensive system. Your left forward is spiking, and your team is covering the spiker. Answer the following questions based on this situation.

_____ 29. The person covering nearest the left sideline would be the
   a. LF
   b. LB
   c. RF
   d. RB

_____ 30. The person covering nearest the net would be the
   a. CB
   b. RF
   c. setter
   d. LF

_____ 31. The player covering nearest the right sideline would be the
   a. RB
   b. RF
   c. CB
   d. setter

_____ 32. The player covering nearest the end line would be the

    a. CB   c. LB

    b. RB   d. RF

_____ 33. The player in the middle of the semicircle of players covering the spiker would always be

    a. RB   c. setter

    b. LB   d. CB

_____ 34. The main reason why you cover a spiking teammate is to

    a. be able to spike immediately again if the first attempt is blocked

    b. pick up any blocked ball that drops quickly

    c. block your opponent's spike attempt

    d. cover the opponent's view of the spike

Note: 35 through 39. The next five questions should be answered based on the following situation: The opposing left forward is spiking. Your team is defending against his spike, using the 2-1-3 defense.

_____ 35. The two players who form the block for your team will be the

    a. CF and RF   c. LF and RF

    b. CF and LF   d. RF alone

_____ 36. The player who covers the power alley would be the

    a. LF   c. LB

    b. CB   d. RB

_____ 37. The player who is the key person for covering against a dink is the

    a. RB   c. LB

    b. setter   d. CB

_____ 38. The player who defends against a spike down the line would be the

    a. CB   c. LF

    b. RF   d. RB

_____ 39. The player responsible for dinks to the center of your court, dinks close to the net, or junk off the net would be the

    a. LF   c. CF

    b. CB   d. LB

_____ 40. One of the advantages of the 2-1-3 defensive alignment is

    a. it provides good coverage of dinks and balls that come off the blocker's hands

    b. it is excellent when you have short blockers

    c. it is easy to learn because it is similar to the serve reception formation

    d. the backcourt coverage is strongest, especially against a strong spiking team

Fill-In Directions: From the following list, fill in the blanks with the word or phrase that best completes the statement. Some phrases or words may be used more than once.

Word or Phrase List

dink	specialization		
right forward	left back	junk off net	serve reception
setter	strong, consistent	free ball	strong blocking
good digging	hitting	opening up	good quick hitting
attacker	quickness	power alley	kill
crosses the net	side out	attackers	right back
ace	just after	reading	switch
roll	left	lateral movement	serve
sprawl	setters	excellent leadership	attacking
W	left forward	dink to the middle	left side
	spike		

1. An offensive shot that is put over the block and drops quickly to the floor is called a
   _____.

2. The W-formation in volleyball is used during _____ and _____.

3. The crosscourt territory where most spikers place their hits is called the _____.

4. In serve reception formation, the one player who should not receive the serve is the
   _____.

5. When one player is receiving the serve, all her teammates should turn and face that player.
   This action is called _____.

6. When you name an offensive system with two numbers, the first number refers to how
   many (a) _____ you will use, and the second number refers to how many
   (b) _____ you will use.

7. If you are playing on a team of all right-handers, the stronger side of your forward line
   always is the _____ side.

8. If you have a left-hander playing in your forward line, you always try to have that player
   (a) _____ to the (b) _____ position when your team is (c) _____.

9. The _____ formation is used by your team when you are receiving serve.

10. The setter should always face the _____ of the court when in the setting position.

11. A(n) _____ is a lateral movement that allows a player to go to the floor without
    injury and return quickly to his or her feet.

12. The exchange of service is called _____.

13. When taking statistics in volleyball, a serve that is not returned is called a(n) _____.

14. A spike that ends the play as a point or side out is called a(n) _____.

15. In serve reception, the two players who you would like to receive the majority of the serves are the _____ and the _____.

16. The player during serve reception who would call the sideline for the left front player is the _____.

17. When blocking, the blockers should watch the (a) _____ in order to time their jumping so that they leave the floor (b) _____ the attacker.

18. The player who calls for the ball during serve receive should call for it before it _____.

19. The process of analyzing your opponents to decide what they are going to do, in order for your team to counteract their attack, is called _____.

20. When players continuously switch positions so as to play only one position on the court, the process is called _____.

What two characteristics are important in players who play each of the following positions?: middle hitter-blocker (21) _____ (22) _____; outside hitter (23) _____ (24) _____; and setter (25) _____ (26) _____.

27. When a right-handed spiker is playing the _____ position, he or she would be spiking on-hand.

28. In spike coverage, the person in the middle position of the three-person coverage, when using the 6-2 offense, is always the _____.

29. In spike coverage, when using the 4-2 offense, the person closest to the net in the three-person coverage is always the _____.

30. When you use a double block against the opposing left forward, the person who sets the block is the _____.

31. When the ball is served between the left and the right backs, it is better for the _____ to play the ball.

32. You must be in your correct rotational position—that is, with no players overlapping—during _____ and _____.

When you use a two-man block on either side of the court, the off blocker would assume the responsibility of receiving three types of play from the opponents, which are (33) _____, (34) _____, and (35) _____.

Matching Directions: Write the letter of the choice that gives the best definition or best matches the term.

_____ 1. middle-in defense

_____ 2. dig

_____ 3. front row setter

_____ 4. "roof"

_____ 5. off-hand spike

_____ 6. kill

_____ 7. dink

_____ 8. strong side right-hander

_____ 9. strong side left-hander

_____ 10. topspin

_____ 11. W-formation

_____ 12. back set

_____ 13. bump

_____ 14. off-speed hit

_____ 15. free ball

_____ 16. opening up

_____ 17. side out

_____ 18. crosscourt hit

_____ 19. double hits

_____ 20. floater

_____ 21. wrist snap

_____ 22. heel plant

_____ 23. open hand

_____ 24. ace

_____ 25. turn outside hand in

a. 4-2

b. the setter is on the side opposite the hitter's hitting hand

c. offensive drop shot

d. left forward position

e. 2-1-3

f. blockers have their hands over the net

g. one-arm desperation play to save a hard-driven ball

h. the setter is on the hitter's strong-arm side

i. no spin for stabilization

j. a spiked ball that isn't returned

k. ball will float

l. puts topspin on the ball

m. ball will drop

n. right forward position

o. transfers forward momentum into upward momentum

p. setter sends the ball over her head to a player behind her

q. an easy return from the opponents

r. a serve that is not returned

s. serve reception

t. turning to face the player who is playing the ball

u. a spike directed diagonally to the longest part of the court

v. the serve changes hands

w. hand position of the blocker closest to sideline

x. a player plays the ball twice in succession

y. a spike that is hit after the speed of the striking arm is greatly reduced

z. forearm pass

aa. 2-4

bb. 5-1

cc. correct hand position for spike and serve

WRITTEN EXAMINATION ANSWERS

Multiple Choice	Fill-Ins	Matching
1. b	1. dink	1. e
2. d	2. free ball,	2. g
3. b	serve reception	3. a
4. d	3. power alley	4. f
5. c	4. setter	5. b
6. a	5. opening up	6. j
7. d	6. a. attackers	7. c
8. d	b. setters	8. d
9. b	7. left	9. n
10. b	8. a. switch	10. m
11. d	b. right forward	11. s
12. b	c. attacking	12. p
13. a	9. W	13. z
14. a	10. left side	14. y
15. c	11. roll or sprawl	15. q
16. b	12. side out	16. t
17. c	13. ace	17. v
18. a	14. kill	18. u
19. b	15. left back/right	19. x
20. a	back	20. i
21. c	16. left back	21. l
22. b	17. a. attacker	22. o
23. a	b. just after	23. cc
24. c	18. crosses the net	24. r
25. a	19. reading	25. w
26. b	20. specialization	
27. c	21. strong blocking	
28. b	or good quick	
29. b	hitting	
30. c	22. lateral movement	
31. b	23. strong, consis-	
32. b	tent hitting	
33. d	24. good digging	
34. b	25. quickness	
35. a	26. excellent	
36. c	leadership	
37. d	27. left forward	
38. d	28. setter	
39. a	29. setter	
40. a	30. right forward	
	31. left back	
	32. serve/serve	
	reception	
	33. spike	
	34. dink to middle	
	35. junk off net	

Appendices

Appendix A
How to Use the Knowledge Structure Overview

A knowledge structure by definition is a very personal statement about what you know about a subject and how this knowledge guides your decisions in teaching and coaching. This knowledge structure for volleyball has been designed for a teaching environment with teaching progressions that emphasize technique and performance objectives in realistic settings. In a coaching environment, you would need to emphasize more physiological and conditioning factors with training progressions to prepare athletes for competition.

The Knowledge Structure of Volleyball shows the first page or an *overview* of a completed knowledge structure. The selected large categories used for all of the participant and instructor guide books within the Steps to Success Activity Series include the following:

- physiological training and conditioning,
- background knowledge,
- psychomotor skills and tactics, and
- psycho-social concepts.

The physiological training and conditioning category includes two subcategories, warm-up and cool-down. Only the principles and exercises used in carrying out an effective warm-up and cool-down are presented due to time restrictions that most instructors face when teaching. The inclusion of a warm-up and a cool-down is supported by knowledge from exercise physiology and the medical sciences. In a more intense environment, additional categories should be added, in particular, training principles, injury prevention, training progressions, and nutrition principles.

The background knowledge category presents subcategories of information that represent essential background knowledges that all instructors should command when meeting their classes. The volleyball knowledge structure includes playing the game, basic rules, equipment, and volleyball today.

Under psychomotor skills and tactics, all the individual skills in an activity are named. For volleyball, these are shown as movement patterns, forearm pass, serving, overhead pass, attack, blocking, and individual defense. These skills are also presented in a recommended order of introduction. In a completed knowledge structure, each of these skills is broken down into subskills with selected technical, biomechanical, motor learning, and other teaching/coaching points presented that describe mature performance. These points can be found in the Student Keys to Success in this book and the Keys to Success Checklists within the participant book.

Following the identification and analysis of individual skills, selected basic tactics of the activity are presented and analyzed. For volleyball, these include offense tactics (4-2, International 4-2, 5-1, and 6-2) and defense tactics (2-4, and 2-1-3). Notice that they are also arranged to reflect the decision making strategies and capabilities of learners as they become more proficient.

Within each offense three basic formations are discussed: free ball, covering the attacker, and serve reception. Each defense is broken down into two formations: the base defense and the block coverage.

The psychosocial category identifies selected concepts from the sports psychology and sociology literature that have been shown to contribute to the learners' understanding of and success in the activity. These concepts are built into the key concepts and activities for teaching. For volleyball, the concept identified is teamwork.

In order to be a successful teacher or coach, you must convert what you know as a player to a form of knowing that you can present to others. A knowledge structure is designed to help you with this transition and speed your *steps to success*. You should view a knowledge structure as the most basic level of teaching knowledge you possess for a sport or activity. For more information on how to develop your own knowledge structure, see the theory textbook that accompanies this series, *Instructional Design for Teaching Physical Activities*.

Knowledge Structure of Volleyball (Overview)

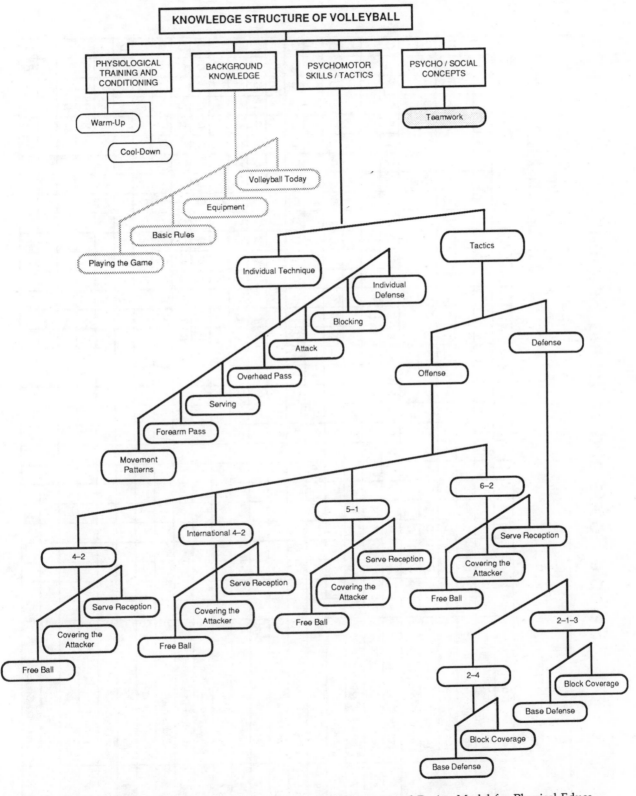

Note. From "The Role of Expert Knowledge Structures in an Instructional Design Model for Physical Education" by J.N. Vickers, 1983, *Journal of Teaching in Physical Education*, 2(3), 25, 27. Copyright 1983 by Joan N. Vickers. Adapted by permission. This Knowledge Structure of Volleyball was designed specifically for the Steps to Success Activity Series by Joan N. Vickers, Judy P. Wright, Barbara L. Viera, and Bonnie Jill Ferguson.

Appendix B.1

Sample Scope and Teaching Sequence

NAME OF ACTIVITY: Volleyball
LEVEL OF LEARNER: Beginner-intermediate

Legend: **N** = New   **R** = Review   **C** = Continue

Steps	Session Number	1	2	3	4	5	6	7	8	9	10	11	12	13	14	15	16	17	18	19	20	21	22	23	24	25	26	27	28	29	30
1	Introduction/Orientation	N																													
2	Movement Patterns		N	R	C																										
3	Forearm Pass		N	R	C	C	C	C	C	C	C	C	C	C	C	C	C	C	C	C	C	C	C	C	C	C	C	C	C	C	C
4	Serve			N	R	C	C	C	C	C	C	C	C	C	C	C	C	C	C	C	C	C	C	C	C	C	C	C	C	C	C
5	Two-Skill Combination			N	R	C																									
6	Overhead Pass				N	R	C	C	C	C	C	C	C	C	C	C	C	C	C	C	C	C	C	C	C	C	C	C	C	C	C
7	Set					N	R	C	C	C	C	C	C	C	C	C	C	C	C	C	C	C	C	C	C	C	C	C	C	C	C
8	Three-Skill Combination						N	R																							
9	Attack							N	R	C	C	C	C	C	C	C	C	C	C	C	C	C	C	C	C	C	C	C	C	C	C
10	Four-Skill								N	R																					
11	Dig									N	R	R	C	C	C	C	C	C	C	C	C	C	C	C	C	C	C	C	C	C	C
12	Five-Skill										N	R																			
13	Spike											N	R	C	C	C	C	C	C	C	C	C	C	C	C	C	C	C	C	C	C
14	Block												N	R	C	C	C	C	C	C	C	C	C	C	C	C	C	C	C	C	C
15	Six-Skill													N	R	R															
16	Advanced Serves														N	R	R	C	C	C	C	C	C	C	C	C	C	C	C	C	C
17	Individual Defense															N	R	C	C	C	C	C	C	C	C	C	C	C	C	C	C
18	4-2 Offense																N	R	R	C	C	C	C	C	C	C	C	C	C	C	C
19	2-1-3 Defense																		N	R	R	R	C	C	C	C	C	C	C	C	C
20	International 4-2																				N	N									
21	6-2 Offense																						N	N	R	R	C	C	C	C	C
22	2-4 Defense																							N	N	R	C	C	C	C	C
23	5-1 Offense																									N	N	R	C	C	C
24	Game Situations																												N	N	R
	Game Play Choices																													N	R

Notes:

Appendix B.2

How to Use the Scope and Teaching Sequence Form

A completed Scope and Teaching Sequence is, in effect, a master plan. It lists all the individual skills to be included in your course, recorded (vertically) in the progressive sequence in which you have decided to present them and showing (horizontally) the manner and the sessions in which you teach them.

The Sample Scope and Teaching Sequence (Appendix B.1) illustrates how the chart is to be used. This chart indicates that in session 3, the class will continue practicing the movement patterns and the forearm pass, will review the serve, and will then combine these skills. It also indicates that the skills in Step 8 (the attack), for example, are introduced, reviewed, and then practiced continuously.

A course scope and teaching sequence chart (use the blank form in Appendix B.2) will help you to better plan your daily teaching strategies (see Appendix D.1). It will take some experience to predict accurately how much material you can cover in each session, but by completing a plan like this, you can compare your progress to your plan and revise the plan to better fit the next class.

The chart will also help you tailor the amount of material to the length of time you have to teach it. Be sure that your course's scope and teaching sequence allots ample time for reviewing and practicing of each area.

Appendix B.2

Scope and Teaching Sequence

New N	Review R	Continue C	Student Directed Practice P

NAME OF ACTIVITY _____

LEVEL OF LEARNER _____

Steps	Session Number	1	2	3	4	5	6	7	8	9	10	11	12	13	14	15	16	17	18	19	20	21	22	23	24	25	26	27	28	29	30
1																																
2																																
3																																
4																																
5																																
6																																
7																																
8																																
9																																
10																																
11																																
12																																
13																																
14																																
15																																
16																																
17																																
18																																
19																																
20																																
21																																
22																																
23																																
24																																
25																																

Note. From *Badminton: A Structures of Knowledge Approach* (pp. 60-61) by J.N. Vickers and D. Brecht, 1987, Calgary, AB: University Printing Services. Copyright 1987 by Joan N. Vickers. Adapted by permission.

Appendix C.1

Sample Individual Program

INDIVIDUAL COURSE IN ___Volleyball___

GRADE/COURSE SECTION ___Freshman___

STUDENT'S NAME _____

STUDENT ID # _____

SKILLS/CONCEPTS	TECHNIQUE AND PERFORMANCE OBJECTIVES	WT* x	POINT PROGRESS** 1	2	3	4	= FINAL SCORE***
1 Movement Patterns	*Technique:* Maintain low body position; block without arm swing; hands high in waiting position.						
	Performance: Continuous movement for 60 seconds doing Mirror Dill. Continuous movement for 30 seconds in medium body posture in Forward and Back Drill. 10 consecutive jumps and rolls without touching the net. 5 floor sits in 30 seconds.	0.5					
2 Forearm Pass	*Technique:* Correct hand position; elbows locked/no arm swing; body positioned behind the ball; shoulders square to target.						
	Performance: Pass 25 held balls in 30 attempts.	1.5	10	15	20	25	
	Make 20 good passes in 25 attempts in partner toss.	1.5	8	12	16	20	
	Make 25 consecutive forearm passes in continuous bumping, while in a 10-foot-square area.	1.5	10	15	20	25	
	Make 20 accurate passes on 25 tosses in Passing to Target Drill (Step 2, Drill 4).	1.5	8	12	16	20	
3 Underhand Serve	*Technique:* Hold ball at waist level; holding hand should not swing; holding hand drops before contact; ball is not tossed; weight transfers forward.	1.0					
4 Overhand Floater Serve	*Technique:* Shoulders square to net; toss is consistently in front of hitting shoulder; ball is contacted at full arm extension; ball is contacted with the heel of an open hand.	1.5					
5 Underhand or Overhand Floater Serve	*Performance:* 9 good serves in 10 attempts in Wall Serve Drill (Step 3, Drill 2).	1.0	6	7	8	9	
	7 accurate serves in 10 attempts of Partner Serve at the Net Drill (Step 3, Drill 3).	to	4	5	6	7	
	9 good serves on 10 attempts of End Line Serve Drill (Step 3, Drill 4).	1.5	6	7	8	9	
	Hit a target at least 5 times in 20 attempts.		2	3	4	5	

(Cont.)

Sample Individual Program (Cont.)

			WT				
6	Overhead Pass	Technique: Hands are 6 inches in front of forehead; hands are on sides of ball with thumbs back; gets to correct position behind the ball; shoulders are square to target.	1.5				
		Performance: 25 consecutive overhead passes in Pass-Bounce-Pass Drill (Step 5, Drill 1).	1.5	10	15	20	25
		8 good passes in Partner Toss and Pass Drill (Step 5, Drill 2).		2	4	6	8
		8 good passes in 10 Tosses of Free Ball Passing Drill (Step 5, Drill 3).		2	4	6	8
		15 consecutive 3-pass sequences in the Short Pass, Back Pass, Long Pass Drill (Step 5, Drill 4).		6	9	12	15
7	Attack	Technique: Waits until ball reaches highest point to begin attack approach; uses two foot takeoff with heel plant; swings both arms to increase jump height; contacts ball at full arm extension with heel of open hand for hard-driven spike.	2.0				
8	Attack	Performance: Will hit the target 5 times on 10 attempts in Dink to Target Drill (Step 8, Drill 1).		2	3	4	5
		Hits 10 good off-speed spikes on 15 tosses in Off-Speed Spike to Center Court Drill (Step 8, Drill 2).		4	6	8	10
9	Block	Technique: Keeps eyes on attacker; jumps after attacker jumps; keeps arms bent on arm swing; penetrates the net with hands.	1.5				
		Performance: 6 out of 10 good blocks in the Toss to Block Drill (Step 13, Drill 1).	1.5	3	4	5	6

*WT = Weighting of an objective's degree of difficulty

**PROGRESS = Ongoing success, which may be expressed in terms of (a) accumulated points (1, 2, 3, 4); (b) grades (D, C, B, A); (c) symbols (merit, bronze, silver, gold); (d) unsatisfactory/satisfactory; and others as desired.

***FINAL SCORE equals WT times PROGRESS

Appendix C.2
How to Use the Individual Program Form

To complete an individual progam for each student, you must first make five decisions about evaluation:

1. How many skills or concepts can you or should you evaluate, considering the number of students and the time available? The larger your classes and the shorter your class length, the fewer objectives you will be able to use.

2. What specific quantitative or qualitative criteria will you use to evaluate specific skills? See the Sample Individual Program in Appendix C.1 for ideas.

3. What relative weight is to be assigned to each specific skill, considering its importance in the course and the amount of practice time available?

4. What type of grading system do you wish to use? Will you use letters (A, B, C, D), satisfactory/unsatisfactory, a number or point system (1, 2, 3, etc.), or percentages? Or, you may prefer a system of achievement levels indicated by colors (red, white, blue), positions (diggers, spikers, blockers), or medallions (bronze, silver, gold).

5. Who will do the evaluating? You may want to delegate certain quantitative evaluations to the students' peers up to a predetermined skill level (e.g., a ''B'' grade), with all qualitative evaluations and all top-grade determinations being made by you.

Once you have made these decisions, draw up an evaluation sheet (using Appendix C.2) that will fit the majority of your class members. Then decide whether you will establish a minimum level as a passing/failing point. Calculate the minimum passing score and the maximum attainable score, and divide the difference into as many grade categories as you wish. If you use an achievement-level system, assign a numerical value to each level for your calculations.

The blank Individual Program form is intended not to be used verbatim (although you may do so if you wish), but rather to suggest ideas that you can use, adapt, and integrate with your own ideas to tailor your program to you and your students.

Make copies of your program evaluation system to hand out to each student at your first class meeting. Be prepared to make modifications for students who need special consideration. Such modifications could include changing the weight assigned to a particular skill or substituting one skill for another, or varying the criteria used for evaluating those students. Thus, individual differences can be recognized within your class.

You, the instructor, have the freedom to make the decisions about evaluating your students. Be creative. The best teachers always are.

Appendix C.2

Individual Program

INDIVIDUAL COURSE IN _____ GRADE/COURSE SECTION _____

STUDENT'S NAME _____ STUDENT ID # _____

SKILLS/CONCEPTS	TECHNIQUE AND PERFORMANCE OBJECTIVES	WT* ×	POINT PROGRESS** =				FINAL SCORE***
			1	2	3	4	

Note. From "The Role of Expert Knowledge Structures in an Instructional Design Model for Physical Education" by J.N. Vickers, 1983, *Journal of Teaching in Physical Education, 2*(3), p. 17. Copyright 1983 by Joan N. Vickers. Adapted by permission.

*WT = Weighting of an objective's degree of difficulty

**PROGRESS = Ongoing success, which may be expressed in terms of (a) accumulated points (1, 2, 3, 4); (b) grades (D, C, B, A); (c) symbols (merit, bronze, silver, gold); (d) unsatisfactory/satisfactory; and others as desired.

***FINAL SCORE equals WT times PROGRESS

Appendix D.1
Sample Lesson Plan

Lesson plan _____2_____ of _____30_____ Activity _____Volleyball_____

Class ___1:00–1:50___

Objectives:
1. Student will move continuously in the Mirror Drill for 60 seconds.
2. Student will complete 10 consecutive jumps and rolls without touching the net.
3. Student will complete 20 accurate forearm passes in 25 tosses.
4. Student will make 9 accurate tosses in 10 attempts.
5. Student will make 9 good wall serves in 10 attempts with both the underhand serve and the floater serve.

Equipment:
- 2 courts
- 2 nets
- 1 ball per player
- 12-inch-square targets (1 per player)
- tape for net line on wall

Skill or concept	Learning activity	Teaching points	Time (min)
1. Outline objectives			
2. Warm-up	• Court sprints with partner • Over-net ball exchange	• Don't leave until after ball exchange. • Do not touch net. Land on two feet.	5
3. Movement patterns	• Mirror Drill (Step 1, Drill 1) • Block and Roll Drill (Step 1, Drill 3)	• Quick movement. Low position • Quick withdrawal of hands. • Buttocks hit floor first. • Quick roll and return to feet.	5
4. Review forearm pass	• Passing to Target Drill (Step 2, Drill 4)	• Call for every ball. • Shoulders square to target. • Use body to impart force.	15

5. Introduce underhand serve, overhand floater

- Ball Toss Drill (Step 3, Drill 1)
  - Concentrate on ball. 3
  - Reach high with placing arm.
  - Be consistent.

- Wall Serve Drill with underhand serve (Step 3, Drill 2)
  - Contact ball at waist. 12
  - Holding hand does not move.
  - Follow-through to net line on wall.

- Wall Serve Drill with overhand floater serve (Step 3, Drill 2)
  - Shoulders square to net
  - Place ball into position.
  - Do not wait for ball.
  - Poking action at contact.
  - Point hand to target.

6. Review questions, bridge to next lesson.

Appendix D.2
How to Use the Lesson Plan Form

All teachers have learned in their training that lesson plans are vital to good teaching. This is a commonly accepted axiom, but there are many variations in the form that lesson plans can take.

An effective lesson plan sets forth the objectives to be attained or attempted during the session. If there is no objective, then there is no reason for teaching and no basis for judging whether the teaching is effective.

Once you have named your objectives, list specific activities that will lead to attaining each. Every activity must be described in detail—what will take place and in what order, and how the class will be organized for the optimum learning situation. Record key words or phrases as focal points as well as brief reminders of the applicable safety precautions (see Appendix D.1).

Finally, set a time schedule that allocates a segment of the lesson for each activity to guide you in keeping to your plan. It is wise to also include in your lesson plan a list of all the teaching and safety equipment you will need, as well as a reminder to check for availability and location of the equipment before class.

An organized, professional approach to teaching requires preparing daily lesson plans. Each lesson plan provides you with an effective overview of your intended instruction and a means to evaluate it when class is over. Having lesson plans on file allows someone else to teach in your absence. You may modify the blank lesson plan form shown in Appendix D.2 to fit your own needs.

Lesson Plan

LESSON PLAN _____ OF _____		OBJECTIVES:
ACTIVITY _____		
CLASS _____		

SKILL OR CONCEPT	LEARNING ACTIVITIES	TEACHING POINTS	TIME

References

Goc-Karp, G., & Zakrajsek, D.B. (1987). Planning for learning: Theory into practice. *Journal of Teaching in Physical Education,* **6**(4), 377-392.

Housner, L.D., & Griffey, D.C. (1985). Teacher cognition: Differences in planning and interactive decision making between experienced and inexperienced teachers. *Research Quarterly for Exercise and Sport,* **56**(1), 45-53.

Imwold, C.H., & Hoffman, S.J. (1983). Visual recognition of a gymnastic skill by experienced and inexperienced instructors. *Research Quarterly for Exercise and Sport,* **54**(2), 149-155.

Suggested Readings

American Alliance for Health, Physical Education, Recreation and Dance. (1988). *NAGWS Volleyball Guide*. Reston, VA: Author.

American Alliance for Health, Physical Education, Recreation and Dance. (1969). *Skills test manual: Volleyball for boys and girls*. Reston, VA: Author.

Bertucci, B. (Ed.) (1987). *The AVCA volleyball handbook*. Grand Rapids, MI: Masters Press.

Bertucci, B. (Ed.) (1982). *Championship volleyball by the experts*. Champaign, IL: Leisure Press.

Bertucci, B., & Hippolyte, R. (Eds.) (1984). *Championship volleyball drills: Volume I*. Champaign, IL: Leisure Press.

Bertucci, B., & Korgut, T. (Eds.) (1985). *Championship volleyball drills: Volume II*. Champaign, IL: Leisure Press.

Cox, R.H. (1980). *Teaching volleyball*. Minneapolis, MN: Burgess.

Doughtery, N.J. (Ed.) (1987). *Principles of safety in physical education and sport*. Reston, VA: AAHPERD.

Fraser, S.D. (1988). *Strategies for competitive volleyball*. Champaign, IL: Leisure Press.

International Volleyball Federation Coaches Manual. (1975). Vanier, ON: Canadian Volleyball Association.

Scates, A.E. (1984). *Winning volleyball drills*. Boston, MA: Allyn and Bacon.

Schaafsma, F., & Heck, A. (1971). *Volleyball for coaches and teachers*. Dubuque, IA: Wm. C. Brown.

True, S.S. (Ed.) (1988). *1988-89 Official high school volleyball rules*. Kansas City, MO: National Federation of State High School Associations.

Viera, B.L., & Markham, S.A., Jr. (1978). *Volleyball strategy lessons: A drill and practice lesson dealing with the 4-2 offensive and 2-1-3 defensive strategies used in volleyball*. Newark, DE: University of Delaware.

Viera, B.L., & Markham, S.A., Jr. (1978). *Volleyball strategy lessons: Five situation drills dealing with the 4-2 offensive and 2-1-3 defensive strategies used in volleyball*. Newark, DE: University of Delaware.

About the Authors

Barbara L. Viera is an associate professor of physical education and the head volleyball coach at the University of Delaware. She has coached and taught volleyball at all levels for over 25 years. Barbara's teams at Delaware have competed successfully at the Division I level, achieving a win/loss record that places her in the top 10 of all-time active Division I winning coaches in the country. Along with her college coaching, Barbara has established and successfully run a junior volleyball program for high school and junior high school players in the state of Delaware.

In addition to teaching and coaching in Delaware, Barbara has written several articles and chapters in books, journals, and newsletters and has made presentations at the regional, national, and international levels. She has taught volleyball in Costa Rica, Guatemala, Panama, Mexico, and Argentina, working with teachers, coaches, national teams, and players of all age levels. Her teams have competed in St. Lucia and Barbados.

Bonnie Jill Ferguson is an assistant professor of physical education and the head coach of the women's softball and tennis teams at the University of Delaware. For over nine years, her responsibilities have included teaching the skills, techniques, and knowledge of volleyball to those studying to be physical education teachers. Bonnie Jill and Barbara have established a competency-based model for teaching volleyball. Through 5 years of competitive playing experience at the collegiate and USVBA levels, Bonnie Jill developed a knowledge and understanding of volleyball, giving her insight into the various aspects of the game from a player's point of view.